# THE MANAGERS

## FOOTBALL'S GREATEST MANAGERS

## JON REEVES

NEW
HOLLAND

## DEDICATION

For my beautiful wife Katie and my precious son George.

## ACKNOWLEDGEMENTS

I would like to thank Alan Whiticker for commissioning this book, Diane Ward for providing advice, Kate Sherington for the initial concept and all at New Holland Publishing for their assistance throughout the writing and editing process. Thanks must also go to Laura Wagg at Press Association Images for her assistance with sourcing the fantastic photographs that adorn the front and back cover, as well as those that capture 10 of the managers featured in the book.

As with my other previous titles, it quite simply would not have been possible to complete this project without the understanding of my family, particularly my wife Katie who has been so supportive throughout the process.

The research for this book has been extensive and enjoyable and featured many hours reading various managers' biographies and other titles and articles celebrating the great bosses and great teams from the past. Some of the most useful autobiographies have been those of Sir Matt Busby (*Soccer at the Top*), Sir Alex Ferguson (*Managing My Life*) and Brian Clough (*Cloughie—My Life - Walking on Water*). Additionally, watching footage of some of the awesome teams these fantastic managers created and recalling their great style and achievements has helped contextualise each manager's legacy.

In many ways, selecting the greatest managers of all time and the order in which they should be placed is an impossible job. Judging bosses from different eras, different countries and gauging levels of success between club and international football has made this an extremely tricky task. For example, how can you compare the achievements of managers who have succeeded in South America with those celebrating glory in Europe? The style of football, infrastructure and expectations vary so much between both continents but the prominence of the European game and the number of South American players traditionally playing within it, has been a major factor in the more subjective European focus in the book.

It's unlikely that you will agree with the order in which the managers have been ranked or even with the top 30 that have been selected, but that's the beauty of football. It's a game full of opinions, many clouded by club allegiance, but all of which contribute to making it the world's most popular sport.

I hope that you enjoy this title and that it brings back memories of some of the greatest characters and greatest moments in football history.

# THE MANAGERS

First published in 2014 by
New Holland Publishers
London • Sydney • Cape Town • Auckland
www.newhollandpublishers.com

The Chandlery, Unit 114, 50 Westminster Bridge Road, London, SE1 7QY UK
1/66 Gibbes Street Chatswood NSW 2067 Australia
Wembley Square First Floor Solan Road Gardens Cape Town 8001 South Africa
218 Lake Road Northcote Auckland New Zealand

A catalogue record of this book is available at the British Library and the National Library of Australia.

ISBN: 9781742574622

10 9 8 7 6 5 4 3 2 1

Managing director: Fiona Schultz
Publisher: Alan Whiticker
Project editor: Jason Mountney
Designer: Kimberley Pearce
Production: Sandy Jones
Printer: Toppan Leefung Printing Limited

Follow New Holland Publishers on
Facebook: www.facebook.com/NewHollandPublishers

# C O N T E N T S

# INTRODUCTION

There was one clear inspiration behind this book; the retirement of the legendary Sir Alex Ferguson in May 2013 after a peerless managerial career that spanned four decades and delivered 49 trophies. The fiercely driven Scotsman's impact on the game is significant and indelible, and many years before he finally departed the dugout, he was already being touted as the greatest manager of all time.

This book explores to what extent Sir Alex merits that standing and assesses some of the other contenders, considering club and international managers from various different eras and nations. From the philosophic 'total football' coaching methods of the likes of Rinus Michels and Johan Cruyff and the expansive ultra-attacking yet disciplined models instilled by Louis van Gaal and Pep Guardiola, to the uncompromising 'catenaccio' defensive styles of Helenio Herrera and the team-building expertise of Arrigo Sacchi, the greatest managers to have ever lived all feature in the next 11 chapters.

Some of the most captivating characters that football has produced, including Bill Shankly, Brian Clough and José Mourinho, are showcased, as well as often underrated bosses that have achieved notable success with lesser clubs and nations, such as Otto Rehhagel and Ernst Happel. The records and methods of even the most prolific managers have been assessed and scrutinised and, of course, extensively celebrated.

When selecting the 30 greatest managers of all time, a number of different elements need to be considered. More than just sheer trophy-accumulation, success has been judged by the manager's impact on the clubs and teams they have led, their longevity in the game and their ability to create more than one great team. Other factors that were assessed include the philosophies managers implemented, their flexibility to succeed with different clubs and in different countries, as well as their tactical awareness and man-management skills.

Many of the greatest managers have been responsible for revolutionising and shaping clubs, giving them a new identity and placing them at the top of the game, often following years in the wilderness; men such as Sir Matt Busby, Bill Shankly and Jock Stein, through their vision, principles, hard work and sheer personality, have become synonymous with the creation of some of the biggest clubs in the world.

The greatest players are usually the game's most celebrated characters, and in many ways, rightly so. But the managers and coaches who have the vision, intelligence and bravery to implement their philosophies upon teams and individuals certainly deserve a huge amount of credit.

Working in such highly pressurised environments and carrying the hopes of thousands, and in some cases millions, of fans is often a thankless task. In the instant results-driven world of modern football, a manager can be judged as a success just by retaining his role for more than a season or by lifting a single trophy, which makes the achievements of the men mentioned in the following pages even more notable.

Over the next 11 chapters you will discover which managers feature in the top 30, the notable bosses that have missed out, who made the top 10 and, most importantly, the identity of the greatest football manager of all time.

# C H A P T E R   1 :
## T H E   O T H E R   C A N D I D A T E S

The following chapter is filled with some of the finest football managers to have graced the beautiful game. Yet despite their impressive achievements and renowned reputations, they have missed out, some more narrowly than others, on being named in the top 30.

Many of the men detailed in the forthcoming pages are serial winners and prolific trophy gatherers, while others are recognised for their considerable contributions to the clubs and countries they have worked for, as well as being revolutionary tacticians, captivating characters and truly remarkable ambassadors for the game.

### VITTORIO POZZO

A staunch tactician, Vittorio Pozzo remains the only manager to have won two World Cups, after leading his native Italy to consecutive world crowns in 1934 and 1938. He also guided the Azzurri to success in the Central European International Cup, a forerunner to the current European Football Championship, in 1930 and 1935, and an Olympic Gold Medal in 1936.

Known as Il Vecchio Maestro—the old master—Pozzo crafted a philosophy and national identity for the Italian national side and Italian football in general that has remained to this day, creating a pragmatic and steely defensive unit that could also play with attacking precision and guile. As well as his impressive trophy haul for the Azzurri, Pozzo's 63 victories in 95 games as Italian boss remain a national record.

### VICTOR MASLOV

Operating in a similar era to Pozzo, Victor Maslov was one of the game's early innovators and a pioneer of the universally popular 4-4-2 formation. The Russian was the first manager to introduce a pressing style of play, based on speed and fitness, which has been copied by many of the game's most successful teams. Maslov enjoyed plenty of domestic success, winning USSR Championships with Torpedo Moscow, Dynamo Kiev and Ararat Yerevan.

## HERBERT CHAPMAN

A legendary English manager who won two consecutive league titles with Huddersfield Town, before guiding Arsenal to two league titles and the FA Cup, Herbert Chapman was an expert team-builder whose tactical acumen and ability to find the most functional formation for the players at his disposal made him arguably the first great manager of the British game.

He took charge of Huddersfield in 1921 and at the end of his first season, guided the team to FA Cup glory with a 1-0 win over Preston North End. Huddersfield won their first League titles in 1924 and 1925. Chapman moved to Arsenal and soon transformed the Gunners' fortunes, adapting to the new offside rules brought in ahead of the 1925/26 season to field his fabled 'WM' formation, which comprised of a 3-4-3 line-up.

Arsenal claimed its first trophy under Chapman in 1930, beating his former charges Huddersfield in the FA Cup Final. A year later, he guided the Gunners to their first League title, with a record 66 points. Arsenal were league and FA Cup runners-up in 1932, but reclaimed the title in 1933.

## ROBERTO SCARONE RIVERA

One of the most prolific club managers in the South American game, Roberto Scarone Rivera had domestic success in three countries, winning nine league titles and leading Peñarol, the powerhouse of Uruguayan football, to Copa Libertadores and Intercontinental Cup glory.

Scarone Rivera took charge of his first club, Gimnasia, in 1948 and went on to manage in several countries, including Colombia, Chile and Peru. He enjoyed Peruvian league title success with Centro Iqueño and Universitario, lifting the trophy on three occasions with the latter club. A Mexican league title was claimed in 1965 with America, but Scarone Rivera's most prolific spell came while in charge at Peñarol, who he managed between 1959 and 1962, winning six major honours, including three consecutive Uruguayan league titles, a pair of Copa Libertadores trophies and the 1961 Intercontinental Cup, defeating Benfica 5-1 over two legs.

His team developed into a powerful, battle-hardened unit and only missed out on a treble of Copa Libertadores titles after being denied by Santos in 1962. Ten years later, the Uruguayan taskmaster came close to an even more remarkable feat, when he inspired Universitario to the final of the same competition. His team narrowly lost 2-1 on aggregate to Independiente, but became the first Peruvian side to reach the South American showpiece.

## LUIS CARNIGLIA

Managerial success came quickly for Luis Carniglia, whose first club Nice won the

1955/56 French Ligue 1 title during his first season in charge. Spanish giants Real Madrid noted his potential and enticed the Argentine to the Bernabéu midway through the 1956/57 campaign.

At Madrid, Carniglia inherited a team filled with some of the greatest names in world football including Alfredo Di Stéfano, Francisco Gento and Raymond Kopa, with the awesome talents of Ferenc Puskás arriving a year into the manager's spell in Spain.

Noted for his defensive acumen, Carniglia helped ensure a stable base for Puskás and Di Stéfano, who were assisted by the likes of Gento, Kopa, Héctor Rial and José Santamaria, to ensure Madrid was one of the greatest teams of all time.

Real played breathtaking, attacking football and, mixed with Carniglia's pragmatism, continued to dominate in Europe. They won the European Cup in 1958, following a 3-2 victory over AC Milan, and retained the trophy a year later thanks to a 2-0 defeat of Reims. The 1958 La Liga title was also added but the controversial decision to leave star man Puskás out of the 1959 European Cup Final, alongside the failure to retain the Spanish title, cost Carniglia his job. Luis also won the 1961 European Fairs Cup with AS Roma and narrowly lost the 1963 Intercontinental Cup to Santos.

## OSVALDO ZUBELDIA

Osvaldo Zubeldia built one of Argentinean football's most successful teams with Estudiantes de La Plata, winning the national league title in 1968 and following it up with Copa Libertadores and Intercontinental Cup success. He also enjoyed domestic glory with another relatively small Argentine side, San Lorenzo de Almagro, and claimed two Colombian league titles with Atlético Nacional.

## BILL NICHOLSON

Bill Nicholson enjoyed a remarkable run with English side Tottenham Hotspur, guiding the north London outfit to a league and FA Cup double in 1961, as Spurs became the first English team to achieve the feat. Nicholson claimed another first in 1963 when Tottenham became the first English club to lift a European trophy, scoring 115 goals in a 42-game season and captured the FA Cup for good measure.

Just three seasons after becoming manager in 1958, Nicholson had transformed the team into champions, winning its first 11 games, scoring 115 goals over the course of a 42-game season and capturing the FA Cup for good measure.

Tottenham's double success of 1961 was followed up by further FA Cup glory in 1962, with Nicholson's Spurs reaching the European Cup semi-final, losing to eventual winners Benfica.

Nicholson got his hands on European silverware when the 1963 Cup Winners' Cup was delivered to White Hart Lane following victory over Atlético Madrid. A third FA Cup in seven years came in 1967, with two League Cups being claimed in 1971 and 1973, and a UEFA Cup in 1972.

## JOE MERCER AND MALCOLM ALLISON

During the same period that Bill Nicholson enjoyed so much success with Tottenham Hotspur, the managerial partnership of Joe Mercer and Malcolm Allison led Manchester City during the club's golden era, winning the league title, several FA and League Cups and conquering Europe by claiming the 1970 Cup Winners' Cup. After the pair left the club, it took City another 35 years to win a major honour.

## ALBERT BATTEUX

The most successful domestic manager in the French game, having won an impressive nine Ligue 1 titles, Albert Batteux also reached two European Cup Finals and coached the French national side to third place at the 1958 World Cup. As well as the trophies he collected, Batteux was a visionary. Passionate about bringing through young talent, such as Raymond Kopa, Just Fontaine and Michel Hidalgo, at Stade de Reims. His teams played a fast-paced, one-touch passing style, that took European football by storm. At Reims he built a side capable of competing with the very best and would have surely won a European Cup had he not been up against the great Real Madrid team that defeated them in the 1956 and 1959 finals.

Batteux later replicated Reims's domestic success at Saint-Étienne, creating another attractive, flair-filled team that won four consecutive Ligue 1 titles and two French Cups between 1967 and 1970.

## HENNES WEISWEILER

A serial winner who demanded attacking football from his players and enjoyed great success in his native Germany, as well as claiming domestic titles in Switzerland and the United States, Hennes Weisweiler is one of the most successful German coaches of all time.

Weisweiler's first great managerial success came with Borussia Mönchengladbach in the 1970s, when he won three Bundesliga titles, one German Cup and experienced glory in Europe by lifting the 1975 UEFA Cup. Borussia had only claimed one major honour until that point and were stranded in the second tier, but the club was transformed into a relentless winning machine following Weisweiler's appointment in 1964. His ability to develop youngsters became renowned and led to Mönchengladbach being christened 'the Foals', a nickname that has remained since.

Following a disappointing two-year spell in charge of Barcelona, Weisweiler returned to his first club, FC Köln, winning another Bundesliga title and two German Cups. He spent a single season in the United States, guiding New York Cosmos to the North American Soccer League Championship before winning a Swiss League and Cup double with Grasshopper Zürich in 1983.

## DETTMAR CRAMER

Known as the 'Football Professor' due to his obsessive attention to detail, Dettmar Cramer was another vastly successful German manager. As boss of Bayern Munich, Cramer won back-to-back European Cups in 1975 and 1976 as well as the Intercontinental Cup. He also coached at international level for Germany and is credited for helping Japanese football to develop, having coached the national side at the 1960 Olympics.

## SIR ALF RAMSEY

Sir Alf Ramsey guided England to their only ever World Cup win—the country's singular success in a major tournament—so the mild-mannered former Ipswich Town boss came extremely close to being named in the top 30.

Ramsey retired from playing in 1955 and took over at Ipswich Town in the Third Division South. His first two seasons in charge resulted in promotion and the club stabilised in the Second Division for another three years before winning the title in 1961 and reaching the top flight. Amazingly, in their first season at the highest level of English football, Ipswich's tactics and industry surprised the country's biggest clubs, and Ramsey's side won the First Division title, despite being widely tipped for relegation.

Ramsey took over as England manager in 1963 and immediately proclaimed England would win the 1966 World Cup, which was to be held on home soil. He implemented the system that had brought him so much success at Ipswich, and England became famed for playing a narrower formation, which saw the team labelled as the 'wingless wonders'.

In 1966, the manager was true to his promise and following vital wins over Portugal and Mexico, England went on to defeat West Germany 4-2 after extra time in the final, signalling the most famous moment in English football history.

As well as the World Cup win, England reached the quarter-finals of the 1968 and 1972 European Championships under Ramsey. The side also came close to defending their title as World Champions in 1970, when they withered in the Brazilian heat and lost 3-2 to West Germany in the quarter-final, despite being 2-0 ahead at one stage.

## STEFAN KOVÁCS

The man who maintained the success of the great Ajax side of the 1970s and arguably the best Romanian manager of all time, Stefan Kovács lifted 11 major honours in his career, including two European Cups. Kovács managed in his homeland in the early 1950s, going on to taste his first sustained success with Steaua Bucharest, a club he led to the league title and two Romanian Cups.

In 1971, Kovács took over a hugely talented Ajax side crafted by the great Rinus Michels. He inherited a team filled with flair and an extremely well-run club that had just lifted the European Cup for the first time in its history. He went on to enjoy remarkable success, leading the Dutch giants to consecutive European Cups in 1972 and 1973, with the treble of Dutch League title, Dutch Cup and European Cup claimed in his first season. Stefan also won the Intercontinental Cup and European Super Cup.

Kovács remained in Amsterdam for just two trophy-filled years, then became manager of the French national side. He later coached Romania and achieved Greek Cup success with Panathinaikos.

## RAYMOND GOETHALS

A distinctive character in and out of the dugout, Raymond Goethals began his coaching career in Belgian lower-league football, before taking charge of Sint-Truiden and guiding them to second place in the First Division in 1966. Two years later, he was named head coach of the Belgium national team and went on to ensure the nation's qualification for the 1970 World Cup before inspiring them to third place in the 1972 European Championships.

Goethals returned to club football in 1976 with Brussels-based Anderlecht and reached the final of the European Cup Winners' Cup during his first season in charge. Anderlecht lost to SV Hamburg, but having reclaimed their national cup, returned to the final the following year and defeated FK Wein.

Raymond went to France with Bordeaux then to Brazil with São Paulo, but after limited success he returned to Belgium as manager of Standard Liège, with whom he lost the 1982 European Cup Winners' Cup final to Barcelona. Under Goethals, Liège won two Belgian Championships, including the 1982 title that was later shrouded in controversy after the manager had been linked with bribing players from Anderlecht's final opponents of the season. Forced to resign, Goethals went on to manage in Portugal before returning to his homeland and eventually taking charge of Anderlecht for the second time, winning two Belgian Cups.

He later led Bordeaux to second place in the French top flight, finishing below champions Marseille, a club he went on to manage the following season. Goethals plotted the club's journey to European glory, reaching the 1991 European Cup Final before losing to Red Star Belgrade on penalties. His team went one better in 1993 and defeated AC Milan in the final. Goethals then returned to Anderlecht, winning another league title in 1994.

## LUIS ALONSO PÉREZ

Brazil's most successful club manager, Luis Alonso Pérez won five successive

Brazilian championships between 1961 and 1965 and consecutive Copa Libertadores crowns during a 12-year spell with Santos. During this time, Pérez had the good fortune of being able to call upon the considerable services of one of the game's all time greats, Pelé. His record of five successive Brazilian Championships remain unequalled, as does his feat of winning the hugely competitive Copa Libertadores two years in a row. Pérez also presided over consecutive Intercontinental Cup glories in 1962 and 1963.

## DON REVIE

A man whose managerial talent is often overshadowed by his great Leeds United side's combative reputation, as well as the controversial circumstances that surrounded his exit as England manager, Don Revie remains one of the most successful British bosses of all time.

Revie was named Leeds United player-manager in 1961 and made radical changes at the club, introducing a youth team and changing the team's home kit from blue and yellow to all-white, mirroring the image of the great Real Madrid.

Within three years, Revie won the Second Division title and took Leeds into the First Division, where he began to reap the rewards of the youth system he had implemented. Despite his Leeds United side being criticised in many quarters for their aggressive nature and applying pressure to referees during the 1970s, Revie's men also played with style, dominating the English game for a number of years and winning the European Inter-Cities Fairs Cup twice. In 1968 Leeds won the League Cup and European Fairs Cup. The First Division title followed a year later, with another Fairs Cup in 1971 and the FA Cup in 1972.

Leeds won back the league title in 1974 under the forthright and proud Revie, who famously endured an almost toxic rivalry with the charismatic Brian Clough. After claiming the 1974 First Division crown, Revie became England manager; taking the one job Clough craved above all others. Under Revie, England failed to qualify for the 1976 European Championship and the 1978 World Cup. He then secured a lucrative role in the United Arab Emirates.

## TOMISLAV IVIC

An innovative tactician and strategist, Tomislav Ivic managed in 14 different countries during a distinguished career that also saw him coach four national sides. Ivic's early success came in his native Yugoslavia where he led Hajduk Split to three league titles and four Yugoslav Cups during the 1970s.

Ivic went on to win top-flight titles in Holland, Belgium, Greece and Portugal, also achieving European Super Cup and Intercontinental Cup glory with FC Porto in 1987. His last domestic trophy came in Spain, when he guided Atlético Madrid to the 1991 Copa del Rey.

## AIMÉ JACQUET

The phlegmatic Frenchman guided his country to its first ever World Cup victory when Les Bleus lifted the trophy on home soil in 1998. Jacquet began his managerial journey at Olympique Lyonnais, going on to enjoy great domestic success with Bordeaux during the 1980s, winning three French titles, two French Cups and leading the club to two European Cup semi-finals. In 1991 he accepted a position at the French Football Federation's National Technical Training Centre, becoming assistant manager of the French national side a year later. In 1994 Jacquet became caretaker and eventually full-time manager.

Jacquet introduced a group of hugely talented youngsters, including Zinedine Zidane, Youri Djorkaeff and Bixente Lizarazu, taking a relatively inexperienced squad to the 1996 European Championships. There France reached the semi-finals, only losing on penalties to the Czech Republic. Two years later, the experience gained by his well-organised and energetic young team served them well when the team reached the final of the 1998 World Cup, which was held on home soil, emphatically defeating reigning world champions Brazil 3-0.

## MIRCEA LUCESCU

Mircea Lucescu has enjoyed great success at a number of European clubs and is currently in charge of an emerging Shakhtar Donetsk team that has become the dominant force in Ukrainian football. Lucescu first came to prominence as manager of the Romanian national side in 1981 and with Dinamo Bucharest in his homeland, which he guided to league and cup success, as well as the semi-finals of the European Cup Winners' Cup. He spent much of the 1990s in Italy, claiming the Serie B title with Brescia and achieving stability with the likes of Reggiana and Pisa before managing Inter Milan. Title successes in Romania and Turkey followed before he claimed 13 Ukrainian League titles, five Ukrainian Cups and the 2009 Europa League with Shakhtar.

## EMERICH JENEI

Just like Lucescu, Romanian manager Emerich Jenei enjoyed prolific success in his homeland, winning four league titles with Steaua Bucharest and the 1986 European Cup, defeating Barcelona in the final. He later took charge of the Romanian national side on two occasions and achieved qualification for the 1990 World Cup; the first time the nation had reached the tournament in 20 years. Under his charge, Romania later progressed to the quarter-finals of Euro 2000.

## GUUS HIDDINK

The much-travelled Dutch manager won multiple league titles in his homeland with PSV Eindhoven before continuing the winning habit in Spain and England and enjoying international success while in charge of Holland, South Korea, Australia and Russia.

Hiddink's first managerial role came with PSV Eindhoven where he created a team fit to dominate both domestically and in Europe. His side claimed the treble of Eredivisie, Dutch Cup and European Cup in 1988. Less-successful spells in Turkey with Fenerbahçe and in Spain with Valencia followed before Hiddink was named manager of the Dutch national side in 1995.

Hiddink built a team unit that allowed many different personalities and talents to flourish, reaching the quarter-finals of the 1996 European Championship and the World Cup semi-finals two years later. After the World Cup, Hiddink endured two disappointing and short-lived spells with Spanish clubs, losing his job at both Real Madrid and Real Betis. Next stop on the Hiddink managerial world tour was South Korea, as he took charge of the joint World Cup hosts ahead of the 2002 tournament. Putting together a team filled with pace and endurance, which fed off the enthusiasm of the South Korean public, Hiddink's side defeated Poland and Portugal, before eliminating Italy and Spain and eventually losing to Germany in the semi-finals.

After the World Cup, Hiddink returned to PSV Eindhoven and added another three Dutch league titles, the 2005 Dutch Cup and reached the semi-finals of the 2004/05 Champions League. In 2005 Guus became head coach of Australia, guiding the Socceroos to the World Cup for the first time in 32 years. At the tournament, the side battled hard to reach the second round. Another international post followed, as Hiddink became manager of Russia and reached the semi-finals of the 2008 European Championships, their best showing at a major championship for 20 years. Hiddink also won the 2008 English FA Cup during an interim role with London club Chelsea.

## SVEN-GÖRAN ERIKSSON

Sophisticated Swede Sven-Göran Eriksson first impressed in his homeland with IFK Göteborg, winning the 1979 Swedish Cup and the treble of Swedish League, Swedish Cup and UEFA Cup in 1982. Eriksson then won the Portuguese Primeira Liga and the Portuguese Cup with Benfica, and reached the finals of the UEFA and European Cup.

Eriksson won the Coppa Italia with Roma before returning to Benfica, reaching another European Cup Final in 1990 and winning another league title in 1991.

A return to the Italian Serie A came in 1992 when Eriksson won the 1994 Coppa Italia with Sampdoria before being appointed Lazio boss in 1997, where he crafted a dangerous attacking side that won the Coppa Italia, Italian Super Cup and European Cup Winners' Cup, before capping it all by winning the 2000 Serie A title, claiming the Scudetto for only the second time in the club's history.

In 2000, Eriksson was named England boss, becoming the first man from outside of the country to manage the national side. He enjoyed an impressive record of qualification for major championships, with England reaching the 2002 and 2006 World Cups, as well as Euro 2004. However, each tournament ultimately ended in disappointment at the quarter-final stage, with a second consecutive penalty shootout defeat to Portugal at the 2006 World Cup signalling the end of Sven's journey with England.

## LUIZ FELIPE SCOLARI

Luiz Felipe 'Big Phil' Scolari began his managerial career in Brazil, winning the Alagoano state championship with Centro Sportivo Alagoano, moving on to gradually bigger to clubs and managing in Saudi Arabia before taking charge of Grêmio where he won the Gaucho state championship. He later recaptured the same trophy with Goiás.

After a two-year spell in Kuwait, Scolari returned to his homeland to coach Criciúma, which he led to its first major national title, the Copa do Brasil. Big Phil endured further success in the Middle East and in Brazilian club football throughout the 1990s, winning six major trophies with Grêmio in just three years, including the 1995 Copa Libertadores.

Scolari later tasted further domestic success in his homeland with Palmeiras, where he claimed another Copa Libertadores and reached the final of the 1999 Intercontinental Cup.

Scolari was named head coach of the Brazilian national side in June 2001 and created a cohesive and consistent unit, harnessing the huge potential of the likes of Ronaldo, Rivaldo and Ronaldinho to bring home the 2002 World Cup, defeating Germany 2-0 in the final.

Scolari later took charge of the Portuguese national side, guiding them to the final of the 2004 European Championships, the semi-finals of the 2006 World Cup and the quarter-finals of Euro 2008, his last major championships in charge.

Short spells with Chelsea and Uzbekistani champions Bunyodkor preceded a return to Brazil with Palmeiras, where he won the Copa do Brasil. Scolari was re-appointed coach of the Brazilian national team in November 2012 and defeated Spain to win the 2013 Confederations Cup.

## CARLOS ALBERTO PARREIRA

Brazilian Carlos Alberto Parreira guided the 'Seleção' the 1994 World Cup. While he enlisted a more pragmatic approach than usually implemented by Brazilian sides, he also utilised the considerable attacking talents of Romário and Bebeto. In a second spell as national boss, he won the 2005 Confederations Cup. As a club manager, Parreira won league titles and cup competitions in his homeland, Spain, Turkey and the Middle East.

## ARSÈNE WENGER

Known as 'the professor' due to his advanced theories and considered approach to the game, Arsène Wenger has revolutionised Arsenal and had a major bearing on the modernisation of English football, winning several league titles for the Gunners while playing free-flowing, attractive football.

Wenger's first managerial success came with AS Monaco, winning the Ligue 1 title at the end of his first season in charge. He went on to secure the 1991 French Cup and reach the final of the European Cup Winners' Cup, losing 2-0 to Werder Bremen.

Monaco reached the semi-finals of the 1994 European Champions League, but following a poor start to the 1994/95 season, Wenger was sacked. After a year coaching in the Japanese J League with Nagoya Grampus Eight, Wenger joined Arsenal in 1996 and soon transformed the club, improving preparation for games, the players' diet and training techniques. At the end of his second season in charge, the 1997/98 campaign, Arsenal became Premier League Champions and clinched the double following a 2-0 FA Cup Final defeat of Newcastle United.

Further second place finishes followed, with Arsenal also losing in the 2000 UEFA Cup and 2001 FA Cup finals as Wenger continued to develop the squad. Another double success was achieved in 2002 when the team pipped Manchester United to the title and defeated Chelsea 2-0 in the FA Cup Final.

More FA Cup success came in 2003 but the league was again lost to Manchester United. However, it proved to be a prelude to arguably the best campaign in the club's history as Arsenal went through the entire 2003/04 season unbeaten in the league, lifting the Premier League crown. On their way to lifting the trophy, the north London side played mesmerisingly fluid, attacking football.

The Gunners continued their unbeaten record into the following season, eventually clocking up 49 league games without defeat. Another FA Cup was sealed in 2005, but that has proved to be Arsenal's last major trophy under Wenger to date. The Gunners reached the final of the 2006 Champions League but lost 2-1 to Frank Rijkaard's Barcelona in Paris.

It is testament to Wenger's ability to sign lesser-known and lesser-paid players, while still blending them into an entertaining attacking unit, that he has managed to continuously participate in European football's premier competition, finance the move to a new purpose-built 60,000-capacity stadium and remain competitive with bigger-spending clubs.

## CARLOS BIANCHI

The most successful club manager in South American history, Carlos Bianchi has enjoyed multiple glories in South America, also winning the Intercontinental

Cup on four occasions; a record. The Argentine started coaching in France with Stade de Reims and Nice. His first period of sustained success came in his homeland with Vélez Sarsfield, winning Primera División glory in the Clausura in 1993 and 1996 and Apertura in 1995. He added a treble of cup trophies in 1994, with the Copa Libertadores, Intercontinental Cup and Interamerican Cup.

A meticulous planner and lucid tactician, renowned for bringing former greats of South American football back to their best, Bianchi's achievements with Vélez are all the more notable when considering that the club's last major honour before his appointment had come back in 1968.

After a short and ultimately fruitless spell in Italy with AS Roma, Bianchi returned to his homeland with Boca Juniors in 1998 and the constant flow of trophies continued. He won two Copa Libertadores, three Primera Divisions and one Intercontinental Cup, before leaving the club for a short period and claiming another treble of league, Copa Libertadores and Intercontinental Cup upon his return. A failed spell with Atlético Madrid was followed by six years out of club management before Bianchi returned as Boca Juniors' boss in 2012.

## KENNY DALGLISH

A supremely talented footballer, Kenny Dalglish also enjoyed an impressive managerial career, starting his journey in the dugout as a player-boss with Liverpool in 1985, guiding the English club to the league and cup double at the end of his first season in charge.

Dalglish added another league title in 1988, as Liverpool topped the table for almost the whole season and went 37 games unbeaten in all competitions, eventually losing just two of their 40 league games. The Reds also reached the FA Cup Final that season, memorably losing 1-0 to rank outsiders Wimbledon.

However, the tragic story of that season's competition came at the semi-final stage, when Liverpool faced Nottingham Forest at Sheffield Wednesday's Hillsborough Stadium. The game had to be abandoned after overcrowding in the Leppings Lane end of the ground crushed hundreds of Liverpool fans. The disaster led to 96 Liverpool fans losing their lives, with many others injured. Dalglish attended many of the victims' funerals, providing a heroic presence during the club and the city's darkest days.

Liverpool went on to lift the Cup a year later, defeating Merseyside rivals Everton 3-2 in the final, but the league title was lost to Arsenal. Liverpool reclaimed the First Division crown in 1990 at the end of what proved to be the last season of Kenny's first Liverpool reign. Dalglish returned to management in 1991, taking charge of Second Division Blackburn Rovers. Bankrolled by owner Jack Walker's millions, the Scotsman took the Lancashire club into the top flight via the play-offs, then guided Rovers to the 1994/95 Premier League title. Disappointing roles with Newcastle United and Celtic followed, before a romantic return to the Liverpool dugout in 2001. Dalglish claimed another major trophy for the Reds in 2011 when they defeated Cardiff City to lift the League Cup. However, Dalglish's second tenure proved to be short-lived and he was given his marching orders in May 2012.

## WALTER SMITH

Walter Smith enjoyed almost unparalleled success with Rangers, ensuring the Glasgow club were Scotland's dominant force for the best part of a decade, winning 10 Premier League titles during his two spells at the helm, including seven on the bounce in the 1990s. This completed a total of nine consecutive Scottish Championships in a row, equalling a record previously held by Celtic. During that time, Rangers won a domestic treble of league, Scottish Cup and League Cup in 1992/93 and also impressed in the European Champions League.

## FATIH TERIM

Turkey's most successful manager of all time, Fatih Terim has won multiple league titles with Galatasaray. His career began with modest success at club level before he became the Turkish national side's assistant manager and coach of the under-21s in 1990. He was promoted to head coach of the senior side in 1993 and successfully guided Turkey to the 1996 European Championships; the first time the nation had reached a major tournament.

Terim then took charge of Galatasaray, winning four consecutive Turkish league titles and the 2000 UEFA Cup, defeating Arsenal in the final. Known as 'the Emperor' in Turkey, Terim also had short-term spells with Fiorentina and AC Milan.

Fatih was reunited with Galatasaray in 2002, but with the club struggling financially their boss was unable to recapture the magic of his first spell in charge and quit in 2004. He returned to international management in 2005 with Turkey and guided the team to the semi-finals of the 2008 European Championships. In 2011, Terim agreed to a third spell with Galatasaray and won the Turkish Super League in 2012 and 2013.

## MANUEL PELLEGRINI

Manuel Pellegrini's enjoyed club success with Universidad Católica in his native Chile and became assistant coach of the national team in 1990. Having lifted the Chilean Cup and the Copa Interamericana and finished as league runners-up, Manuel won the Ecuadorian national tile with Liga Deportiva Universitaria de Quito and added further domestic honours in Argentina with San Lorenzo and River Plate. In Europe he impressed with Spanish La Liga sides Villarreal and Malaga, taking both clubs into the later stages of the Champions League. Pellegrini also experienced a season as Real Madrid boss when his team amassed a record 96 points but were pipped to the title by a brilliant Barcelona team that hit the 99-point mark. Manuel was appointed Manchester City manager in the summer of 2013.

## VANDERLEI LUXEMBURGO

The most successful manager in the history of the Brazilian Serie A, having claimed five league titles, Vanderlei Luxemburgo has also won 13 State Championships and guided the Brazilian national side to Copa America glory. Like Pellegrini he had a short spell with Real Madrid, lasting just over a season with the Spanish giants and leading them to a La Liga runners-up spot behind Barcelona.

## RAFA BENÍTEZ

Famed for his penchant for rotating teams and obsessive attention to tactical detail, Rafa Benítez enjoyed great success in Spain, winning the La Liga and the UEFA Cup with Valencia before lifting the 2005 Champions League with an unfancied Liverpool side.

Benítez started coaching at Real Madrid, taking charge of the B team before managing a number of smaller Spanish sides, leading both Extremadura and CD Tenerife to promotion. His first big job came with Valencia in 2001, inheriting a talented team built by former boss Héctor Cúper that had reached the previous two Champions League Finals. Benítez achieved what his predecessor could not do and finished above Real Madrid and Barcelona to win La Liga, both in 2002 and 2004. The earlier league success marked Valencia's first league title in 31 years, with the latter also being accompanied by the 2004 UEFA Cup.

Rafa was appointed as Liverpool manager in 2004 and his first season ended in a miraculous Champions League Final victory over AC Milan when Liverpool overcame a 3-0 first half deficit to eventually win on penalties. Benítez became only the third Liverpool manager to win the European Cup as the Merseysiders lifted the trophy for the fifth time.

Benítez gradually improved Liverpool's standing in the Premier League, claiming the FA Cup in 2006 and going on to reach another Champions League Final a year later, this time losing 2-1 to AC Milan. Liverpool finished the 2008/09 Premier League campaign as runners-up to Manchester United, marking their most consistent league campaign for over a decade. However, with boardroom issues clouding the picture, the Spaniard left the club by mutual consent following a disappointing 2009/10 campaign.

Rafa moved on to Inter Milan where he won the UEFA Super Cup and the World Club Championship, but was sacked halfway into his first season after struggling in the league and the Champions League.

Benítez was named Chelsea's interim manager in 2012 and went on to deliver a third-place finish as well as the 2013 Europa League before taking charge of Napoli.

## JOE FAGAN

Like Rafa Benítez, Joe Fagan won the European Cup at the end of his first season in charge of Liverpool. The Englishman managed his hometown club for two seasons in the 1980s, having been assistant manager for a decade. He lifted a treble of trophies in 1984 as the League title and League Cup were added to Europe's premier club accolade.

## ROBERTO MANCINI

A three-time Italian Serie A winner with Inter Milan, Roberto Mancini also claimed the English Premier League title with Manchester City in 2012, sealing the club's first championship victory after a 44-year drought.

As well as his league title successes, the Italian has gained a reputation as a cup specialist, reaching the semi-final or final of a major national cup competition in all of his seasons as a manager between 2002 and 2013.

## MARCELO BIELSA

Famed for his revolutionary formations and extreme analytical approach, while advocating a fast-paced attacking brand of play, Marcelo Bielsa has been labelled as the "best manager in the world" by Pep Guardiola, a man he heavily influenced. Bielsa had domestic success in South America and Europe, winning Primera División titles in his native Argentina and reaching the finals of the Copa del Rey and Europa League with Athletic Bilbao. He also led Argentina to Olympic gold.

# CHAPTER 2

## MANAGERS 30 – 26

# 30.NEREO ROCCO

**Born:** December 20, 1912 in Trieste, Austria-Hungary
**Died:** February 20, 1979, aged 66
**Clubs Managed:** Triestina, Treviso, Padova, AC Milan, Torino, Fiorentina
**Major Honours:** 10

One of the most successful Italian managers of all time, Nereo Rocco established AC Milan as Serie A's first domineering, premier club during three spells at the San Siro. An advocate of the 'catenaccio' tactical system originally implemented during his time at Padova and later used to great effect by Milan's city rivals, Internazionale, Rocco built a pragmatic yet sophisticated team that took the Rossoneri to new heights.

The catenaccio system, when translated from Italian means 'the chain', sees a deeper-lying defender or sweeper operate behind a defensive back three. It inspired a whole host of Italian clubs to play extremely conservatively, protecting the most slender of winning margins by playing a low-risk, slow-tempo style of play focused on ball retention and overloading the middle of the pitch.

Rocco enjoyed a 13-year playing career, representing top-flight Italian clubs such as Napoli and Padova and made a single international appearance for Italy. His first coaching role came with one of the lesser lights of Italian football, Triestina, which he took charge of in 1947.

Rocco guided Triestina to a highly unlikely and unprecedented second place finish in Serie A, toppling some of the biggest names in the division and achieving a league standing that remains the highest in the club's history. Following a disagreement with the northern Italian club's chairman, Rocco left the club for a brief spell with Treviso in 1951, before returning to Triestina two years later. It proved another short tenure, as Padova appointed him as their manager during the 1953/54 season.

At the time Padova were languishing at the wrong end of Serie B, Italian football's second tier, but Rocco transformed the club, avoiding relegation before achieving promotion to Serie A in 1955. The pragmatic coach went on to enjoy achievements similar to those he had realised at Triestina during a seven-year spell that is remembered as the most successful in Padova's history. With the catenaccio system the foundation of the club's success, the club established itself as a fixture in the top flight for the remainder of the 1950s and into the '60s, peaking with a third-place finish in 1958.

Rocco's ability to get the best out of relatively modest resources while building a cohesive and productive team unit saw his reputation enhanced season on season, culminating in his appointment as manager of AC Milan in 1961. That club had been successful domestically before Rocco's arrival, winning the Serie A title as recently as 1959, but had constantly failed in European competitions.

The supremely organised Rocco had an instant impact at the San Siro, leading AC Milan to the Serie A title at the end of his first season in charge in 1962. He went one step better the following year, guiding the Rossoneri to their first European Cup success.

In the 1963 final, held at Wembley Stadium, Milan faced the supremely talented Portuguese champions Benfica and largely kept the considerable attacking abilities of Eusébio, José Torres and António Simões quiet, despite the former opening the scoring just 18 minutes into the game. Showing the competitive spirit and resilience that Rocco's teams were famed for, Milan came back into the game in the second half, equalising and taking the lead through their Brazilian marksman José Altafini. Once the second goal went in, the Italians played stereotypical defensive football and held out to win the trophy by a single goal.

Rocco then left Milan for Torino to fulfil a promise he had made to the Turin club's president that he would become manager. This left AC's rivals Inter Milan and their own expert of the catenaccio style, Helenio Herrera, to dominate domestically and enjoy success in Europe. Rocco impressed at Torino, achieving the club's best results for years before a highly anticipated return to AC Milan in 1967.

Back at the San Siro, Rocco wasted no time in his continued pursuit of trophies, accumulating another Scudetto, as well as the European Cup Winners' Cup, when Hamburg SV were dispatched 2-0 in the final thanks to a brace from Swedish star Kurt Hamrin. In 1969, he guided Milan to another European Cup, when they played a more expansive game and destroyed an emerging Ajax side, containing a young Johan Cruyff, 4-1. The Milan hero on the day was Italian striker Pierino Prati, who scored a hat-trick.

More trophies followed for Milan and Rocco, with both the European Super Cup and the Intercontinental Cup delivered in 1969, the latter following a brutal two-legged victory over a combative Estudiantes side. The European Cup Winners' Cup was again lifted in 1973 with a 1-0 over Leeds United. This proved to be Rocco's last major honour at the San Siro, as he departed for the second time at the end of the season.

A single trophyless season with Fiorentina followed before Rocco returned for a third spell with AC Milan, becoming technical director and assistant to new manager Nils Liedholm.

As well as his almost unrivalled trophy success, the indomitable Rocco remains Milan's longest-serving manager, having led the club for 459 matches, comprising 323 as head coach and 136 as technical director. His critics would lambast the often defensive style of play that accompanied his successes, with many alleging that he cajoled his players into playing with an ultra-competitive attitude that verged on the combative.

In an era when physical contact was an accepted and expected element of the game, Rocco embraced that physicality to steamroller opponents. His teams had both the skill and cohesion to win games with attacking football and also the bloody-minded, fierce defensive nature and will to win, to grind out results when required.

Inter Milan boss Helenio Herrera may have perfected the catenaccio approach, but it was Nereo Rocco who first implemented it to garner success in Italy. He is as responsible as anybody for giving Italian football an identity and reputation, both good and bad, that has remained for generations. Rocco was a manager capable of getting the best out of limited resources at smaller clubs and later maximising the potential of bigger clubs, creating a winning mentality at AC Milan in his three spells at the San Siro, which came to form the club's philosophy. A single-minded innovator, expert motivator and a winner, Nereo Rocco oozed managerial class.

# 29. SIR BOBBY ROBSON

**Born:** February 18, 1933 in County Durham, England
**Died:** July 31, 2009, aged 76
**Clubs Managed:** Fulham, Ipswich Town, PSV Eindhoven, Sporting Lisbon, FC Porto, Barcelona, Newcastle United
**International:** England: 1982-1990 (Reached the semi-final of the 1990 World Cup)
**Major Honours:** 10

Affectionately remembered by players, managers and supporters, Sir Bobby Robson was a true English gentleman and a football man through and through. A rarity for an English manager and something of a trailblazer, Robson was happy to ply his trade away from his homeland, going on to enjoy success with some of the biggest clubs in Europe. Tactically astute, a good communicator—despite his penchant for mixing players' names up—and a canny judge of a footballer, Bobby Robson was an expert team builder who understood how to get the very best out of individuals and shape them into a cohesive formation.

A large proportion of his managerial career was spent as the head coach of the England national side, which he led to three major championships, enjoying particular success at the World Cup. His ability to adapt his methods in different footballing cultures, combined with his longevity and a fair few trophies along the way, made him one of the most successful English coaches of the last 30 years.

A talented footballer, Bobby Robson spent the majority of his playing days as an inside forward with Fulham and West Bromwich Albion in the English First Division. He went on to play 20 times for England and experienced a short spell as player-manager of Canadian side Vancouver Royals before he became Fulham manager in 1968.

Robson inherited a struggling team and, unable to keep Fulham in the First Division, he was later sacked with the team sitting eighth in the second tier. His next role came with Ipswich Town and it was this job that helped him make his mark. The Suffolk club had been in decline since England's World Cup-winning manager, Sir Alf Ramsey, had left in 1963. Robson took four seasons to turn them around, leading them to an impressive fourth place finish in the First Division and lifting the Texaco Cup during the 1972/73 campaign.

Robson continued to ensure that the Tractor Boys punched above their weight for the best part of a decade, with Ipswich only finishing lower than sixth in the top flight once in nine seasons. The 1977/78 campaign saw Ipswich lift the FA Cup for the first time in their history, following a tough 1-0 victory over Arsenal at Wembley.

As well as that cup final success, the most notable feats from the Geordie's time in charge of Ipswich were the two First Division runners-up spots he achieved in 1981 and 1982, and winning the UEFA Cup in 1981. In his 13-year spell in charge of the club, Robson built a team filled with graduates from a successful youth team, supplemented with astute foreign signings, such as the Dutch pair, Arnold Mühren and Frans Thijssen. In an era when few players from outside of Britain and Ireland plied their trade in England, Robson embraced the different style offered by continental players, whose enhanced tactical awareness and technique on the ball gave Ipswich another dimension.

While Mühren and Thijssen, and the likes of Paul Mariner and Bryan Hamilton, proved to be great additions by Robson, they were four of just 14 players he brought into the club during his 13 years in charge. The shrewd manager preferred to develop the considerable young talent at his disposal, establishing the likes of Terry Butcher, George Burley, John Wark and Kevin Beattie in the first team.

Robson's tactical nous bore fruit during the 1981 UEFA Cup win, as his team operated with a more continental style of play and enjoyed an impressive run to the final, which included a 7-2 aggregate quarter-final victory over a Saint-Étienne team featuring Michel Platini. German side FC Köln were dispatched 2-0 on aggregate in the semi-finals to set up a two-legged final with AZ Alkmaar of the Netherlands. After two thrilling encounters, the English team ran out 5-4 winners, thanks to a 3-0 victory at Portman Road, which featured goals from Wark, Thijssen and Mariner.

Bobby's superb record with Ipswich saw him offered the England manager's job in 1982. Robson began with a solid qualifying campaign for the 1984 European Championships, but a single loss in 28 matches against Denmark saw the Three Lions miss out on the tournament. The qualification process for the 1986 World Cup was successfully negotiated and despite a slow start during the tournament proper, which was being held in Mexico, Robson's men reached the quarter-finals of the competition.

England's progress owed heavily to the goalscoring exploits of prolific striker Gary Lineker, who Robson had chosen to pair with Peter Beardsley rather than Mark Hateley as the tournament progressed. In one of the most controversial World Cup contests of all time, England gave their all against a talented, Diego Maradona-inspired, Argentina in a quarter-final clash played in oppressive Mexican heat. The South Americans took a controversial lead, when Maradona infamously challenged England goalkeeper Peter Shilton for the ball, made intentional contact with his fist and punched the ball into the net. Despite the appeals of the English players the goal stood. The incident was later labelled the "Hand of God" by the culprit himself.

The Argentines dominated possession for large periods of the game. Maradona was the orchestrator of all of the team's attacking play and went on to double his team's advantage by scoring one of the greatest goals of all time. The stocky number 10 picked up the ball inside his own half before dancing and slaloming past countless English opponents, jinking into the area, deceiving Shilton and guiding the ball home. England rallied thanks to a late goal from Gary Lineker, but was bundled out of the tournament.

Robson's England qualified for Euro 1988 in emphatic fashion, dropping just a single point en route to the championships in West Germany. However, during the tournament itself, the team played poorly and finished bottom of their qualifying group following three straight defeats. The press called for the manager's head, and despite Robson offering his resignation, the FA continued to give him their full backing, a decision they were rewarded for just two years later as England enjoyed their most successful World Cup campaign since lifting the trophy in 1966.

The Three Lions began Italia '90 in an effective but uninspiring manner, producing draws with Ireland and Holland, and a narrow victory over Egypt. During the tournament, Robson made the bold but insightful tactical decision to transform England's traditional 4-4-2 formation to a strategy that featured three central defenders and included a sweeper. The new line-up gave England's experienced and technically gifted players the licence to express themselves and helped the Three Lions play with more fluidity going forward.

England went on to enjoy a last-gasp victory over Belgium, then a topsy-turvy 4-2 win over one of the most impressive sides of the tournament, Cameroon, in the knockout stages to set up a semi-final encounter with West Germany. England gave as good as they got against the Germans, recovering from going a goal behind to take the game into extra-time and eventually penalties, when missed spot-kicks from Stuart Pearce and Chris Waddle sent England out and West Germany into the final, where they defeated Diego Maradona's Argentina by a single goal.

After a third place play-off loss to hosts Italy, England finished in fourth spot. However, the team's performances and the drama associated with it recaptured the nation's pride in its football team, as well as its joy for the game, paving the way for English football's golden era during the 1990s and into the 21st century. Robson remains only the second coach after Alf Ramsey to take England to a World Cup semi-final, and the only coach to do so on foreign soil.

Having been informed by the FA that his contract wouldn't be renewed following Italia '90, Robson opted to take his first managerial job outside of England when he was appointed head coach of PSV Eindhoven. Succeeding Guus Hiddink, who had won the 1988 European Cup and successive Eredivisie titles, Robson inherited a team filled with talented, yet temperamental players, including Brazilian hotshot Romário. The Englishman soon adapted tactically to the Dutch game and the demands of the players, taking PSV to Dutch league titles in both 1991 and 1992. However, after failing to impress in Europe, Robson left the club after just two seasons in charge to take up another continental coaching mission, this time in Portugal with Sporting Lisbon.

Acting as Robson's interpreter at the club was a young José Mourinho, who would go on to follow the Englishman to Barcelona, gradually becoming more and more immersed in the football and coaching side of the game, before carving out his own hugely successful career as a manager.

In Lisbon, Robson discovered a club he later described as being in a "terrible state", and a club president with a habit of signing players without his manager's consent. Despite guiding Sporting to third place in 1993 and to the top of the table during his second season in charge, Robson was sacked in December 1993 following a premature UEFA Cup exit.

Sporting's loss went on to be the gain of their fierce rivals, FC Porto, as Robson was appointed manager and transformed the struggling club into Portuguese Cup winners, beating Sporting in the final. League championships then followed in both the 1994/95 and 1995/96 campaigns. The Englishman soon became a firm fans' favourite at Porto, with supporters referring to him as 'Bobby Five-0' due to the frequency with which his team won games by a 5-0 scoreline. Another league title was delivered in 1996 before Robson was appointed as manager of Catalan giants Barcelona.

Robson made the hugely talented Brazilian striker, Ronaldo, his first major signing. The prodigiously skilled forward went on to play a major role in the three trophies collected by Robson during his single season as coach, as the Spanish Cup, Spanish Super Cup and European Cup Winners' Cup, were delivered. Ronaldo later labelled Robson — as "one of the greatest trainers in the world".

Robson moved upstairs to become Barça's general manager for the 1997/98 season, with Dutchman Louis van Gaal taking over as manager. However, after a single season in that role, Bobby opted to return to the dugout and to Holland with PSV on a short-term, single-season deal. At the end of the 1997/98 campaign, Robson claimed the Dutch Super Cup and guided PSV into the Champions League via a third-placed finish.

After departing Eindhoven, Robson returned to his homeland to take up a technical position with the English FA before becoming manager of his hometown club, Newcastle United, in September 1999. He inherited a team rooted to the bottom of the Premier League and a club in disharmony, with high-profile players such as Alan Shearer having fallen foul of the previous manager, Ruud Gullit. But Robson soon reignited the players' hunger, passion and pride to wear the black-and-white jersey.

He made an immediate impact as Newcastle won his first game in charge 8-0 and went on to finish the season in 11th place, winning 14 games. The following campaign saw Robson add younger, more energetic players, such as Craig Bellamy and Kieron Dyer, to the team and the Magpies responded, finishing fourth in the league and qualifying for the Champions League.

Robson guided the Magpies through the first qualifying group of Europe's premier club tournament in impressive fashion, defeating Italian giants Juventus 1-0, but the team faltered in the second group stage. Newcastle found the Champions League a tough challenge during the 2003/04 campaign and they were knocked out in the play-off stages, dropping into the UEFA Cup, where they reached the semi-final.

Working into his 70s, Robson continued to develop the north-eastern club, with Newcastle playing some of the most entertaining and aesthetically pleasing football seen at St James' Park since Kevin Keegan's time in charge, while also achieving consistent results. In August 2004, Bobby was surprisingly shown the door by Newcastle chairman Freddy Shepherd, a decision that would hamper the club for several seasons. That four-year spell with his local club proved to be Robson's last job as a football manager.

Bobby Robson showed the world of football that English coaches possessed the tactical acumen and knowledge required to succeed in other countries. He is famed for his popularity and loyalty to players, but his adaptability and decision making were just as impressive.

An expert man-manager, the style of play with which Robson's teams operated and his penchant for nurturing young talent are also notable qualities possessed by the likeable Geordie. Robson is also renowned for his ability to make the right signing at the right time, with some of the world's most talented footballers, such as Ronaldo and Ruud van Nistelrooy coming to prominence under his guidance.

Not many managers have been honoured by statues to recognise their achievements outside the stadiums of clubs they have worked for, but Bobby Robson has received that distinction with both Ipswich Town and Newcastle United. His achievements of guiding Ipswich Town to European success and England to the edge of the

World Cup Final, making him the second most successful Three Lions boss of all time, become even more notable as the years go by. A true gentleman of the game, Sir Bobby's impressive achievements are only dwarfed by his popularity.

# 28. MÁRIO ZAGALLO

**Born:** August 9, 1931 in Maceió, Brazil

**Clubs Managed:** Botafogo, Fluminense, Flamengo, Al-Hilal, Vasco da Gama, Bangu, Potuguesa

**International:** Brazil: 1967-1968, 1970-1974 and 1994-1998 (Won the 1970 World Cup and reached the 1998 World Cup Final); Kuwait: 1976; Saudi Arabia: 1981-1984; United Arab Emirates (1989-1990)

**Major Honours:** 8

A man synonymous with Brazilian football and the success of the country's national team at the World Cup, Mário Zagallo, nicknamed 'the professor' due to his tactical knowledge and understanding of the game became the first man to lift the trophy as both a player and a manager.

Following a distinguished playing career, Zagallo's first taste of management came with Botafogo in his homeland, which he took charge of in 1966 following a spell coaching the club's youth team. At Botafogo, Mário lifted his first managerial trophies, leading the club to consecutive Rio state championships and winning the Taça Brasil cup in 1968. Becoming a coach allowed Zagallo to introduce the strategies and philosophies he had thought so deeply about as a player, and his ability was soon noticed by the Brazilian FA, who appointed him as coach for a first and brief spell in 1967. He continued to succeed at club level and was appointed Brazil's head coach on a full-time basis ahead of the 1970 World Cup in Mexico.

Already blessed with a team of players brimming with magical talent, including greats such as Pelé, Jairzinho, Rivelino and Carlos Alberto, Zagallo created a formation and an ethos that allowed them to express their natural talents and flourish as part of a captivatingly brilliant team unit. The Brazilian's took the tournament by storm, winning all six of their matches and scoring 19 times, including some of the most memorable goals ever seen on the world stage.

The 1970 side is still considered by many observers to be the greatest football team of all time. It encapsulated individual brilliance with incisive and pleasing-on-the-eye passing, with every member of the starting 11 at complete ease in possession of a ball they treated with a level of respect and passion that verged on worship.

Key to Zagallo's tactical approach was giving his defensive players, particularly the full-backs, more licence to get forward and join the attack. This meant he could cram more creative talent into the team and seize the initiative more frequently in games. Another strength was his ability to knit such attacking brilliance together, with seemingly similar players, such as Pelé and Tostão, all accommodated and able to link-up to devastating effect. His 5-3-2 formation could became 3-5-2 on the balance of play and left even the most notable of opponents struggling to establish any kind of foothold in games.

The 1970 team's talent was exceptionally illustrated during that year's World Cup Final as they tore a normally resolute Italian side to shreds and won 4-1, with Carlos Alberto's drilled 86th minute effort, following a hypnotically brilliant passing move, later becoming one of the most replayed goals of all time.

Following the World Cup, Zagallo returned to club management in Brazil, while maintaining his role as national team coach. There the trophies continued to flow as he added further honours with both Fluminense and Flamengo. But Zagallo and Brazil struggled to defend their world crown during the 1974 tournament, following the retirement of several key players, and the side was knocked out in the second round by Holland.

That defeat signalled the end of Zagallo's reign in charge and prompted his full-time return to Botafogo before, in 1976, he took on his first coaching assignment outside of his homeland, becoming head coach of the Kuwait national side. He went on to win the Gulf Cup before lifting the Saudi Arabian league title with Al-Hilal, then becoming Saudi national coach and winning the Asian Cup in 1984.

He returned to Brazilian club football in the second half of the 1980s, before resuming his globetrotting coaching experience by becoming manager of the United Arab Emirates in 1989. Under Zagallo the UAE qualified for the 1990 World Cup, before he returned to Brazil for a brief spell in charge of Vasco da Gama.

In 1991, when Brazil's wait for a World Cup trophy had extended to 20 years; Zagallo was drafted in as technical director, alongside manager Carlos Alberto Parreira, ahead of USA 1994. There the team displayed a more defensive and functional approach, more in line with a European style of play. Brazil went on to win the tournament, defeating Italy on penalties in the final to give Zagallo the unique achievement of being involved in four of the nation's World Cup-winning teams.

A year later, Zagallo took over from Parreira and presided over a successful qualification for the 1998 World Cup and also claimed both the Copa America and Confederations Cup in 1997. With the mercurial talent of Ronaldo implemented in the team, ably backed up by the likes of Rivaldo, Cafu and Carlos Dunga, Brazil played some captivating football at the 1998 World Cup and reached the final, where they faced hosts France in Paris.

The build up to that game remains shrouded in controversy. With Ronaldo's physical condition in doubt hours before kick-off, Zagallo selected the striker. With the youngster and his team-mates clearly disrupted, Brazil were ineffectual 3-0 losers to a Zinedine Zidane-inspired France.

Zagallo again returned to club football in Brazil, before taking his final role with the national side in 2003 when he again became assistant coach to Carlos Alberto Parreira. Mário kept his place in the dugout for one last World Cup, the 2006 tournament held in Germany that saw Brazil exit to France in the quarter-finals. In total, he took charge of the Brazilian national side for 154 matches, winning an incredible 110 of them.

Zagallo's coaching career was the embodiment of a man at ease with being a footballing romantic and disciple of the beautiful game. But he was also sensible enough to be pragmatic and select a more defensive style, depending on the players at his disposal. With either approach the wily campaigner was keen to allow his players to express themselves and make tactical decisions on the field of play. Discussing his coaching style, Zagallo once said, "My own approach is to set out a plan and then leave the players complete freedom."

An innovator of many coaching principles and strategies that have remained in the modern-day game, such as the celebration of attacking full-backs, Zagallo was also fundamentally aware of the simplicity of football. One of the Brazilian's greatest attributes was his ability to translate his coaching principles throughout a whole host of different nations, enjoying success with both world class players and those of limited talent, the latter strength being illustrated by the feat of taking the UAE to the 1990 World Cup.

The only Brazilian manager to make the top 30, a statue of the great Mário Zagallo has been erected at the famous Maracanã stadium in Rio de Janeiro and provides a tangible and lasting illustration of how the 'godfather' of Brazilian football is revered in his homeland. His trophy-gathering may not have been prolific but the 1970 Brazil team that he perfected provided sheer sporting beauty.

# 27. JUPP HEYNCKES

**Born:** May 9, 1945 in Mönchengladbach, Germany
**Clubs Managed:** Borussia Mönchengladbach, Bayern Munich, Athletic Bilbao, Eintracht Frankfurt, Tenerife, Real Madrid, Benfica, Schalke 04, Bayer Leverkusen
**Major Honours:** 10

The vastly experienced German manager arguably realised his greatest achievement in what could prove to be his last season in the game, when he guided Bayern Munich to the treble of Bundesliga title, German Cup and European Champions League during the 2012/13 campaign.

After a prolific playing career at club and international level, Jupp Heynckes became assistant and eventually manager of Borussia Mönchengladbach, succeeding Udo Lattek as boss in 1979. Heynckes's first season in charge saw the team reach the final of the UEFA Cup which they lost to Eintracht Frankfurt.

Jupp continued to impress with his hometown club, launching a Bundesliga title challenge during the 1983/84 campaign before eventually finishing third, only losing the championship to VfB Stuttgart on goal difference and later missing out on German Cup success following defeat to Bayern Munich in the final.

Mönchengladbach's 1985/86 campaign under Heynckes included a 5-1 home victory over Real Madrid in the UEFA Cup, but a 4-0 away defeat in the second leg saw them exit on away goals. The following season, which proved to be the emerging manager's last in charge, saw Borussia claim another third-place league finish and reach the semi-final of the UEFA Cup. Despite not lifting a trophy during his time in charge, Heynckes' achievements with a team of such modest resources saw his managerial stock rise significantly and he was labelled "the champion without a title".

It was a tag he would soon shake off, following his appointment as Bayern Munich manager in 1987, where he again succeeded the outgoing Udo Lattek. Heynckes remained with Bayern until 1991, winning back-to-back titles in 1989 and 1990, and reaching the semi-finals of the 1989 UEFA Cup, and the 1990 and 1991 European Cup, losing to the eventual winners of the competition each time.

Despite a more than respectable record, Jupp was shown the door in October 1991 after a poor start to the season. Following his departure Bayern continued to struggle and even flirted with relegation, leading Munich's General Manager Uli Hoeness to describe the decision to remove Heynckes as "the biggest mistake of his career".

In 1992, the German took has first coaching assignment outside of his homeland when he was named manager of Athletic Bilbao in Spain. His first season ended in an eighth place finish before an improved fifth place was achieved in 1994, which saw the Basque club qualify for the UEFA Cup.

A return to Germany with Eintracht Frankfurt came later that year, but he lasted less than 12 months at the club, as clashes with star players such as Tony Yeboah and Jay-Jay Okocha undermined his position. Heynckes' next appointment was back in Spain when he took charge of CD Tenerife. He led the Canary Islands' outfit to fifth place in La Liga and into the UEFA Cup, a competition they reached the semi-finals of in 1997.

Heynckes's efforts with less-prominent Spanish sides, as well as his success with Bayern Munich, saw him offered arguably the biggest job in club football in June 1997, when he took over as Real Madrid manager. Despite leading Real to glory in the 1998 Champions League Final, thanks to a 1-0 victory over Juventus, secured by Pedrag Mijatovic's close range finish, he was sacked after a single campaign. It was Madrid's first European Cup success for

32 years and their seventh in total, but a fourth place La Liga finish, which left Real 11 points behind champions Barcelona, was deemed too much of a failure.

Heynckes took a year out of football before taking charge of Portuguese side Benfica ahead of the 1999/2000 season. It would again prove to be a single-season stay at a club for the German, who led the team to third place and an early UEFA Cup exit, before agreeing to leave by mutual consent at the end of the campaign.

Another short spell came with one of Heynckes's former clubs when he returned to Athletic Bilbao for the 2001/02 campaign. A ninth place finish saw the club narrowly miss out on the UEFA Cup. Bilbao reached the semi-finals of the Copa del Rey the same season before finishing seventh in 2002/2003. At the end of that campaign, Heynckes returned to his native Germany to become manager of Schalke 04, but things didn't work out back in the Bundesliga and after a seventh place standing in 2003/04 was followed by a slow start the next season, the axe fell on Jupp once again.

In May 2006 Heynckes returned to what he knew, taking charge of Borussia Mönchengladbach. Despite a promising start, it didn't prove to be a happy reunion after a second half of the season slump that saw the team go 14 games without victory, leding to his resignation. Following his departure, Mönchengladbach dropped out of the top flight at the end of the season.

Heynckes became caretaker-manager of Bayern Munich in April 2009, inheriting a team whose participation in the following season's Champions League was under threat due to their indifferent league form. Heynckes made a significant impact, leading Bayern to four wins and a draw, claiming second place in the Bundesliga and entry into the biggest competition in European football. In 2009 he signed a two-year deal to manage Bayer Leverkusen, where he made an immediate impact by inspiring the team to a record 24 Bundesliga games unbeaten, challenging Bayern Munich for the league title for much of the season before eventually finishing fourth.

Jupp's Leverkusen improved upon that fourth place with a runners-up spot in 2010/11, achieving the club's highest finish for nine years and reaching the Champions League for the first time since 2005. However, Heynckes opted to leave the club at the end of the season to take up the managerial reins at Bayern Munich for the third time in his career. It would prove a canny decision as the Bavarian giants went on to achieve unprecedented success.

Replacing Louis van Gaal at the helm at the age of 66 made Heynckes the oldest coach in the Bundesliga. He inherited a team that had finished a place below and three points behind his Leverkusen side. Heynckes had an array of talented players, including the likes of Arjen Robben and Franck Ribéry, as well as several German internationals. But his first two seasons in charge saw his side pitted against an extremely progressive and talented Borussia Dortmund team. Bayern battled hard against Borussia during the 2011/12 season but were ultimately unsuccessful, losing the Bundesliga title before suffering a chastening 5-2 defeat to the same opponents in the German Cup Final.

Munich fans could be forgiven for not being too distraught, though, as Heynckes' men had enjoyed an impressive Champions League campaign, culminating in a famous two-legged victory over Real Madrid in the semi-finals that saw Bayern reach their second European Cup Final in three seasons. The final was played at Munich's home ground against English side Chelsea.

The German giants went on to dominate the game, controlling possession and territory against a defensively minded Chelsea, creating chance after chance. Those opportunities were squandered for most of the match, until Bayern took an 83rd minute lead through Thomas Müller. Chelsea showed great spirit and equalised through Didier Drogba with just minutes remaining to take the game into extra-time. Bayern were the better side in the extra period and could've won the trophy had Arjen Robben successfully converted a penalty but Petr Cech saved his effort and the tie went to a penalty shoot-out.

Missed kicks from Ivica Olic and Bastian Schweinsteiger meant that Chelsea lifted the European Cup for the first time and

Bayern had to suffer the ignominy and agony of missing out on the great trophy on their home turf.

Buoyed by that disappointment, Heynckes and Munich went into the 2012/13 season with a renewed sense of purpose and a determination to reach the top of European football. Bayern went on to produce one of the most dominant Bundesliga campaigns in living memory, winning their first eight league matches and only suffering a single reverse all season. It was less a title race and more a procession as Munich built up a nine-point lead at the turn of the year and cruised to the championship, dropping just two further points and winning 14 consecutive matches. Bayern claimed the title on April 6, 2013, the earliest a team had ever won the Bundesliga. The side broke a whole host of records, including most points in a season with 91, the highest league winning points margin of 25, the most wins in a season, with 29, and the best goal difference in a season and fewest goals conceded, with just 18. The team also enjoyed the distinction of scoring in every single league match.

However, during that emphatically successful domestic campaign, it was announced that the highly-coveted former Barcelona boss, Pep Guardiola, would replace Heynckes at the Bayern Munich helm at the end of the season. Rather than unsettling Munich it galvanised the team and their dominant league form was matched by an equally impressive run of form in the Champions League.

Bayern were playing an aggressive and energetic, yet highly skilled and entertaining brand of football. Taking the high-pressing techniques that had given the modern Barcelona and Spain sides such great success, while combining it with the hardworking, uncompromising and highly-organised elements that had made the German game so successful, Bayern hunted in pairs for the ball and were incisive when they won it back. The silky and pacey skills of Arjen Robben and Franck Ribéry were afforded the license to express themselves, with both individuals also buying into the team ethic and committing to the tactical strategy implemented by Heynckes.

This style was demonstrated in stunning fashion during that season's Champions League semi-final tie with Barcelona, European Champions as recently as 2011 and the team that had reached levels of performance that verged on footballing paradise. Undeterred by the reputation of their opponents and riding the crest of a wave of confidence created by their domestic dominance, Bayern out-manoeuvred, out-thought and out-played their Catalan opponents, destroying them 4-0 at home and then 3-0 away to inflict a comprehensive 7-0 aggregate victory and tee up a final clash against fierce German rivals, Borussia Dortmund, at Wembley.

In the final, Bayern found Dortmund

in good form, and despite struggling to exert their usual influence on the game they battled to a 2-1 victory thanks to a late winner from Arjen Robben. Munich lifted their first European Cup since 2001, ensuring that Heynckes became just the fourth manager, after Ernst Happel, Ottmar Hitzfeld and José Mourinho, to have won the competition with two different clubs.

Heynckes and Munich still had one more trophy to add, as they went on to defeat VfB Stuttgart 3-2 in the German Cup Final, becoming the first German club to win the treble of Bundesliga, German Cup and European Cup in a single season. Bayern legend Franz Beckenbauer labelled Heynckes's side as "the best Bayern team ever", indicating the amazing legacy and platform that Jupp created for the incoming Pep Guardiola to build upon.

It's worth considering just what heights Heynckes and Munich could have reached if he had stayed with the club for longer periods and been afforded the opportunity to build an even larger dynasty of trophy success.

---

# 26. OTTO REHHAGEL

**Born:** August 9, 1938 in Essen, Germany
**Clubs Managed:** FV Rockenhausen, FC Saarbrücken, Kickers Offenbach, Borussia Dortmund, Arminia Bielefeld, Fortuna Düsseldorf, Werder Bremen, Bayern Munich, FC Kasierslautern, Hertha Berlin
**International:** Greece: 2001-2010 (Won the 2004 European Championships)
**Major Honours:** 12

An extremely resourceful manager with an ability to maximise the individual and collective talents of lesser teams, notably the Greek national side that he led to European Championship glory in 2004; Otto Rehhagel's longevity and versatility in the game is almost unrivalled.

The outspoken German began his managerial career in his homeland in 1974, taking charge of Kickers Offenbach.

Rehhagel's early experiences of management were unremarkable and he largely struggled to achieve success with the likes of Borussia Dortmund and Arminia Bielefeld, until he carved out a reputation as a shrewd operator during his time at Fortuna Düsseldorf.

During the 1979/80 campaign, his only season at the helm, Rehhagel led Fortuna to an 11th place finish and won the

German Cup, delivering a campaign that remains one of the most successful in the club's history. The achievement was made more notable due to the relatively modest playing squad he had at his disposal.

In 1981 Otto was appointed as Werder Bremen boss and went on to spend 14 years with the club, progressing a small unfashionable team into one of the most renowned in German football, implementing a powerful, high-tempo style of play built upon the foundations of a smothering defensive unit.

Werder regularly vied for Bundesliga and German Cup success during the 1980s but often fell at the final hurdle, until a first league title was claimed in 1988. Another Bundesliga was lifted in 1993, with Bremen also winning two German Cups under Rehhagel in the early 1990s. His side also won the 1992 European Cup Winners' Cup, defeating Arsène Wenger's Monaco 2-0 in the final to experience the club's first ever taste of European glory.

As well as creating several great teams during his Bremen tenure, Rehhagel was also responsible for the development of countless top players and future German internationals, including Rudi Völler, Karl-Heinz Riedle, Dieter Eilts and Mario Basler. The team's significant success was built on a solid defence, signified by their 1988 Bundesliga victory which saw them break the record for fewest goals conceded in a single season, just 22; a feat that remained unbroken until Bayern Munich bettered it

in 2013/14. Bremen also played expansive and adventurous football under Rehhagel, taking the greater creative risks afforded to them by having such a sound defensive foundation to rely on.

Rehhagel ended his tenure with Bremen, the second-longest spell by a manager at a single club in the Bundesliga, in 1995 to take charge of Germany's biggest club, Bayern Munich. Rehhagel and the club invested heavily in the squad, capturing notable talents such as Jürgen Klinsmann and Andreas Herzog as they attempted to dominate both domestically and in Europe. The new manager's first season was fraught with fractious controversy, as Rehhagel's single-minded approach and unique coaching methods saw him clash with some of Bayern's high-profile players. The fallout of the recurring fallouts was a disappointing Bundesliga season that was salvaged by the team's progress to the 1996 UEFA Cup Final. With three weeks to go before the European showpiece, Rehhagel was sacked and Franz Beckenbauer took over, taking his place in the dugout as the team lifted the trophy.

Rehhagel remained in German football, taking charge of a Kaiserslautern side on the decline having just experienced relegation to the second tier. The new boss took the team back into the Bundesliga at the first time of asking before achieving the unthinkable during the 1997/98 campaign and going on to claim the German league title; in a victory that remains the only Bundesliga crown captured by a promoted team. Despite achieving the kind of success that should've made his position at Kaiserslautern untouchable, internal politics and disagreements with players and staff led to Rehhagel's departure in 2000.

Otto took his first job outside of club football and outside of Germany, when he was appointed head coach of the Greek national team in 2001. The Greeks were struggling in their qualifying group for the 2002 World Cup and remained one of European football's poorest relations, but Rehhagel slowly took stock of the talent at his disposal, however limited it may have been, and began to create a competitive and hard-to-beat unit.

The size of his task was illustrated by a 5-1 defeat to Finland in his first game in charge, but a trip to England for a game that would decide the qualification fate of the hosts provided a prelude to what lay ahead. England, shrouded under a cloud of extreme pressure, struggled to express themselves and Greece made matters harder for them, defending in numbers, closing down the space and offering an incisive threat on the counter attack. With just minutes remaining, Rehhagel's men were close to an unlikely victory until David Beckham stepped up to score one of the most memorable and crucial free-kicks of the modern era to rescue a 2-2 draw and send England to the World Cup.

The performance showed what Rehhagel's methods could achieve and in the build up to Euro 2004 he continued to hone his squad, adding younger, more energetic players to his list and building a team that qualified for the European Championships ahead of Spain and Ukraine. Going into the tournament Greece were ranked as 100-1 outsiders to lift the trophy, with few observers expecting them to even progress through a qualifying group that also featured hosts Portugal, as well as Spain and the Czech Republic.

However, showing the defensively strong, counter-attacking and gutsy level of performance that would sum up their tournament, Greece shocked Portugal with a 2-1 victory in their first game, before backing it up by drawing with Spain and reaching the quarter-finals where they amazingly defeated reigning champions France by a single goal. One-nil was again the scoreline in the semi-finals when Greece dispatched the Czech Republic after extra-time and then in the final, when they completed one of the most unexpected successes in international football by defeating the much-fancied Cristiano Ronaldo-inspired Portugal.

There were several key elements in that Greece team, including the defensive prowess of Traianos Dellas and Giourkas Seitaridis, the combative tackling and metronomic passing of holding midfielder, Theodoros Zagorakis, and the aerial threat of target man Angelos Charisteas. But the primary factor behind the Greeks' success was their ability to perform as a complete entity, defending and attacking as a unit and understanding entirely how to mask their weaknesses as individuals and maximise their strengths as a team.

Criticism of Greece and Rehhagel for their perceived negative style of play was prevalent in the international media, but within the game itself there only remained huge respect for what they had achieved. Defending his philosophy after the tournament, the German said, "No-one should forget that a coach adapts the tactics to the characteristics of the available players. People tell me my tactics are not modern. But modern football is about winning."

Despite being offered the chance to coach Germany, Rehhagel stayed loyal to Greece. He failed to inspire qualification to the 2006 World Cup but took the team to Euro 2008 where they attempted to defend their crown. However, with opposing teams prepared for the Greek's style of play and several veteran performers having retired from the international game, the team struggled and exited at the group stage following three straight defeats.

Rehhagel remained in charge into his 70s and took Greece to the 2010 World Cup, their first since 1994, following 1-0 aggregate play-off victory over Ukraine. The team went on to lose all three group stage games and were knocked out of the competition, but Dimitris Salpingidis did score his country's first ever goal at World Cup during a 2-1 loss to Nigeria.

Otto tendered his resignation and retired following the tournament, spending two years out of the game before being coaxed back into management by Hertha Berlin in 2012. The team Rehhagel had begun his playing career with were struggling in the Bundesliga and he was unable to save them from relegation at the end of his first season in charge, in what proved to be an ultimately short return to the dugout.

Many observers try to pigeonhole Rehhagel as a defensive coach, but he was innovative enough to deploy a range of different tactics depending on the players at his disposal.

Other notable strategies adopted by the formidable German during his career include the insistence upon building attacking pressure down the wings and maximising the abilities of a strong, physically imposing centre-forward, who also possessed great technical ability.

He had a keen eye for a player, scouting many of the stars who would become key elements in his teams, such as Marco Reich, Miroslav Klose and Angelos Charisteas. Rehhagel is also renowned as an inspirational motivator, particularly adept at fostering team spirit within most of the teams he created. His achievements at club level were extraordinary but guiding Greece to European Championship glory in 2004 was nothing short of a footballing miracle.

# CHAPTER 3

## MANAGERS 25 – 21

# 25. FABIO CAPELLO

**Born:** June 18, 1946 in San Canzian d'Isonzo, Italy
**Clubs Managed:** AC Milan, Real Madrid, AS Roma, Juventus
**International:** England: 2008-2012 and Russia 2012-present day
**Major Honours:** 13

An iron-fisted disciplinarian who possesses the tactical nous and ability to inspire maximum fitness and effort from his players, Fabio Capello has enjoyed a lengthy and successful career that has seen him manage some of the biggest club sides in Europe, win domestic league titles with each of them, and also try his hand at international management.

A talented midfielder who won several domestic titles and became a full international for Italy, Capello's first venture into coaching saw him take charge of the AC Milan youth team, which included notable performers such as Paolo Maldini and Alessandro Costacurta.

He later became assistant manager to Nils Liedholm at the San Siro, taking charge of the first team as caretaker boss at the end of the 1986/87 season. He remained at the club following the appointment of a new Rossoneri manager, Arrigo Sacchi, a man whose influence and ability to create a winning team would eventually leave Capello with an impressive legacy to build upon.

Sacchi went on to achieve Serie A and double European Cup success before he departed to become manager of the Italian national team in 1991, leaving the door wide open for Capello to succeed him. With the basis of an extremely talented group of players already used to playing as a fluid and successful unit, Fabio had no problem making an early impact in the San Siro dugout. In his first five seasons as a manager he won four Serie A titles, before presiding over one of the most one-sided European Cup Finals ever, when his Milan team hammered a much-fancied Barcelona side, labelled the 'dream team' and managed by Johan Cruyff, 4-0.

The Catalan giants were famed for their attacking style and many pundits expected Milan to play a defensive, containing game. But Capello's team came out and attacked their opponents, playing with great pace and fluidity to build a lead before exploiting the counter-attack to add some gloss to the scoreline.

In fact, Capello's Milan generally played with a more expansive style than what had become customary under Sacchi, and Fabio ensured the constant evolution of the team by bringing through talented youngsters such as Demetrio Albertini. The Italian wasn't afraid to splash the cash, though, hence his then world-record £15m signing of Gianluigi Lentini. And while the Lentini deal eventually proved a flop, Capello would make plenty of shrewd signings, including the likes of Jean-Pierre Papin, Dejan Savicevic, Zvonimir Boban and Marcel Desailly.

A team already including the attacking riches of Marco van Basten and Ruud Gullit remained one of the most dangerous and revered sides in European football and its domestic record continued to justify that reputation, as Milan claimed further league titles, before reaching successive Champions League Finals; losing narrowly to Marseille in 1993, before overcoming Barcelona in the aforementioned emphatic victory a year later.

Capello's team also clocked up a 58-match unbeaten record in the league and went on to lift the 1994 European Super Cup and reach another Champions League Final in 1995. However, they were defeated by an Ajax side filled with youthful exuberance and class. The manager's last season at the San Siro, the 1995/96 campaign, again ended in Scudetto glory before Capello opted to leave Italy for a new challenge, taking over as Real Madrid boss in the summer of 1996.

Capello again inherited a squad bursting with talent, including considerable attacking resources that he would soon embrace, opting to play three strikers to maximise the abilities of Davor Šuker, Predrag Mijatovic and Raúl. The latter was often played out of position on the left-wing, a move that angered supporters and the Spanish press.

It proved to be a brief but successful first spell in Spain as Capello led Real to the La Liga title, pipping fierce rivals Barcelona by two points. However, despite that success and some shrewd moves in the transfer market, Fabio left the club after a single season, having fallen out with the club's chairman, Lorenzo Sanz.

Capello returned to AC Milan, but possessing an ageing squad that struggled to compete with an emerging Juventus side, he failed to recapture the glory years. Fabio again spent heavily to rebuild the squad, but only a few of his signings made the grade and the team went on to finish the 1997/98 campaign in 10th place, winning just 11 games. Capello moved on before the season was out. The team that the departing manager had largely built did go on to lift the Serie A crown the following season. If afforded more time to complete his rebuilding job, there's every chance that Capello may have led the Rossoneri to further glory.

Fabio remained in Italy for his next role, taking charge of AS Roma in 1999. The shrewd Italian again made some extremely successful moves in the transfer market, capturing the Argentinean pair of combative defender Walter Samuel and prolific striker Gabriel Batistuta, whose goals transformed the team's fortunes.

His first campaign in charge was steady rather than spectacular with a sixth place finish made harder to swallow for the Roma fans as their local rivals Lazio lifted the league title. However, they wouldn't have to wait too long before the Scudetto was captured by their team, when, despite a slow start to the 2000/01 campaign that led to violent protests at the club's training ground and many supporters to call for the manager's resignation, Capello led Roma to the title to secure the club's first Serie A crown in 18 years and their first major honour for a decade.

He followed that up with Supercoppa Italiana success in 2001 before guiding the team to a second place finish in the defence of their title in 2002. Unable to build on his Scudetto success with Roma and after struggling to make an impact in the Champions League, Capello departed for Juventus in 2004.

With the Turin giants, Capello again made significant additions, including the likes of Emerson from Roma and the enigmatic, yet effusively skilled, Zlatan Ibrahimovic from Ajax. In 2005 and 2006 he led Juventus to the latter stages of the Champions as well as consecutive Serie A titles, but following their involvement in the Calciopoli scandal—when several teams, including Juventus were involved in a police investigation that unearthed the rigging of games through referee selection—the club was stripped of both Scudetto crowns.

The club was later demoted from the top flight and Capello, although never implicated in the scandal, tendered his resignation in favour of a second spell with Real Madrid. The Italian's second tenure in Spain was ultimately just as controversial as his first, as his hard-line, often defensive approach and decision to drop superstar players such as David Beckham, proved particularly disruptive.

Despite a whole host of stellar names and an abundance of attacking talent, Madrid were struggling when Capello returned to the Bernabéu, with the club enduring one of their longest spells without a trophy, having failed to win La Liga for three seasons. The Italian insisted results were more important than playing beautifully, a philosophy in direct contradiction with the Madrid mantra. But as results started to improve 'Don Fabio', as he was christened in Spain, managed to transform the views of a selection of his critics.

An early Champions League exit didn't help his cause and with the team struggling for form domestically, Capello opted to recall Beckham. The team's fortunes began to improve as the energetic Englishman linked up superbly with his former Manchester United team-mate Ruud van Nistelrooy. Real soon overtook Barcelona and went on to lift their 30th league title on the final day of the season, following a 3-1 home victory over Real Mallorca. Despite ending Los Merengues' trophy drought, Capello was again given short shrift by the Madrid directors and was sacked at the end of the season.

Fabio's next role saw him move into international football, taking charge of the English national side in December 2007,

inheriting a squad on its knees following a disastrous Euro 2008 qualifying campaign under Steve McClaren.

Capello signed a four-and-a-half year deal and began transforming the culture of the England set-up, bringing in more structure and discipline and commanding the respect of the players. England enjoyed an impressive qualifying campaign for the 2010 World Cup, topping their group and achieving a 100 per cent winning record. A revitalised Wayne Rooney flourished under Capello, as did Steven Gerrard and John Terry, who was appointed the Italian's captain.

In the build up to South Africa 2010, as is the case ahead of most major tournaments, much was expected of the England team that had previously been dubbed the 'golden generation'. And following such a prolific run of form under Capello, hopes were high that the Three Lions would reach the latter stages. However, it turned out to be a disastrous tournament for England and their manager, as the team looked tired—with many pointing the finger at Capello's intensive fitness regime and methods of preparation—and played with no freedom or fluidity in a regimented 4-4-2 formation, struggling against lesser nations the USA, Algeria and Slovenia.

Two uninspiring draws were followed by a narrow 1-0 win over Slovenia that saw England gain qualification to the knockout stages where they met an expressive, young German side. England's performance against the Germans was tactically inept and despite having a Frank Lampard goal wrongly ruled out with the scores at 2-1 to the Germans, Capello's men were, in truth, lucky to come out of the match with a 4-1 defeat.

Capello remained in his role for England's Euro 2012 campaign and again sealed qualification for a major tournament, with the Three Lions topping the group. However, all wasn't well between the manager and the FA and following the governing body's decision to remove the captaincy from John Terry, after his alleged racial abuse of Anton Ferdinand, Capello resigned his post in February 2012.

Later that year the Italian took his second international job, becoming manager of the Russian national team. His new national side went on to qualify for the 2014 World Cup, where Capello will be keen to improve upon a dubious record at major tournaments.

A master of achieving consistency and building for a sustained domestic programme, Capello boasts a formidable and almost unrivalled league record. In his 15 seasons managing at club level, including the two Serie A crowns that Juventus were docked under his stewardship, the Italian has led teams to the top of the table on nine occasions.

An expert club manager, who has succeeded under sustained pressure and taken great teams to even greater heights, Capello's record at international level remains the only blot on an extremely impressive copybook.

# 24. CARLO ANCELOTTI

**Born:** June 10, 1959 in Reggiolo, Italy
**Clubs Managed:** Reggiana, Parma, Juventus, AC Milan, Chelsea, Paris Saint-Germain, Real Madrid
**Major Honours:** 12

Another prolifically successful Italian coach, Carlo Ancelotti edges out Capello having claimed a similar number of honours in a shorter managerial career, which has also included a trophy-filled spell with AC Milan.

Following a stellar playing career, which included domestic dominance with Milan and international recognition with Italy, Ancelotti's first steps in management came with Serie B side Reggiana, which he led to the top flight in 1995 before being snapped by Parma a year later. His Parma team, including the young talents of Gianluigi Buffon and Fabio Cannavaro, excelled, going on to finish second at the end of his first season in charge and qualifying for the Champions League.

Not traditionally one of Italy's most prominent clubs, Parma maintained a consistent record under Ancelotti, qualifying for the UEFA Cup in 1998, before he was appointed Juventus boss a year later. He was met with an ageing side whose greatest achievements were behind them. Despite winning the Intertoto Cup and claiming two runners-up spots for the Turin club, he left his role in 2001 to return to the scene of so many successes during his playing career, as he became manager of AC Milan.

The Rossoneri had been devoid of success since their last Serie A title in 1999 and had struggled to make an impact in Europe, but Ancelotti went on to address both these failings. First he reached the semi-finals of the 2001/02 UEFA Cup, then continued to improve the team's league form, despite being derided by club owner, Silvio Berlusconi, for his defensive tactics.

The calm yet confident young manager continued to put his own mark on the team, converting attacking midfielder Andrea Pirlo to a deep-lying playmaker and soon reaping the rewards as the likes of Rui Costa, Filippo Inzaghi and Ukrainian goal-machine Andriy Shevchenko benefited in front of him. A solid defensive base filled with hugely experienced Italian defenders, such as the great Paolo Maldini and the emerging Alessandro Nesta, provided the ideal platform for the team's attacking players to flourish.

Milan went on to enjoy a successful 2002/03 Champions League campaign, reaching the final and defeating Ancelotti's former club Juventus on penalties following an edgy, tactical chess battle of a 0-0 draw. Consistency was achieved in the league with the 2004 Serie A title claimed and followed up with runners-up spots in 2005 and 2006, as the team continued to impress in Europe.

The Rossoneri reached two more Champions League finals under Ancelotti's guidance, losing the first in 2005 to Liverpool, despite being 3-0 up at half-time and teaching the English giants a footballing lesson. AC were pegged back to 3-3 by a spirited second half performance from Rafa Benítez's men before eventually being defeated 3-2 on penalties. That defeat was avenged in 2007, when Carlo and Milan defeated Liverpool 2-1 in the Athens final thanks to the creative brilliance of key-performer Kaká and a predatory double by veteran finisher, Inzaghi. It provided the manager with a double double, as he had lifted the trophy on two occasions as both Milan player and manager.

The FIFA Club World Cup was claimed in 2007, but following successive trophyless campaigns in 2007/08 and 2008/09, Ancelotti departed the San Siro to undertake his first coaching assignment outside of his homeland, becoming Chelsea manager in June 2009.

His appointment followed a spell of instability at the English club, with the Italian becoming the fourth permanent manager in 21 months and succeeding temporary boss Guus Hiddink. Ancelotti settled quickly, clocking up an impressive run of early form and enjoying a season-long battle for the title with reigning champions Manchester United. The Italian went on to lift the biggest trophy in English domestic football on the final day of the season as the London club finished ahead of United by a single point. Ancelotti wasn't finished there and subsequently added the FA Cup to the Blues' trophy cabinet, thanks to 1-0 victory over Portsmouth at Wembley that saw Chelsea achieve the English League and Cup double for the first time. Ancelotti became only the second foreign manager to lift both trophies in a single season; a feat first achieved by Arsène Wenger at Arsenal. The tactically astute boss also became the first Italian manager to win the English title and presided over the first team to score more than 100 goals in a single Premier League season.

Despite such impressive form at home, the team struggled abroad, losing to Inter Milan, led by former Chelsea boss José Mourinho, in the knockout stages of the Champions League. The following season saw Chelsea again in direct competition with Manchester United for major trophies, but this time Ancelotti's men lost out on both occasions with United knocking them out of the Champions League in the quarter-finals and winning the title as the Blues finished second. During the season, Chelsea spent a British record £50 million to snare Fernando Torres from Liverpool and £22 million on Brazilian defender David Luiz and saddled by the pressure of these investments as well as owner Roman Abramovic's desperation to win the Champions League, Ancelotti was harshly sacked at the close of the campaign.

Following a short break from management, Carlo returned to the dugout with ambitious French Ligue 1 side, Paris Saint-Germain in December 2011, taking over a team challenging at the top of the table and a club backed by potentially billions of euros' worth of investment.

The 2011/12 campaign eventually ended in a runners-up spot, but Ancelotti's first full season in Paris the following year saw PSG win the Ligue 1 title and reach the quarter-finals of the Champions League, losing to Barcelona on away goals.

Ancelotti was able to entice top drawer performers such as Zlatan Ibrahimovic and Thiago Silva and created one of the most exciting French teams of the modern era, providing the coaching expertise to transform the club to the next level, before announcing his intention to leave France in the summer of 2013 to take charge of Real Madrid.

The Italian now finds himself at another

club where the expectations are excessively high but a man of Ancelotti's profile and quietly assured self-confidence should be able to flourish at the Bernabéu. A supreme organiser, controller of big egos and considered strategist, Carlo Ancelotti is young and talented enough to continue to amass major honours at a prolific rate and eventually become the greatest Italian manager ever.

# 23. LOUIS VAN GAAL

**Born:** August 8, 1951 in Amsterdam, Netherlands
**Clubs Managed:** Ajax, Barcelona, AZ Alkmaar, Bayern Munich
**International:** Netherlands: 2000-2002 and 2012-present day
**Major Honours:** 19

A well-organised coach with an authoritarian style, Louis van Gaal brought European glory back to Ajax in the modern era after presiding over a decade of domestic dominance with the Amsterdam giants. The Dutchman also won league titles in Spain and Germany and has managed his country on two occasions.

A workmanlike midfielder who never hit great footballing heights, van Gaal's coaching and managerial career has been in great contrast to his days on the pitch. An intelligent, deep-thinking tactician, whose insistence on discipline has seen his relationships with many players suffer; the determined Dutchman began his coaching career with an assistant's role at AZ Alkmaar before starting his managerial apprenticeship under Leo Beenhakker at Ajax.

Louis took take charge of the Amsterdam giants in 1991 and went on to preside over two great teams during his six-year spell at the helm. The first impressive 11 included the likes of Dennis Bergkamp, Aron Winter and Wim Jonk before a second notable side that featured an almost unrivalled generation of talented youngsters, even by Ajax's great standards, as the likes of Patrick Kluivert, Edgar Davids and Clarence Seedorf progressed into a team that also included emerging talents such as Edwin van der Sar, Frank and Ronald de Boer, Marc Overmars and Jari Litmanen as well as the experience of Danny Blind and Frank Rijkaard.

Keeping true to the club's traditions of developing youth and playing attacking, 'total football' that featured a passing style bordering on the telepathic, van Gaal went on to lift three Dutch Eredivisie titles and the domestic cup, as well as tasting success in Europe, claiming the UEFA Cup for the first time in the club's history, then lifting the Champions League in 1995.

That European Cup triumph, the fourth won by Ajax, was achieved thanks to a narrow 1-0 victory over Fabio Capello's much fancied AC Milan. The winning goal was scored by the precociously talented teenage striker, Patrick Kluivert, who showed composure beyond his years to tuck the ball away in the 85th minute.

Champions League success ensured that van Gaal's team completed the 1994/95 campaign without experiencing defeat in either the league or in Europe, with 1995 continuing to be a fruitful year for Ajax, as the team claimed both the UEFA Super Cup and the Intercontinental Cup. The team continued to progress and again reached the final of the Champions League in 1996 where they lost on penalties to an equally talented Juventus side.

The trophy-laden manager left his homeland to take over at another European giant, Barcelona, in 1997. Inheriting a team built by Bobby Robson that included great attacking talents such as Brazilian striker Ronaldo, van Gaal stuck to his adventurous attacking principles and went on to win two La Liga titles. The first came at the end of his debut campaign in Spain and the second in 1998/99. Adding the Copa del Rey he lifted in 1998, the Dutchman won a major trophy in each of his first three seasons at the Nou Camp.

However, van Gaal's combustible character didn't go down well with the demanding Spanish media and he often struggled to implement his footballing philosophy on a group of big-name players that had equally large egos and hadn't been schooled in the Ajax traditions. The manager's response was to bring in Dutch players that he had worked with before, but it only served to create divisions within the camp and, with the media continuing to call for his head, van Gaal stepped down in May 2000 famously remarking to the press, "I am leaving. Congratulations."

Louis' next job was his first at international level as he took charge of the Netherlands national side in preparation for the 2002 World Cup. However, the Dutch failed to qualify and van Gaal stepped down. His next appointment saw him reprise his role at Barcelona for the 2002/03 season but as the old La Liga demons returned, he left his position halfway through the campaign, taking some time out of the game before returning to Ajax in 2004. Van Gaal became the club's technical director but following disagreements and internal conflict he resigned later that year.

A return to the dugout came in January 2005 when van Gaal became manager of unfashionable AZ Alkmaar. Working under less pressure and with less high-profile players, the Dutchman successfully implemented his coaching techniques, as he guided AZ to third place in the

Eredivisie and the final of the Dutch Cup in 2007, narrowly missing out on a place in the Champions League.

A less impressive 2007/08 season was the catalyst for Louis to announce his intention to leave AZ, but after the players campaigned for him to stay, he pledged to remain with Alkmaar. The manager promptly guided his team to an unlikely Dutch league title in 2009, as the team went unbeaten for the majority of the season, consistently achieving a higher placing than Ajax, before being crowned champions and finishing with the best defensive record and second highest rate of goalscoring. AZ's title was sealed by an 11-point margin and saw them become the first club other than Ajax, PSV Eindhoven or Feyenoord to take the Eredivisie crown for 28 years.

Van Gaal's team included few star names and was built on the principles of a strong team ethic, progressive passing football and tactical diligence. Their Eredivisie success is all the more noteworthy as it represented just the second league title in the club's history. With the manager's reputation and arguably his love for the game rekindled, Louis was again hot property on the managerial market and became Bayern Munich boss in 2009.

The Dutchman labelled the German giants as his "dream club" but the first few months were more like a nightmare, as Bayern claimed just one win in his first four games and came close to an early exit from the Champions League. Speculation surrounded the manager's future as he struggled to implement his tactical beliefs. However, as his new signings, including the explosively skilled Arjen Robben, found their feet, and the emerging talents of Bastian Schweinsteiger, who he converted from a winger into a holding midfielder, and the versatile Philipp Lahm, responded to his methods, van Gaal's men soon looked the part and began to storm up the Bundesliga table, eventually claiming the title following an impressive end-of-season run.

Bayern also won the German Cup, meaning that van Gaal had won the two biggest domestic honours in Holland, Spain and Germany, and went on to reach the final of the Champions League, following an away goals victory over Manchester United following a 4-4 aggregate draw. Van Gaal faced his former assistant at Barcelona, José Mourinho and his experienced Inter Milan side in the final, and was tactically outmanoeuvred by the charismatic Portuguese coach as the Italians ran out 2-0 winners. The Dutchman remained at the Munich helm into the 2010/11 campaign, winning the German Super Cup, but the team struggled in their defence of the Bundesliga and eventually finished in third place, a full 10 points adrift of champions Borussia Dortmund.

Louis was sacked at the end of the campaign but had left an impressive legacy by instilling several talented youngsters in the team, including Thomas Müller, David Alaba, Toni Kroos and Holger Badstuber, who would all go on to play a major role in the club's 2012/13 Champions League, Bundesliga and German Cup success. Van Gaal, meanwhile, took charge of the Netherlands for the second time in July 2012 and went on to secure qualification for the 2014 World Cup in Brazil.

Although famed for his indignation and single-minded approach to the game, Louis van Gaal has also proved that he is able to adapt to different countries and players of varying abilities and still achieve success on a consistent basis. He once said, "The coach is the team's focal point, so preparing the tactical formation is essential. Every player must know where he has to be and support his teammates.

There has to be absolute discipline and mutual understanding. Discipline is the basis of creativity and flexibility."

The Dutchman demands complete respect for the tactical systems he instils, providing a clear mental picture of the game and the way his players should approach it. Such foresight and planning has led to his teams playing with beautiful fluidity and rather than being constrained by his tactics, their willingness to embrace them has seen them express themselves with great tempo and attacking prowess. A passionate believer in 'total football' and a lucid possession game, akin to what has been deployed so effectively by the modern day Barcelona, van Gaal didn't simply rely on the talents of his players to succeed, he prepared them with obsessive intensity.

# 22. VALERIY LOBANOVSKYI

**Born:** January 6, 1939 in Kiev, Soviet Union
**Clubs Managed:** Dnipro Dnipropetrosvk, Dynamo Kiev
**International:** USSR: 1975-1976, 1982-1983, 1986-1990 (Reached 1988 European Final), United Arab Emirates: 1990-1993, Kuwait: 1994-1996, Ukraine: 2000-2001
**Major Honours:** 30

A giant of the game in the former Soviet Union and in modern-day Ukraine, Valeriy Lobanovskyi enjoyed unprecedented success with Dynamo Kiev, winning 13 league titles, nine domestic cups and two European Cup Winners' Cups. He also coached the USSR side that reached the 1988 European Championship Final.

A pioneer and a philosopher of the theoretical side of the game, Lobanovskyi was a deep-thinking tactician. He studied football intensely and was keen to experiment with science and apply it to his preparations for games and the conditioning of his players. He implemented approaches considered during his time studying engineering in Kiev and discussed ideas with statistician Anatoliy Zelentsov. He also had a thorough scouting network and was ahead of his time when it came to assessing the strengths and weaknesses of opponents, while also using technology to evaluate the form and performance statistics of his own players.

He ensured that his players were also athletes. A combination of fitness and conditioning with the technical brilliance of several generations of talented footballers, heralded decades of success. All of these methods were revolutionary during the 1970s and '80s but are common place today, ensuring the progressive Ukrainian has left a hefty footballing legacy.

Orchestrating minuscule attention to detail, he was a passionate believer in the strength of the team unit over the individual and obsessively searched for the most productive formations to achieve the best connections between his players. Despite the structured theories, Lobanovskyi certainly saw his players as more than functional robotic athletes and vehemently believed footballers should be capable of operating in any role, rather than restricting them to being labelled in one position. Taking a Soviet slant on 'total football', he famously once stated, "There is no such thing as a striker, a midfielder, a defender... only footballers."

A decorated colonel in the Red Army, Lobanovskyi was a naturally skilled left-winger capable of individual brilliance as a player. He spent most of his career with teams in his homeland, including his hometown club, Dynamo Kiev, who he would go on to manage during two separate spells that totalled 21 years. However, Valeriy's first managerial role came with Dnipro Dnipropetrovsk, where he coached for four years before taking up the reins at Kiev in 1974.

His first spell with Dynamo lasted 15 years, during many of which he also enjoyed a dual role as head coach of the USSR national side. At club level he created a team that successfully broke the Russian dominance of Soviet football, winning the Soviet Super League on eight occasions and the Soviet Cup six times. Lobanovskyi's team also conquered European competition, winning the European Cup Winners' Cup following a memorable 3-0 destruction of Atlético Madrid in the 1986 final.

The '86 Final was an eloquent 90-minute showcase of Lobanovskyi's football theory being incisively put into practice, as the combination of a ferocious pressing game with an energetic counter-attacking style, saw Kiev burst forward in numbers to ruthlessly exploit the space between the midfield and defence as they used the width of the pitch to devastating effect. The game was won by playing fluid football at a rapid tempo and with ruthless efficiency.

The manager's great USSR teams of 1986 and 1988 were built around the framework of talented Ukraine players. His first success at international level saw him lead the Soviet Union to a bronze medal at the 1976 Olympic Games but his later achievements in the late 1980s were much more notable. Lobanovskyi was appointed USSR head coach just days before the 1986 World Cup, but led a skilful and functional side, which featured a plethora of the Dynamo Kiev players he knew so well, through the qualifying group and into the knockout stages, a feat the Soviets seldom realised at World Cup level.

Remaining at the helm for the 1988 European Championship, the Ukrainian developed an extremely competitive squad that played with great fitness and finesse to top its group, beating Holland along the way. The team excelled in the knockout stages and reached the final. The Soviets' opponents in the showpiece were a Marco van Basten-inspired Holland who comprehensively won the game 2-0.

The 1990 World Cup was a rare black mark in Lobanovskyi's notebook, as he failed to inspire a USSR side, filled with significantly less Dynamo Kiev players, to qualify out of their group, eventually finishing bottom of the table. He subsequently stepped down from his

roles with the national side and Dynamo to coach the United Arab Emirates for three years before a two year spell with Kuwait and an eventual return to Dynamo in 1997.

He found a club that had dramatically fallen from the heights it had scaled during his previous tenure, with Dynamo now struggling in the Ukraine league following the break-up of the Soviet Union and banned from European competition for attempting to bribe an official.

However, Lobanovskyi used his vast experience and unrivalled knowledge of the Ukrainian game to build a team featuring a generation of hugely talented performers, which included the barnstorming defender Oleg Luzhnyi and the lethal strike pairing of Serhiy Rebrov and Andriy Shevchenko. His team went on to win five consecutive league titles and regularly reach the later stages of the Champions League, including the semi-finals of the 1998/99 competition.

Recapturing club success with Kiev led to a return to international management with Ukraine, but with the nation's lowly world ranking making qualification for major tournaments more challenging, Lobanovskyi struggled and was relieved of his duties following defeat to Germany in a play-off to reach the 2002 World Cup. In May 2002, shortly after his Kiev side had defeated Metalurh Zaporizhzhya in a domestic fixture, Lobanovskyi suffered a serious stroke and died later that month during surgery on his brain. He was 63.

Viewed as an intense, stern and downbeat character, who often downplayed his achievements, Lobanovskyi once responded when questioned about achieving the dream of Kiev fans to win the Super League title by saying, "A realised dream ceases to be a dream." Elaborating on this, the analytical manager, eluded to his view of that feat as just the beginning of a series of achievements. He was proven emphatically correct as he went on to become the most successful manager in the history of both Soviet and Ukrainian football.

# 21. UDO LATTEK

**Born:** January 16, 1935 in Bosemb, East Prussia
**Clubs Managed:** Bayern Munich, Borussia Mönchengladbach, Borussia Dortmund, Barcelona, FC Köln, Schalke 04
**International:** Germany (Assistant Manager): 1965-1970
**Major Honours:** 16

The most successful manager in the German game, Udo Lattek won 14 major trophies in a career that spanned 35 years and included spells with Bayern Munich and Barcelona. Alongside Giovanni Trapattoni, Lattek is one of only two coaches to have won all three major European club titles, and the only coach to have done so with three separate clubs.

A relatively limited footballer who ended his playing days prematurely in 1965 to join the coaching set-up with the German national side, he led the youth team and formed part of the senior side's backroom staff as the Mannschaft reached the final of the 1966 World Cup. His first role in club football came with Bayern Munich in 1970.

Although his appointment was recommended by club legend Franz Beckenbauer it remained a controversial one due to Udo's lack of managerial experience. But he was aided by the inheritance of a hugely talented side, including Beckenbauer, Gerd Müller and Sepp Maier, and the young manager soon proved the doubters wrong.

The introduction of younger players such as Paul Breitner and Uli Hoeness helped to evolve a hugely successful side and ensured Bayern remained one of the strongest teams in Europe during Lattek's tenure. Munich went on to win three successive Bundesliga titles; becoming the first German club to do so, as well as lifting the German Cup, before becoming the first German team to win the 1974 European Cup following a 4-0 replay victory over Atlético Madrid in the final.

The following season saw Munich struggle in domestic football and with Lattek appealing to the Bayern president that the club needed some changes, he was promptly told changes were afoot, including his dismissal as manager. With his considerable achievements still fresh in the memory, Lattek had no problem getting another job and succeeded Hennes Weisweiler at Borussia Mönchengladbach ahead of the 1975/76 campaign.

In a four-year spell in Mönchengladbach, the progressive coach lifted two more German league titles, only losing out on a third by goal difference and won the 1979 UEFA Cup thanks to a 2-1 aggregate victory over Red Star Belgrade. Lattek also guided Borussia to the 1977 European Cup Final, but his team were out manoeuvred by a dominant Liverpool side.

Following the '79 UEFA Cup victory, Udo resigned his post with Mönchengladbach to become Borussia Dortmund boss. There he spent two relatively unsuccessful seasons before taking over at one of Europe's premier clubs in 1981, when Barcelona came calling.

At the Nou Camp, Lattek succeeded another top manager, taking up the reigns from Helenio Herrera and went on to guide Barça, where he was labelled 'El Professor', to European Cup Winners'

Cup glory at the end of his first season in charge, following a 2-1 final victory over Standard Liège.

Lattek added to an already impressive squad of internationals, which included his compatriot Bernd Schuster and Allan Simonsen, who he'd managed at Mönchengladbach, with the significant signing of the mercurial talents of Argentine play-maker, Diego Maradona. However, after Barcelona struggled domestically during the 1982/83 season and failing out with Maradona over his discipline and work ethic, Lattek was replaced at the end of the campaign by the Argentine's coach at national level, César Luis Menotti.

A return to Bayern Munich followed as Lattek discovered a squad of players whose talents were significantly lower than during his previous spell in charge. However, after introducing the likes of Lothar Matthäus, Klaus Augenthaler and Søren Lerby into the team, success soon followed as two more German Cups and amazingly another hat-trick of Bundesliga titles, including the league and cup double in 1986, were delivered to the club's bulging trophy cabinet. Another European honour also came within touching distance for Lattek, as Bayern lost the 1987 European Cup Final 2-1 to FC Porto.

Following that defeat, Lattek decided to step away from the game for a few years, eventually returning as manager and later technical director with Köln in

1991, then as manager of Schalke 04 a year later. However, it appeared that some of the magic and probably the hunger had gone, and the manager that had been a consummate winner during his prime again drifted out of coaching.

His second spell of retirement lasted seven years before he answered the desperate call of a Borussia Dortmund team staring relegation in the face. The team were just a point above the drop zone with five games remaining of the season. Lattek came in and made an instant impact, gaining two wins and two draws to steer the 1997 Champions League winners to safety. He departed the club at the end of the season but had done enough to preserve Dortmund's future.

A popular figure with the players, perhaps down to the simplicity of his methods and his propensity to trust them tactically, Lattek was famed as an excellent motivator who inspired great loyalty. Jürgen Kohler, who played under Udo at Köln and Borussia Dortmund, once said,

"Udo Lattek is my idol as both a manager and a person."

One of Lattek's major assets was his ability to manage a selection of truly great players and big characters, instilling and maintaining a winning mentality. He wasn't afraid of conflict and encouraged his players to have a voice, famously saying, "Where there is friction there is energy."

Critics may opine that Lattek's tenures at each of the clubs he managed were too brief and that despite his considerable success, he was never responsible for building a great team, rather building on what had been created before him. But winning in such a prolific manner and maintaining success is a talent that should not be underestimated. Neither should Lattek's ability to integrate talented youngsters into a winning system and to replicate domestic and European glory with a succession of clubs. As a pure trophy gatherer, Lattek's record of 16 major honours in 16 years, between 1971 and 1987 takes some beating.

# CHAPTER 4

## MANAGERS 20 – 18

# 20. PEP GUARDIOLA

**Born:** January 18, 1971 in Santpedor, Spain
**Clubs Managed:** Barcelona B, Barcelona, Bayern Munich
**Major Honours:** 15

The architect of arguably the greatest football team the world has ever seen, Pep Guardiola enjoyed almost unrivalled success at Barcelona, lifting two Champions League and three La Liga crowns in his four years at the Nou Camp.

Immaculate in everything he does, from his stylish appearance, command of multiple languages and his huge attention to detail, Pep Guardiola has the substance to back up the tailored suits that have spawned countless copycat managers. Many have recreated the look, but seldom are fit to lace the Spaniard's designer Italian shoes when it comes to success.

A product of Barcelona's fabled youth academy, La Masia, having joined the club at the age of 13 before progressing through the ranks to make his first team debut in 1990, Josep 'Pep' Guardiola went on to enjoy a glittering playing career that featured countless domestic honours with the Catalan giants and success in Europe as part of Johan Cruyff's hugely successful and aesthetically pleasing 'dream team'. The latter stages of Guardiola's career saw him play in Italy, Qatar and Mexico, as he prepared for his evolution from player to coach.

His first role in a coaching capacity

came with the Barcelona B side, where he was responsible for developing the club's most talented youngsters. Assisted by his eventual successor as first team coach, Tito Vilanova, the team topped their Tercera División group and went on to achieve promotion after winning the 2008 Segunda División B play-offs.

His talents and excellent relationships with the younger players were soon recognised and Pep became Barcelona head coach in 2008, succeeding fellow Dutchman Frank Rijkaard, who had claimed the club's second European Cup victory in 2006.

Despite Rijkaard's team being full of hugely talented performers and plenty of big personalities, Guardiola wasted little time putting his imprint on the squad, announcing the likes of Ronaldinho and Deco would not be part of his plans and letting several players leave the club. Another performer who appeared to be set for the exit door was sharp-shooting striker, Samuel Eto'o, but the new manager later had a change of heart and put his faith in the Cameroonian forward.

Working alongside Barça's director of sport, Txiki Begiristain, Pep brought in his own players, reducing the age of the squad by capturing the likes of Dani Alves and Gerard Piqué. He also promoted youngsters such as Sergio Busquets, Pedro and Jeffrén, who he'd nurtured in the B team, into the senior set-up. These players, added to the hypnotically rhythmic passing ability of the stunning midfielder Xavi Hernández; the creative genius of his sidekick Andrés Iniesta and emerging brilliance of the magical Lionel Messi, left Guardiola possessing one of the most exciting teams in Europe and one bursting with huge potential.

That potential was instantly realised in emphatic style during Guardiola's first season in charge as he led his breathtakingly entertaining Barcelona to a treble of trophies, including La Liga success, in a campaign that saw an undefeated 20-plus match run and a thumping 6-2 victory over nearest rivals, Real Madrid. Barça also won the Copa del Rey and the Champions League, following a comprehensive 2-0 victory over Manchester United in the final, which featured goals from the increasingly talismanic Messi and the reprieved Eto'o.

The following campaign saw Barcelona claim the Spanish Super Cup, UEFA Super Cup and the FIFA Club World Cup to complete the accumulation of six trophies in the calendar year of 2009. Guardiola, who became the first manager to have achieved that feat, swapped Samuel Eto'o for Inter Milan's Zlatan Ibrahimovic and trimmed his squad by releasing and loaning out several players as he focused on developing younger talent.

In January 2010 Guardiola amazingly became Barcelona's longest-serving Spanish coach, overtaking the record previously held by Josep Samitier, and his immediate future seemed secure after he agreed another year's extension to his contract. Later that year he became the first Barça coach to win four consecutive 'El Clásico' clashes against Real Madrid as the Catalan outfit went on to retain their title, their 20th as a club, by accumulating 99 points.

Pep's first disappointment as a manager came that season, as Barcelona lost out to José Mourinho's Inter Milan in the semi-finals of the Champions League, following a controversy-filled 3-2 aggregate defeat that saw the opening exchanges in what would become a fierce rivalry with Mourinho, particularly when the outspoken Portuguese took charge of Real Madrid the following summer.

Ahead of the 2010/11 campaign, Guardiola's third in charge, further big name players departed Barcelona, including marauding midfielder Yaya Touré, as well as Ibrahimovic and Thierry Henry, who were both casualties of the brilliance of Lionel Messi who had become the fulcrum of the team and had the ability to play in a free role as a lone 'false nine' striker that saw him score with prolific regularity.

The likes of David Villa and Javier Mascherano were added to a team that was now playing with such style that it had become renowned all over the world. Another Spanish Super Cup was snared, as were Real Madrid in a 5-0 La Liga thumping. Barça also faced their fierce rivals in the semi-finals of that season's Champions League, completing a third successive campaign of reaching the last four under Guardiola. After two enthralling ties, which featured plenty of pre-match bluster from Mourinho, including the scrutinising of the officials, some brutal tactics by Madrid and some exaggerated simulation from both sets of players, Barcelona progressed thanks to 3-1 aggregate victory.

Barça would later lose to Real in the Copa del Rey Final, signifying Pep's first defeat in a major showpiece, but emerged victorious in La Liga to claim their third successive title under his guidance. The Catalans won another Champions League, again defeating Manchester United in the final, securing an emphatic 3-1 victory that featured goals from Pedro, Messi and Villa. Guardiola showed his tactical nous in the Wembley final, placing Villa and Pedro on each touchline to widen the pitch and stretch the English club's midfield, giving Xavi and Iniesta the time and space to control possession and dictate the tempo of the game.

Guardiola's fourth season in charge of Barça proved to be less fruitful, despite the signings of Cesc Fàbregas and Alexis Sánchez and the continually brilliant football played by his charges. The campaign began with more trophies, as the Spanish Super Cup, UEFA Super Cup and World Club Cup were delivered. However, the two biggest tournaments, La Liga and the Champions League, both ended in disappointment. Real Madrid wrestled the league title from the Nou Camp and Chelsea achieved an against-all-odds Champions League semi-final victory over Barça, following a determined rearguard action and countless squandered chances from the Catalans.

The Copa del Rey was later claimed to provide some consolation but Guardiola still faced the first major criticism of his Barcelona era, with many viewing his insistence on playing the same tactics as inflexible and a little naïve. The journalistic platitude of having 'no plan B' was frequently aimed in his direction, but when your plan A has been so devastatingly successful, the patience to persevere with it is is both understandable and admirable.

However, citing the pressures involved and his tiredness of the all-encompassing job of being Barcelona manager as the reasons, Pep stepped down as manager at the end of the 2011/12 campaign.

During his tenure Barça dominated in all aspects, succeeding domestically, in Europe and on the world stage, winning with an unrivalled entertaining style and absolutely dominating opponents in terms of possession, territory and chances created in almost every game they played. Guardiola crafted something beautiful but it was simply the end result of meticulous preparation, astute man-management, tactical awareness and the intense work-ethic that accompanies all of the greatest managers.

The players relished playing under Pep and his relaxed-yet-focused approach, as Gerard Piqué explained, "He has a natural, extraordinary authority. He doesn't have to raise his voice or bang on the table—the players just trust him."

Under Guardiola, Barcelona became more disciplined tactically and placed greater focus on possession and operating with an aggressive pressing style, which incorporated a high-defensive line, attacking players hunting down opponents in pairs and adventurous full-backs.

He used the ultra-reliable and incisive passing talents of Xavi and Iniesta to dominate possession with all elements of the team building to service a brilliant crescendo of attacking talent at the fulcrum of the team, the miracle-making Argentine, Lionel Messi. Guardiola also experimented with a 3-4-3 system in an attempt to negate the defensive tactics his team often encountered.

He departed the Nou Camp with the unprecedented record of winning 14 trophies in his four years in charge, including three La Liga crowns and two Champions Leagues. He missed out on just five of the competitions he could've won, marking him down as the most successful coach in Barcelona's history. But it's not just the excess of these successes, but the mesmerising manner in which they were achieved that marks the Spaniard out. The football created by Guardiola's philosophy and his belief in the tiki-taka system produced pure sporting theatre.

The middle two seasons of his reign, in particular, saw Barcelona take the game to another level and rediscover and evolve a football philosophy admired globally. Barça's boldness and its achievements also helped inspire Spain to World Cup and European Championships success.

After leaving Barcelona, Pep took a year's sabbatical away from the game before being named as coach of reigning European Champions, Bayern Munch, in 2013. In Germany, Guardiola has again inherited a remarkably talented team accustomed to success, but he has made moves to put his own stamp on the club, developing a style in line with his principles and already claimed the 2013 European Super Cup.

The biggest test of his abilities will be whether he can recreate the glories he has already experienced at a club other than Barcelona; a club he understood, loved and which seemed to fit perfectly with his vision of the way football should be played.

# 19. BILL SHANKLY

**Born:** September 2, 1913 in Glenbuck, Scotland
**Clubs Managed:** Carlisle United, Grimsby Town, Workington, Huddersfield Town, Liverpool
**Major Honours:** 11

An inspirational figure and expert motivator, Bill Shankly built the traditions that saw Liverpool enjoy three decades of dominance. On the face of it, his 11 major honours, including three English First Division titles, two FA Cups and one UEFA Cup, is impressive but not remarkable.

To appreciate Shankly's managerial abilities the impact he had on Liverpool as a whole should be considered. He transformed the Reds from a second-tier outfit to a team that dictated the world's footballing landscape, created an identity that would later become a worldwide brand and laid the foundations for years of success under his successors.

Like many of Britain's finest managers, Bill Shankly grew up in a small mining community in working-class Scotland, where football provided an escape route for many young men. An accomplished right-half or modern-day full-back, as a player, Shankly was an expert tackler whose work ethic and dedication to his profession saw him maximise every last ounce of his footballing ability.

In his autobiography, Shankly later wrote that he had long prepared himself for the day when he would become a football manager by absorbing different coaching systems, giving him the confidence to succeed as a manager.

His first managerial role came with Carlisle United in 1949. A struggling Third Division North side were transformed into an extremely competitive team that came close to promotion in 1951. He worked to involve supporters and the local community in the team, giving them a sense of ownership of the club; an approach that would serve him well for the remainder of his career.

However, the principled Scotsman resigned from the club, accusing the board of reneging on a bonus promise made to the players. He took up a role with Grimsby Town, having applied for the vacant Liverpool manager's job but failed to get the nod. With Grimsby, Bill led the team to second place in the Third Division South at the end of his first season in charge. Presiding over a side that played flowing football and developed more tactical awareness, Shankly took the club to fifth place in 1954 and pressed the board to invest further in an ageing team.

When funds weren't forthcoming, he resigned his position and went on to manage Workington, another team struggling in the lower echelons of English football, again in the Third Division North. He again improved the team's fortunes, despite working on a shoestring budget and almost running the club single-handedly. The frustrations of the role caught up with Shankly and in 1955 he departed to become assistant manager and reserve team coach of Second Division Huddersfield Town.

When Andy Beattie resigned in 1956, Shankly was promoted to manager and began blooding some of the younger players he'd worked with in the reserves, such as 16-year-old striker Denis Law, who became one of the great players of his era, and future England World Cup winner Ray Wilson. Despite progressing the team, Shankly couldn't mastermind promotion to the top flight, particularly as the club's board sold many of his better players. So when the opportunity to become Liverpool's manager came along in November 1959, he jumped at the chance.

Liverpool had been in the Second Division for five years having suffered top flight relegation in 1954, but Shankly recognised the club's huge potential and went on to revolutionise the Anfield outfit. The fiery Scotsman inherited a Reds side apparently marooned in the second tier that had recently been defeated by non-league Worcester City in the FA Cup. Liverpool's soon-to-be-renowned Anfield ground was in a state of disrepair, with the club's training facilities described by the manager as "a shambles". His playing staff was also suitably modest, indicating the enormity of the task that faced the ambitious manager.

He almost immediately took the city of Liverpool and the club's supporters to his heart, feelings that were soon reciprocated as a great bond of mutual affection developed. Shankly's coaching staff, which included future managers Bob Paisley and Joe Fagan, helped him to build a new a team and a new culture at the club. Paisley was often seen as the tactician and Shankly credited as the master psychologist and man-motivator. The coaching staff famously met in the fabled Anfield boot room to discuss tactics and plot future glories.

Shankly oversaw development of the club's Melwood training ground, as well as the Anfield Stadium and implemented major surgery to his first-team squad, enlisting an impressive network of scouts to search for players from various levels of the game and all over Britain. He signed the likes of Ron Yeats and Ian St John from Scotland, who would both transform the team. Young talent was also developed with the likes of Ronnie Moran, Gerry Byrne and Roger Hunt flourishing in the first team.

The Scotsman was heavily involved in the coaching set-up, improving players' endurance and introducing better warm-up exercises. He encouraged players to use the ball more during training sessions and introduced fiercely competitive five-a-side matches, where the famed 'pass and move' techniques were honed.

Two third-placed finishes in Shankly's first two seasons were followed by the championship-winning 1961/62 season, in which Roger Hunt scored an impressive 41 goals to guide Liverpool back into the First Division. The 1962/63 campaign was one of consolidation as the Reds finished eighth in the First Division and Shankly continued to improve his team with astute signings such as Peter Thompson and again put his trust in youth by introducing the considerable talents of Ian Callaghan and Tommy Smith. The 1963/64 Football League title was claimed following a final-day 5-0 victory over Arsenal at Anfield, confirming Liverpool's return as a major top flight force.

The initial trickle of trophies at the beginning of Shankly's Liverpool career would soon become a tidal wave of glory, both under the Scotsman and his successors, with the team he had built going on to enjoy great consistency. Famed for their fitness and ability to overrun teams, Liverpool also played a patient passing style that was pleasing on the eye and extremely affective. The 1965 FA Cup was claimed thanks to a 2-1 extra-time victory over Leeds United. The same year Liverpool and Shankly made their debut in the European Cup reaching the semi-finals, before losing to Helenio Herrera's well-drilled Inter Milan.

Earlier in the competition, Shankly famously introduced another innovation that would have a lasting legacy on the future of Liverpool FC. Ahead of a second-round tie against Anderlecht, the manager decided to experiment with Liverpool's traditional kit of red shirts with white shorts and hooped socks, as he and Ian St John had the idea of playing in an all-red kit that would emulate the all-white of Real Madrid. The club have appeared in an all-red home strip ever since.

The Reds failed to defend their league title in 1965. During an era when the race for the championship was much fiercer and involved several clubs, this wasn't surprising, particularly when considering the extra demands placed upon the Reds during extended FA Cup and European Cup runs. However, a year later, Shankly's Liverpool were again league champions and went on to reach the final of the European Cup Winners' Cup. They were denied in extra-time by Borussia Dortmund, but both Shankly and Paisley were learning quickly about the different tactical styles showcased in continental football.

Apart from lifting the Charity Shield, the 1966/67 season ended trophyless for the Reds, as a once-successful team started to struggle with the demands of league and European competition. Shankly added promising teenager Emlyn Hughes to the side and he soon become an Anfield great, but did little else to redevelop the squad. This is one of the few aspects of the Scot's Liverpool tenure to receive criticism.

Third-, second- and fifth-place league finishes followed in the forthcoming seasons as Shankly attempted to refresh the team. However, some of his signings, including the club record £96,000 deal for Tony Hateley didn't work out. Liverpool's emergence as a constantly dominant force in the First Division was delayed as an established team grew old together.

The turning point came during a shock FA Cup quarter-final defeat to Watford in 1970, when the younger generation of players, including Ray Clemence, John Toshack and Steve Heighway were added to the nucleus of Smith, Callaghan and Hughes to form the Scotsman's second great team at Anfield.

While the 1960s provided a taste of Liverpool's success, the '70s would see Shankly's vision for the club come to fruition, as he moulded a talented group of young players into a hugely successful team unit.

In 1971, Liverpool reached the semi-final of the European Inter-Cities Fairs Cup in a run that featured a 4-1 aggregate victory over Bayern Munich. The team also appeared in an FA Cup Final, losing in extra time to Arsenal.

Then, another superbly scouted player from the lower leagues, an energetic striker called Kevin Keegan, joined the club and became the crucial final piece of Shankly's second Liverpool jigsaw. Skilful, strong and with the heart of a lion, Keegan formed a devastating strike partnership with John Toshack and Liverpool came within a point of winning the 1971/72 First Division title.

The Reds didn't have to wait too long

for another championship, however, as Shankly's side lifted the 1973 title before going on to taste their first success on the continent, defeating Udo Lattek's Borussia Mönchengladbach, whom Shankly rated as the best in Europe. Liverpool won 3-2 over two legs in the final, largely thanks to a 3-0 home victory inspired by the Keegan-Toshack axis. It was the first time an English club had claimed the league title and a European trophy in the same season.

European and league success was harder to come by in the following campaign, as Red Star Belgrade knocked Liverpool out of the European Cup in the second round, with the Reds going on to finish runners-up to Don Revie's emerging Leeds United in the First Division. There was some consolation, though, as Shankly claimed his second FA Cup thanks to one of the most one-sided finals of all time, when a Keegan-inspired Liverpool destroyed Newcastle United 3-0.

That victory amazingly proved to be Shankly's last as Liverpool managed as he stunned the Anfield faithful by retiring from the game in the summer of 1974. The Scotsman was 60 years old but later admitted that he felt jaded from all of the years he'd spent in the pressure-cooker world of professional football.

A man completely in tune with the Liverpool supporters, Shankly understood the passion of football fans, identified with it and used it as a method of motivating his players even further. In his autobiography, *Shankly: My Story*, the Scotsman wrote: "Right from the start as a manager I tried to show that the fans are the people that matter. You've got to know how to treat them [and] have them on your side."

Despite the entertaining patterns of possession play that his teams weaved, Shankly viewed football in its simplest terms as a team game that required the complete cohesion and understanding of a group of people sharing a similar goal and set of values. But he also accepted that brilliant individuals were needed to complement his teams, famously once saying, "A football team is like a piano. You need eight men to carry it and three who can play the damn thing."

He instilled a relentless winning ethic at Liverpool that would go on to become the norm and the very fabric of everything that the club was based on, ensuring a plethora of league titles and European Cups would follow in future seasons. Not one of those achievements could have been realised without Shankly's influence and his revolutionary methods. Former Liverpool chairman John Smith summed up Shankly's gargantuan influence on the club by saying, "In my opinion, he was the most outstanding and dynamic manager of the century."

Following Shankly's death in 1981, Liverpool erected the 15-foot high cast-iron Shankly Gates in front of the Anfield Road stand with the inscription of the club's famous 'You'll Never Walk Alone' motto.

There was a captivating aura around the man, that many found intimidating and the vast majority found enticing. Shankly was a forerunner in providing memorable quotes and using the media to get messages across to his players and opponents. Arguably the most famous comment of all time, was one made in jest, when he said, "Some people believe football is a matter of life and death, I am very disappointed with that attitude. I can assure you it is much, much more important than that."

One of the first managers to harness the power of psychology in sport, Bill Shankly had the ability to make his own players feel invincible, while notoriously unsettling opponents before matches. The purring Scot once said, "A lot of football success is in the mind. You must believe you are the best and then make sure that you are."

Another innovation implemented by Shankly was the 'This is Anfield' plaque above the players' tunnel, which reminded opponents of the enormity of the task facing them.

Football was Shankly's life. He had been obsessed with the game and ways of improving the teams and players that he managed. He had a vision to create an institution that was more than a football club, but something the local community could embrace and be proud of.

That vision has resulted in Liverpool Football Club becoming one of most successful and popular club sides in the world. Leading by inspirational example, the brilliance and purest enthusiasm of the incomparable Bill Shankly created pretty much everything that has come to symbolise the club.

# 18. ARRIGO SACCHI

**Born:** April 1, 1946 in Fusignano, Italy
**Clubs Managed:** Parma, AC Milan, Atlético Madrid, Real Madrid (Director of Football)
**International:** Italy: 1991-1996 (Reached the 1994 World Cup Final)
**Major Honours:** 8

The man who laid the foundations for a decade of AC Milan success, Arrigo Sacchi won back-to-back European Cups with the Rossoneri in 1989 and 1990, as well as the Serie A title in 1988. The Italian also managed his country at the European Championships and the World Cup, reaching the final of the latter in 1994.

As well as these notable achievements, the Italian maestro's place in the top 30 managers of all time is justified due to his revolutionary high-pressing, attacking 4-4-2 tactical approach. His system transformed the identity of the Italian game and acted as the template for many of the great European teams that followed, including recent Champions League victors Bayern Munich.

Sacchi remains the last coach to have won consecutive European Cups, a feat he achieved by playing blistering attacking football. Opinionated, forthright and a fierce defender of his football philosophy, the Italian remains one of the most knowledgeable and quoted personalities in football.

An amateur footballer in his youth, Sacchi decided to quit the game at an early age. As he later explained, "I stopped playing football when I was 19 because I soon realised that I'd never be a champion." That pragmatic approach would serve him well in the future as he dedicated his life to becoming a successful football coach. After he stopped playing, he held down a job as a shoe salesman, which saw him travel around Europe watching as many top-flight matches as time allowed.

Passionate about the game throughout his youth, Sacchi enjoyed the attacking style of play implemented by the great, Budapest Honvéd, Real Madrid, Brazil and Dutch teams, with Ajax and the Netherlands national side and their 'total football' principles having a particularly strong influence on the budding coach.

After managing his local club, Baracca Lugo, and then Bellaria, Sacchi was employed by AC Cesena to work with their youth team. A managerial role with Serie C1 side Rimini followed. There he almost won a league title before being appointed as youth team coach of Serie A side Fiorentina.

Impressing in Florence by creating a talent-filled, progressive youth system, Sacchi was appointed manager of Serie C1 side Parma in 1985. With Parma he earned his first promotion, taking the club into Serie B. He almost sealed back-to-back promotions when his team fell just three points short of reaching Serie A. During his reign with the club, Sacchi famously recorded two 1-0 Coppa Italia victories over the giants of Italian football, AC Milan. The results and the manner of Parma's performances caught the attention of AC Milan owner, Silvio Berlusconi, who promptly appointed him as the club's manager in 1987.

It was a shock decision for many. Sacchi's lack of experience and major honours, as well as the fact that he'd not played professionally, caused uncertainty inside and outside of the club. The media were particularly critical, prompting the Italian's memorable quote: "A jockey doesn't have to have been born a horse." In his first press conference, Sacchi gave journalists even more tantalising insight, including a view into the theories he hoped to implement. "The football of the future will be more intellectual than muscular," he said. "The mind counts for more than athletic preparation... the opponent that I fear the most is time."

Abundantly aware that he'd be afforded little time to make an impact, Sacchi spent significantly and astutely on the Dutch trio of Marco van Basten, Ruud Gullit and later Frank Rijkaard. This trio would fulfil a specific system that would also celebrate the talents of a group of emerging Italian youngsters such as Roberto Donadoni and Paolo Maldini. Arrigo had an immediate impact with the Rossoneri, going on to lift the Serie A title at the end of his first season in charge.

More was to follow, as he led Milan into a dominating 1988/89 European Cup campaign, including a 6-1 aggregate victory over Real Madrid that featured a 5-0 humiliation at the San Siro. The campaign culminated in a 4-0 thumping of Steaua Bucharest in the final. Milan dominated the Romanians, who had been European champions just three years earlier and hadn't lost a domestic league game during that time, from the kick-off. Gullit and van Basten went on to score two goals apiece in one of the most one-sided European Cup Finals of all time.

It was a game that beautifully showcased Sacchi's revolutionary tactical approach. The 4-4-2 formation was certainly nothing new, but the way the Italian instructed his players to operate within it had never been attempted before. In many ways the intelligent coach struck the perfect balance between the catenaccio and total football styles, playing an extremely bold, high defensive line, a narrow midfield with little width and two strikers that were comfortable with dropping deep to ensure a compact and cohesive unit that allowed the team to press opponents aggressively and higher up the pitch. This great understanding between his players was not instinctive or simply down to chance, it was honed on the training ground after hours and hours of 'shadow training', which involved the team moving around the pitch without the ball, reacting to different situations.

The base was an organised defence that worked and moved as a unit, communicated efficiently and operated a zonal marking system. This was completely at odds with the fervently tight man-marking philosophy customarily implemented by Italian defenders. Sacchi's system strangled the life out of some of the most creative talents in Serie A, which was at the time arguably the strongest division in world, as well as in the European Cup.

It was a style that put intense pressure on their opponents and quite simply meant that when the ball was won back, Milan were further away from their own goal and closer to the one they were attacking. All of those elements were present during Milan's 4-0 masterclass against Steaua. "The morning after we beat Steaua Bucharest 4-0 I woke up with a feeling I had never experienced before," said Sacchi later. "I realised it was the apotheosis of my life's work."

Sacchi relentlessly trained his players, attempting to indoctrinate them into the style he desired. This often led to conflict and when Marco van Basten questioned his methods, Sacchi promptly challenged 10 attacking players to score against his well-drilled defensive unit in a 15-minute period. They failed.

Sacchi's belief in the strength of the team over the individual was evident in his approach to the game and the way he treated his players. He wanted men of responsibility that were aware of their duty to their colleagues. Sacchi's resounding faith in the team unit was once eloquently described by the man himself, who said, "It is a question of having a team which is ordered, in which the players are connected to one another, which moves together, as if it was a single player."

It wasn't uncommon for an Italian side to be strong defensively, but Sacchi's Milan was a million miles away from the catenaccio style implemented by the great Serie A sides of the past. The importance of that defensive unit cannot be underestimated, as it allowed the attacking players to express themselves and play on the front foot, but Arrigo was a forward-thinking coach, both in literal and metaphorical terms, and sought to play in a positive and entertaining manner.

The manager advocated his team should always set the tempo and take the game to their opponents in a proactive way. He encouraged positive, short and rapid passing, believing the more direct style would find opponents less prepared and more likely to be out of position. It wasn't a system merely based on high-energy pressing, rather one that featured intelligence of movement. As Sacchi later explained, "We didn't run more than the others. We just ran better."

While AC Milan failed to defend their Serie A title in 1989/90, they again enjoyed success in Europe, with Frank Rijkaard scoring the only goal to defeat Sven-Göran Eriksson's Benfica 1-0 in the 1990 European Cup Final. It meant that the Rossoneri had become the first team since Brian Clough's Nottingham Forest in 1980 to retain the trophy. Sacchi's supreme Milan side also lifted consecutive Intercontinental Cups in 1989 and 1990, defeating Atlético Nacional and Club Olimpia respectively.

The domestic title again eluded Sacchi in 1991 and so did Europe's biggest prize as the reigning champions were knocked out by Marseille in the quarter-final. Ending the season without a trophy, coupled with an increasingly disillusioned set of players weary of the manager's fierce training regime, hastened Sacchi's exit from the San Siro. In 1991, he instead became head coach of the Italian national side.

Italy had missed out on the 1992 European Championships, but Sacchi soon had an impact, comfortably achieving qualification for the 1994 World Cup. Replicating his successful methods at Milan, Sacchi selected a strong defence which included mainly Rossoneri-based players he had worked with. Using the experience of Franco Baresi and the significant talents of Paolo Maldini in the backline, Sacchi selected players ahead of them with the licence to express themselves, including the sumptuously talented Roberto Baggio.

Following a disappointing start to USA 1994, when the Italians lost 1-0 to the Republic of Ireland in their first game, Sacchi soon turned things round as Italy progressed through the group as one of the best third-placed teams, before finding their feet in the knockout stages. There, inspired by the free-scoring Baggio, Italy defeated Nigeria, Spain and Bulgaria to reach the World Cup Final.

Italy met Brazil in the showpiece, but it was a Brazilian side that played in a different style to that which had made the South Americans so entertaining to watch for decades. The game, played in intense heat, became a tactical battle, as both sides packed the midfield and created few chances. The game ended 0-0 after extra-time, meaning the World Cup would be settled by penalties for the first time. The spot-kicks proved to be disastrous for Sacchi's men as Baresi, Baggio and Daniele Massaro missed to hand the trophy to Brazil.

Sacchi ensured qualification for Euro 1996, but following an impressive victory over Russia in their opening fixture he opted to rest key players for the clash with the Czech Republic. It was a game the Italians ultimately lost to the eventual finalists, and a subsequent draw with the team that would win the tournament, Germany, signalled an end to Italy's involvement in the competition.

Arrigo left his role with Italy for a brief and ultimately fruitless return to AC Milan, spending a single season at the San Siro before taking his first coaching assignment outside his homeland with Atlético Madrid. However, after finishing 13th in La Liga and advancing to the final of the Copa del Rey in his first season, Sacchi departed the club. Following a two-year break, a return to Parma beckoned in 2001. But it was another short-lived role, this time just 23 days, as he began to realise his strict and intensive coaching methods weren't necessarily suited to the modern game and that the demands of management and his unquenchable passion for football was affecting his health.

Another sabbatical from the game, this time for three years, followed before Sacchi was appointed as Real Madrid's director of football in 2004. During a season that saw the Spanish giants recruit four managers to work alongside the Italian, Real failed to lift a trophy. Sacchi left the club in 2005, effectively retiring from the game at the relatively young age of 59.

Perhaps if the innovative Italian had

been flexible enough to adapt his style, he may have achieved more success. The brilliance of his methods, which were so beautifully realised during his time with AC Milan, are now being utilised by the Italian Football Federation, who enlisted him to overhaul Italian youth football in 2010. His theories are also in practice in the modern game and have been regularly used by the likes of José Mourinho, with his overachieving Porto side, Roberto Mancini with Manchester City, Jupp Heynckes at Bayern Munich and Pep Guardiola with his peerless Barcelona side.

Sacchi once described a manager as, "A maestro who has his own style. He needs to aim for quality, not the superficial and what comes easy. A maestro is someone who demands the best, who demands rigour." Sacchi was clearly a man who demanded the highest of standards and, for two seasons at AC Milan, he came as close to footballing perfection as any of his peers.

# CHAPTER 5

## MANAGERS 17 – 15

# 17. JOHAN CRUYFF

**Born:** April 25, 1947 in Amsterdam, Netherlands
**Clubs Managed:** Ajax, Barcelona
**International:** Catalonia: 2009-2013
**Major Honours:** 14

It's extremely rare for one of the greatest footballers of all time to have enjoyed an equally impactive coaching career, but the Dutch master, Johan Cruyff, provides an emphatic exception to that rule. As a coach he helped establish the celebrated Barcelona style of play, building on the principles of 'total football' that served him so well as a player and as Ajax manager.

Cruyff created one of Barça's greatest ever teams that featured the attacking brilliance of Romário and Hristo Stoichkov and went on to lift the Catalan club's first European Cup in 1992. Although the Dutchman's trophy record has recently been eclipsed by Pep Guardiola, a man he previously coached, his managerial achievements reach a broader spectrum than such a quantitative evaluation.

As a player, Johan Cruyff was one of the finest attacking talents of his generation. The star of the Ajax, Barcelona and Netherlands teams of the 1970s Cruyff was a flying winger or attacking midfielder. He was famed for his balance, technique and ability to turn defenders inside out and went on to win three Ballon d'Or accolades, three European Cups and multiple domestic titles, as well as appearing in the 1974 World Cup Final.

After ending his playing career with Feyenoord, Cruyff went on to succeed his mentor, Rinus Michels, as Ajax manager a year later. Maintaining his predecessor's passion for 'total football' and the development of youth, Johan guided the Dutch giants to the 1987 European Cup Winners' Cup Final. Ajax won the match thanks to a single goal from Marco van Basten; a player Cruyff had spotted and nurtured through the ranks. That European success came after back-to-back Dutch Cup victories for Cruyff's men, who also finished the 1985/86 campaign as Eredivisie runners-up to PSV Eindhoven, despite scoring 120 goals.

At Ajax Cruyff developed and perfected his favoured formation of three defenders and a sweeper, with two holding, deep-lying play-making midfielders flanked by a pair of touchline-hugging wingers, supporting a second striker and then a centre forward. It was a simple system but one that relied upon the flexibility, intelligence and natural footballing ability of the players. It worked spectacularly, both during his tenure with the club and, more notably, after his departure when Ajax went on to win the Champions League; a fitting tribute to the Dutchman's legacy as coach. Cruyff revolutionised the way the Ajax youth academy trained its top footballers, implementing 'The Cruyff Plan', which emphasised individualised training in line with the manager's 'four points of innovation'.

In 1988, Cruyff made the same move that he had experienced as a player, when he departed Amsterdam to become manager of Barcelona. Johan, who had been known as 'El Flaco'; 'the Skinny One' during his playing days at the Nou Camp, reprised a similar approach and brought through a whole host of young talent, including the likes of Pep Guardiola and José Mari Bakero. He added to that local talent with intelligent transfer dealings that included the captures of Ronald Koeman, Michael Laudrup, Romário and Stoichkov. Barcelona had been a club drenched in mediocrity, with just two La Liga titles lifted in the 28 years before Cruyff's appointment. The Catalans were still yearning for that ever elusive first European Cup.

Barcelona went on to dominate La Liga under the Dutchman, winning four consecutive titles between 1991 and 1994, the European Cup Winners' Cup in 1989 and then realising the club's holy grail by lifting the European Cup for the first time in their history. The win came thanks to a 1-0 victory over Sampdoria at Wembley in 1992, delivered courtesy of a Ronald Koeman thunderbolt. It was also the first time that any Spanish club other than Real Madrid had lifted the famous trophy and, coupled with Barcelona's continued domestic dominance, upped the stakes in a rivalry between the two clubs that would be renowned all over the world and lead to their clashes, known as 'El Clásico', to become box-office encounters.

The manager also ensured the club's youth teams were all playing in a similar style. So when the conveyor belt of naturally talented individuals started to click into action, the players would be ready to fit into the first-team system and make an immediate impact.

Cruyff's Barcelona also won the Copa del Rey, European Super Cup and three Spanish Super Cups, and reached the final of the 1991 European Cup Winners' Cup, where they were narrowly defeated by Alex Ferguson's emerging Manchester United. Johan's early days in the Nou Camp dugout where characterised by his chain-smoking during matches, but following double bypass heart surgery in 1991, Cruyff famously traded the cigarettes for a lollypop.

The biggest blot on the Dutchman's managerial record came in 1994 when his Barcelona 'dream team' reached another European Cup Final. Facing a well-drilled AC Milan side, built by Arrigo Sacchi and improved by Fabio Capello, Cruyff's team were tactically and physically dominated by a Milan side playing with an attacking swagger that took their opponents by surprise. The final 4-0 scoreline was only slightly generous to Milan as Barça had been ruthlessly exploited on the counter-attack. The result signalled the beginning of the end for Cruyff as the club's manager.

Ahead of the 1994 World Cup, the Dutchman was close to trying his hand at international management, having discussed the head coach's role of the Netherlands national side with the country's football federation, but Dick Advocaat was eventually appointment in the role.

Despite a then-record trophy haul of 11 major honours and becoming Barcelona's longest-serving manager, following two trophyless seasons, Cruyff fell out with the club's chairman, Josep Lluís Núñez, and departed the Nou Camp in 1996. He later went on to fulfil an advisory role with the club.

The successful implementation of Cruyff's football vision transformed the culture of Barcelona, maintaining what is often referred to as the 'Dutch influence' on the club. His fast moving, beautifully intricate passing game become known as 'tiki-taka' and signalled the birth of a new identity for the Catalan giants that led to decades of success.

In 2008, the Dutch master almost returned to Ajax, with Cruyff coming close to taking a technical director's role with the club. It took until 2011 for him to rejoin the Amsterdam club, this time in an advisory role similar to the relationship he'd enjoyed with Barcelona. Another advisory role, this time with Mexican side, Chivas de Guadalajara, began in 2012, with Cruyff becoming the club's sport consultant for nine months.

Cruyff also managed the Catalonia national team between 2009 and 2013, mostly taking charge of the side during friendlies. Nevertheless it was an appointment that signalled the affection with which the Dutchman was held within the region.

As well as Johan Cruyff's impressive trophy haul and his ability to take Barça to the holy grail of European Cup success, the Dutchman's innovation and revolutionary tactical approach is likely to be his most significant legacy. His principles have influenced so many managers and coaches that have followed him, marking him out as one of the most renowned football visionaries of all time. A man with similar attacking principles, former Manchester United star, Eric Cantona, once commented, "Cruyff was the best. He was a creator. He was at the heart of a revolution with his football. Ajax changed football and he was the leader of it all."

It's a view echoed by Spanish football expert, Graham Hunter, who places huge emphasis on Cruyff's influence on Barcelona. "Without him there would be no Lionel Messi, Xavi, Iniesta or Pep Guardiola—Barcelona's modern success is thanks to Johan Cruyff. From player to coach to advisor, Cruyff is a Barça legend in all three roles."

Cruyff's influence on Guardiola cannot be underestimated, as his decision to develop Pep into a more defensive, play-making midfielder, revolutionised the Spaniard's understanding of the game.

His manager's principles remained with Guardiola into his coaching career, with the man himself saying the following of his mentor, "Johan Cruyff painted the chapel, and Barcelona coaches since merely restore or improve it. I learned a lot of things from him. To some extent, we're all disciples of his style."

The Dutchman's strong belief in nurturing home-grown talent and producing players possessing both technical and tactical expertise, has borne fruit in spectacular fashion with both Ajax and Barcelona, and provided a blueprint for developing youth all over the world. Without Cruyff, Barça's fabled 'La Masia' academy and Ajax's equivalent, the 'Toekomst', wouldn't be nearly as prolific.

That particular legacy was perhaps summed up the best when Spain faced the Netherlands in the 2010 World Cup final, with both teams containing a significant number of players produced from both academies. Quite simply, without Johan Cruyff, Pep Guardiola's Barcelona and the heights they reached would have remained a literal fantasy, rather than a metaphorical one, and the Catalan giants wouldn't have produced two dream teams filled with attacking brilliance and individual flair seldom witnessed in the game. In a sport often dubbed as the 'beautiful game', Johan Cruyff has done more than most to make that description a reality.

# 16. GIOVANNI TRAPATTONI

**Born:** March 17, 1939 in Cusano Milanino, Italy
**Clubs Managed:** AC Milan, Juventus, Inter Milan, Bayern Munich, Cagliari, Fiorentina, Benfica, Stuttgart, Red Bull Salzburg
**International:** Italy: 2000-2004; Republic of Ireland: 2008-2013
**Major Honours:** 22

A veteran of European club and international management who has lifted more than 20 trophies in a career spanning four decades, nine clubs and two national teams, Giovanni Trapattoni has succeeded at the likes of AC Milan, Juventus and Bayern Munich, remaining one of the most prolific coaches of this or any other generation.

Trapattoni is one of only four managers, alongside Ernst Happel, José Mourinho, and Tomislav Ivic, to have won league titles in four different countries. Alongside Udo Lattek, he is the only coach to have won all three major European club titles. He has also won the UEFA Cup three times, more than any other manager. Following a successful playing career with AC Milan, where he won two Serie A titles and two European Cups, Trapattoni began his coaching career at the San Siro in 1972. He took up a role coaching the youth team before becoming caretaker manager and finally being appointed first-team coach in 1975. However, Trapattoni only lasted a single trophyless season at the Milan helm and took up the reins at Juventus a year later. He went on to build two extremely talented teams in Turin, creating tactically astute and fluid sides that included the likes of Liam Brady, Zbigniew Boniek, Michael Platini, Marco Tardelli and Paolo Rossi. Trapattoni's early years in Turin saw him develop an ultra-fit and organised side that operated with a deadly form of 'catenaccio' football, using devastating counter-attacks.

During his 10-year spell at Juventus, Trapattoni enjoyed great domestic and European success, winning six Serie A titles, including his first in 1977 in a campaign that saw Juventus suffer just two defeats. The side bettered that record the following season with just one reversal. Giovanni also added two Italian Cups, each of the major European trophies, including the club's first continental trophy, the 1977 UEFA Cup, thanks to a 2-0 win over Athletic Bilbao—dispatching Manchester City and Manchester United along the way.

Juventus's first ever European Cup was also delivered in 1985, when his charges overcame Joe Fagan's Liverpool 1-0 in the final thanks to a Michel Platini penalty. However, the game was overshadowed by tragedy, after fighting between rival supporters in Belgium's Heysel Stadium where the game was held led to a wall collapsing, killing 39 supporters. His fourth league title, claimed at the age of 43, saw Trapattoni established as one of his country's most successful managers, but the determined, driven and forward-thinking coach still had much to achieve.

Trapattoni's side went on to win the European Super Cup, Intercontinental Cup and the 1984 Serie A title, ensuring Juventus became the first club to have won the Italian league on 20 occasions. He had also led the club to the 1983 European Cup Final, the first in their history, only to lose to Ernst Happel's SV Hamburg. Trapattoni got the very best out of one of the most talented players of his generation, the hugely skilled Michel Platini, who was named European Footballer of the Year in three successive years between 1983 and 1985. Trapattoni's team of the early 1980s also formed the backbone of the Italian national side that won the 1982 World Cup with Paolo Rossi and Marco Tardelli putting in star turns for their country.

Giovanni signed off his 10-year stint in Turin with another league title in 1986 before returning to the San Siro, this time to manage Inter rather than his old club

AC Milan. His Juventus legacy included six Serie A titles and guiding the Old Lady to their first European Cup, UEFA Cup, Cup Winners' Cup, UEFA Super Cup and Intercontinental Cup.

The fiery and forthright manager went on to spend five seasons with Inter, winning the Serie A title in 1989—the club's first for nine years—thanks to the talents of German pair, Andreas Brehme and Lothar Matthäus, and Argentine Ramón Díaz. Another top-class foreign recruit, Jürgen Klinsmann was added following the title success and Inter claimed the 1989 Supercoppa Italia. However, further league success proved hard to come by, and with an emerging AC Milan side dominating the division, Trapattoni returned to Juventus.

The man who had enjoyed unprecedented success at the Stadio delle Alpi found trophies harder to come by as he started to rebuild the team, introducing the likes of Dino Baggio, Antonio Conte, Fabrizio Ravanelli and Angelo Peruzzi. He also made shrewd signings such as Andreas Möller and Gianluca Vialli to complement the mercurial skills of the 'divine ponytail', Roberto Baggio. The majority of those players would go on to form the basis of the Juventus side that dominated Italian football for the remainder of the 1990s, reaching three European Cup Finals and winning the trophy once under Marcello Lippi.

During Trapattoni's second spell, Juventus claimed just a single trophy, the

1993 UEFA Cup. The Turin side defeated Ottmar Hitzfeld's Borussia Dortmund 6-1 on aggregate in the final thanks to goals from Roberto and Dino Baggio and Andreas Möller. Having triumphed over a German club, the Italian went on to manage one of the Bundesliga's finest when, in 1994, he was named as Bayern Munich boss.

It was Trapattoni's first foreign assignment and he inherited a Bayern team that, while in possession of the Bundesliga, was far from being one of the club's vintage sides. Following high-profile disagreements with the press and having struggled to assert his authority on the dressing room, the Italian left Munich after a single season.

He returned to his homeland to take charge of Cagliari, the smallest club he had managed in terms of stature, and went on to lead them to a respectable 10th-place finish before unexpectedly returning to Bayern Munich at the end of the season. Trapattoni's second spell in Germany proved to be a happier one as he lifted the Bundesliga and German League Cup double in 1997, before adding the German Cup a year later. As well as his trophy success, the Italian's latter tenure with Bayern is remembered for an infamous outburst during a press conference when he was particularly critical of the attitudes of players such as Mehmet Scholl and Mario Basler. At the time Bayern had been nicknamed 'FC Hollywood' due to political infighting and regular off-field stories surrounding the players.

In 1998 Trapattoni departed Bayern for Italy for the second time, this time taking charge of Fiorentina. Inspired by the manager's guidance and the explosive goalscoring ability of Gabriel Batistuta, the Viola challenged for the title during Trapattoni's first season, eventually finishing third to secure a rare appearance in the Champions League.

The team from Florence reached the group stages of the tournament during the 1999/2000 campaign and recorded a famous 2-0 victory over holders Manchester United, as well as a 1-0 win at Arsenal. However, their league form suffered and Trapattoni opted to leave the club at the end of the season to become head coach of the Italian national team

Having enjoyed such sustained success at club level, much was expected of Trapattoni on the international scene. Things began well when he led the Italians to the 2002 World Cup, but the tournament itself proved to be a minor disaster. Following an opening victory over Ecuador, Trapattoni's men slumped to a controversial defeat to Croatia, in a match where refereeing decisions went against them, before salvaging a draw with Mexico to qualify for the knockout stages.

Further controversy followed in the second round of the tournament after Italy lost to hosts South Korea following an extra-time golden goal. Italy had a goal ruled out for offside, which was later proven to be the wrong decision and Francesco Totti was harshly sent off for a dive. The manner of the exit riled Trapattoni who later accused FIFA of attempting to fix the tournament to ensure the host nation advanced to the latter stages.

Trapattoni remained in charge as Italy again comfortably qualified for a major tournament, reaching the 2004 European Championships. Italy went on to draw with Sweden and Denmark in the group stages before defeating Bulgaria to finish on five points. However, Denmark and Sweden, playing each other in the last game, knew a draw would be enough for each of them to advance at the expense of the Italians and the match ended level, prompting Trapattoni to again speculate about a conspiracy.

Despite some harsh treatment at the hands of referees and not receiving much luck, Italy failed to play with fluency under the experienced manager. However, his consistency in selection and ability to pair Alessandro del Piero and Francesco Totti in games, while also implementing a sound defensive unit, created a legacy that helped his country win the 2006 World Cup under Marcello Lippi, two years after 'El Trap's' departure.

Following his exit from international football in 2004, Trapattoni was named manager of Benfica. He spent just a single season in Portugal, opting to return home to be closer to his family, but it was a single season of success as he guided Benfica to their first league title in 11 years and into the Portuguese Cup Final, where they were defeated by Vitória de Setubal.

A man whose love for the game bordered on obsession, it wasn't long before Trapattoni returned to the dugout, this time with German side VfB Stuttgart ahead of the 2005/06 Bundesliga campaign. It proved to be a short and unsuccessful spell for the Italian and following a poor start to the season and public criticism from certain players, Trapattoni was sacked in February 2006.

Later that year, Giovanni ventured into Austria to become director of football at Red Bull Salzburg, where his former player at Inter Milan, Lothar Matthäus, worked under him as coach. After a single season, which saw Red Bull win the Austrian Bundesliga, the German was dismissed with Trapattoni taking over team affairs. During Salzburg's defence of the title, the Italian announced his intentions to resign the position at the end of the season to take charge of the Republic of Ireland national side. Trapattoni's final season at Red Bull ended with a second place league finish and early exits from the Champions League, then the Europa League.

Trapattoni installed his former players Marco Tardelli and Liam Brady as part of his coaching staff with Ireland and went on to guide the Republic to an undefeated qualification campaign for the 2010 World Cup, which led to a runners-up spot and a play-off place. Trapattoni's men certainly didn't receive the luck of the Irish in a two-legged tie with France. The first game in Ireland finished 1-0 to the French but a Robbie Keane goal in the Paris return clash forced the tie into extra-time. An extremely well-organised and spirited Ireland side were frustrating France until one of the most controversial goals in the history of international football. The goal was scored by William Gallas, who tapped the ball home on the goal-line having been found by Thierry Henry who had initially received the ball in an offside position before deliberately handling the ball twice and laying on the assist for his team-mate.

Trapattoni again presided over a successful qualifying campaign for the 2012 European Championships, once more finishing second in the group and reaching the play-offs, where they comprehensively defeated Estonia 5-1 over two legs to ensure the Republic's first qualification for a major tournament in 10 years.

Due to their low seeding, the Irish were placed in a tough group during Euro 2012. Facing World Champions Spain and eventual finalists Italy, they exited the competition without registering a single point. Trapattoni remained at the helm until he departed by mutual consent in 2013 as Ireland failed to qualify for the 2014 World Cup.

An indomitable character whose passion for the game is as conspicuous as his tactical awareness, Giovanni Trapattoni is a manger from the old school who adapted his game to succeed in the modern era. Many may argue that his methods haven't progressed enough, but he has maintained relative success in recent years, while coaching teams with limited abilities. The Italian's true genius shone through when he was managing top class players, particularly during his empire building spell at Juventus, where he developed greatness, both in terms of the team and the individuals playing within it.

In his native Italy, Trapattoni is affectionately referred to in a similar manner to the way Sir Bobby Robson was considered in England, due to his often eccentric style and mistake-ridden press conferences. However, he certainly differs from his English counterpart when it comes to making controversial statements. When the Italian feels he has been wronged he becomes a raging, eye-bulging force of nature. His presence commands respect from his players, due to his achievements in the game and his demeanour in the dressing room and on the sidelines, where he famously blows a two-fingered whistle to attract their attention during games.

Trapattoni is a no-nonsense character whose tactical approach of pragmatism first and flair second fitted perfectly with the older generation of Italian football and again in the modern era when he has taken charge of clubs and nations with limited talent and resources. The Italian's philosophy, routed in the catenaccio and zonal approaches adopted by his coaches as player at Milan, Nereo Rocco and Nils Liedholm. Both men influenced his preference of ensuring that teams maintained a rigid formation, defending in numbers and playing on the counter attack. However, his great teams at Juventus and Inter Milan also played with their fair share of attacking swagger.

Trapattoni has shown great durability, coaching into his eighth decade and without having a single season out of the game throughout his 35 years as a manager. During that period he has enjoyed success more often than not, leading 13 different teams and five different countries and lifting a burgeoning tally of 22 major honours. He also remains the most successful manager in Serie A history when gauged on the number of trophies won. 'El Trapp' is unquestionably a proven and emphatically regular winner and one of football's greatest bosses.

# 15. MARCELLO LIPPI

**Born:** April 12, 1948 in Viareggio, Italy
**Clubs Managed:** Pontedera, Siena, Pistoiese, Carrarese, Cesana, Lucchese, Atalanta, Napoli, Juventus, Inter Milan, Guangzhou Evergrande
**International:** Italy: 2004-2006 and 2008-2010 (Won the 2006 World Cup)
**Major Honours:** 17

A suave Italian coach, often seen with a cigar in hand, Marcello Lippi oversaw one of the most successful periods in Juventus's history, building a hugely entertaining winning machine that included the likes of Zinedine Zidane and Alessandro Del Piero. Lippi won Serie A titles and the Champions League before guiding his country to 2006 World Cup glory.

Lippi is one of the most prolific coaches in the modern era, thanks to five Serie A titles, one Champions League, a Coppa Italia and one Intercontinental Cup. When he guided Italy to success in the 2006 World Cup, he became the first coach to have won all of the most prestigious worldwide tournaments both at club and international level; a record he now shares with Spain manager Vicente del Bosque.

A defender during his playing days, Marcello spent most of his career with Sampdoria before later joining Pistoiese and Arancioni and hanging up his boots at Lucchese in 1982. Aged 34, he began a coaching career as part of the youth setup at Sampdoria before taking up roles with a number of lower-league Italian sides and a head-coach post with Serie A side Cesena in 1989. Lippi's early managerial career was less than prolific as he went on to receive the sack three times and coach nine clubs in his first 10 seasons. But his fortunes first changed with Napoli, where he tasted tangible success after leading a club that had been struggling both on and off the pitch, into the UEFA Cup via an impressive sixth-place league finish.

Having succeeded against the odds in Naples, Lippi's potential was noticed by a number of Italy's bigger clubs, including Juventus, who appointed him as manager in 1994. His first season ended in Serie A success, as a team including the notable attacking talents of Fabrizio Ravanelli and Gianluca Vialli, as well as Ciro Ferrara, an uncompromising defender the manager had brought with him from Napoli, stormed to the title. That season Juventus finished 10 points ahead of second-place Lazio and ended the club's nine-year Italian Championship drought. The Turin side also reached the final of the 1994 UEFA Cup under Lippi, but were defeated 2-1 on aggregate by Parma.

Lippi was blessed with a group of extremely talented and mainly Italian players that also included the imagination and creativity of the experienced Roberto Baggio and the emerging Allesandro Del Piero. The team failed to retain their title during the 1995/96 campaign but went on to enjoy great success in Europe, playing some devastating football on their way to a Champions League Final against holders Ajax. Following a 1-1 draw at the Stadio Olimpico, Juventus triumphed 4-2 on penalties to lift just the second European Cup in the club's history.

The manager continued to develop his team, spending significantly on the likes of Zinedine Zidane, Filippo Inzaghi and Edgar Davids to build a squad capable of coping with the demands of domestic and European football and creating the most consistent and entertaining team of the mid 1990s. The Serie A title was reclaimed in 1997 and Lippi's men reached another European Cup Final, but this time they were comprehensively defeated 3-1 by Ottmar Hitzfeld's Borussia Dortmund. A similar pattern reccurred during the 1997/98 season, as Juventus again dominated domestically, lifting the Serie A title thanks to a five point margin, before reaching a second consecutive Champions League Final, where they again missed out, this time 1-0 to Jupp Heynckes's Real Madrid.

The Italians' consistency under Lippi during this period was similar to the dominance enjoyed by AC Milan at the beginning of the decade. It also featured European Super Cup and Intercontinental success in 1996. The Bianconeri were revered by their opponents during this period, with many viewing Juventus as a relentless winning machine and their manager as an extremely decisive and incisive operator. Sir Alex Ferguson notably explained in his autobiography, *Managing My Life*, "Marcello Lippi is one impressive man. Looking into his eyes is enough to tell you that you are dealing with somebody who is in command of himself and his professional domain. Those eyes are sometimes burning with seriousness, sometimes twinkling, sometimes warily assessing you—and always they are alive with intelligence. Nobody could make the mistake of taking Lippi lightly."

Like many of the managers featured in this book, particularly those of Italian descent, Lippi placed huge emphasis on the importance of team spirit and unity. He realised no matter how talented the players at his disposal were, they had to work well together as a group. Lippi later explained these theories, saying, "In this day and age you win if you become a team. It doesn't necessarily mean that you've got to have the best football players in the country. It's possible that the best, all together, don't become a team. It's like a mosaic, you have to put all the pieces together."

The man from Tuscany developed a tactical plan that allowed each of his hugely talented performers to play to their maximum. His approach was less revolutionary, more evolutionary, as illustrated by his modern interpretation of the Italian catenaccio defensive approach. With Juventus and latterly Italy, Lippi ensured his teams were built on an extremely solid and uncompromising defensive unit, aided by world-class goalkeepers and defenders, but also supplemented by a defensive awareness and discipline that was implemented throughout the unit. This produced effective and relentlessly successful teams, featuring beautifully technical players that often played without beauty, to quench Lippi's clear and unwavering ambition to win games and lift trophies.

As the '90s wore on, Lippi continued to strengthen his Juventus squad, capturing to class performers such as Gianluigi Buffon, Pavel Nedved, Lilian Thuram and David Trezeguet. However, he did lose the mercurial Zinedine Zidane to Real Madrid in 1996. Following a couple of seasons without significant trophy success, Lippi left Juventus for Inter Milan in 1999. His stay at the San Siro proved a brief and unsuccessful one, and a return to Turin beckoned just over a year later.

With Lippi back at the helm, Juventus went on to lift the 2002 and 2003 Serie A titles and reach another Champions League Final in 2003. Lippi's men faced Carlo Ancelotti's AC Milan in an all-Italian final. In what proved to be a drab tactical affair the game ended goalless after extra-time, meaning the teams had to be separated by penalty kicks. While Lippi had enjoyed spot kick fortune in the 1996 final, he was in possession of a losing ticket in the 12-yard lottery in 2003, and AC Milan lifted the trophy.

Following a disappointing Euro 2004 under Giovanni Trapattoni, the man Lippi succeeded at Juventus, the Italian national side were on the lookout for a new manager and Marcello's club record made him the standout candidate. In July 2004 he was appointed as Italy's head coach and went on to ensure qualification for the 2006 World Cup.

The Azzurri's preparations for the tournament were thrown into chaos following the revelations around the Calciopoli match-fixing scandal enveloping the Italian game and particularly focusing on the manager's former club Juventus. Many of Lippi's squad were on the books of clubs implicated in the scandal and that, coupled with his long-term association with Juventus, led to intense media speculation about the integrity of those involved in Italy's World Cup campaign and their mindset ahead of the competition.

The head coach responded resolutely and emphatically, vying that the controversies would bring the team together and demanding that his charges play with responsibility. Despite so many odds being stacked against him, Lippi went on to enjoy his finest hour and one that he later described as his "most satisfying moment as a coach", galvanising the entire squad and creating a siege mentally that fostered an intense team spirit, focus and determination to succeed.

The Italians began the campaign steadily, progressing through their group by defeating Ghana, drawing with the USA and overcoming the Czech Republic 2-0. The team's success was largely built on an experienced and hugely solid backline, which included Gianluigi Buffon, Alessandro Nesta and captain Fabio Cannavaro. That defensive nous was again on show during the knockout stages of the tournament as they defeated Australia 1-0 thanks to Francesco Totti's stoppage-time penalty kick. Italy had triumphed despite playing with 10 men for large periods following Marco Materazzi's dismissal; their second red card of the tournament after Daniele De Rossi had been given his marching orders against the USA.

Italy continued to impress, with the combative and controlling defensive midfield pair of De Rossi and Gennaro Gattuso, allowing Andrea Pirlo, who had been afforded the freedom to express himself and dictate possession by Lippi, to become one of the tournament's stars. The manager also succeeded in getting the best out of two of the most talented Italian players of that generation, harnessing the creativity of both Francesco Totti and Alessandro del Piero, either in the same team or rotating them from the bench.

The quarter-finals ended in a much more comprehensive victory as Italy defeated Ukraine 3-0 to set up a semi-final clash with an increasingly impressive German side. Lippi's men went on to defeat the German's 2-0 after extra-time in a captivating end to end tactical encounter that saw the resilience of the Italian's overcome the open, attacking endeavours of the hosts.

Italy faced France in the final in a game made famous by the infamous sending off of Lippi's former charge, Zinedine Zidane, who head-butted Italy's Marco Materazzi in the chest following some intense verbal provocation. The match itself was a largely drab affair that ended 1-1 with the game's two main protagonists, Zidane and Materazzi, scoring the goals. The scores remained level after extra-time, leading to the inevitable penalty shootout which, this time, saw Lippi the benefactor as the Italians won 5-3, scoring five goals in a shootout for the first time in their history.

Lippi's World Cup win had been achieved through his savvy and shrewd ability to rotate his squad, illustrated by the Italians boasting 10 different goal scorers throughout the tournament, with five of their 12 goals scored by substitutes. He later stated that the instillation of an identity and united belief had been key in the team's success; "I tried to give the Italian players the same conviction that I had within myself, which was the conviction that I believed strongly, 100 per cent, that in Italy we had the potential to make a World Cup-winning team."

That potential had been brilliantly realised by Lippi, but just three days after the World Cup Final, he declined to renew his contract and went on to take two years out of the game. However, his successor, Roberto Donadoni failed to inspire the Italians past the quarter-final stages of Euro 2008, leading to Lippi's reappointment.

He guided Italy during the 2009 Confederations Cup, but failed to ensure the team's progression through the group stages. Lippi successfully secured his country's passage to the 2010 World Cup held in South Africa, but after relying heavily on an experienced and ageing squad, Italy struggled to establish themselves on the tournament, going on to suffer an embarrassing group stage exit after failing to register a victory and finishing last in a group that featured Paraguay, New Zealand and Slovakia.

The disappointment of the campaign in South Africa saw Lippi step down as manager and again take a two-year break from coaching. In 2012, the Italian took his first managerial role outside of his homeland, but rather than moving to one of Europe's premier leagues, he opted to take up a role in China with Super League side Guangzhou Evergrande. Lippi signed a lucrative two-year deal with the club and went on to claim the Chinese Super League twice and the Chinese FA Cup.

Despite the financial rewards of coaching in China, few would be surprised to see Marcello Lippi return to club or international management at the highest level in Europe. His track record is favourable to many of his contemporaries, including some of the finest Italian coaches of all time and men that have already been mentioned in this book, such Fabio Capello, Carlo Ancelotti and even Giovanni Trapattoni. Lippi's achievements eclipse all three of his compatriots because he has reached the pinnacle of both club and international management.

Not only did he create and maintain a culture of almost incessant success at Juventus, crafting one of the most devastatingly ruthless winning machines of the modern game, he also went on to guide an unfancied Italy to an unlikely World Cup victory. The trophy was a triumph for the team unit and considered tactical approach over naturally, expressive football. Marcello Lippi's teams were some of the most effective sides in football history, and the perceptive Italian's understated, yet prolifically successful, approach to management, ranks him as one of the greats of the European game.

# CHAPTER 6
## MANAGERS 14 - 12

# 14. JOSÉ VILLALONGA LLORENTE

**Born:** December 12, 1919 in Córdoba, Spain
**Died:** August 8, 1973, aged 53
**Clubs Managed:** Real Madrid, Atlético Madrid
**International:** Spain: 1962-1966 (Won the 1964 European Championship)
**Major Honours:** 10

The man who did as much as anybody to build the great traditions and renowned reputation of Real Madrid all over the world, José Villalonga Llorente guided a supremely talented Madrid side to consecutive European Cup crowns in the 1950s. He also achieved domestic success with Los Merengues and their city rivals Atlético Madrid, before leading Spain to their first major international honour, the European Championships, in 1964.

The Madrid job was the Spaniard's first in professional football and one that he took on midway through the 1954/55 season. He inherited a team assembled by the club's formidable president, Santiago Bernabéu Yeste, who created Europe's first multi-national side, which included greats such as Alfredo Di Stéfano, Francisco Gento and Miguel Muñoz. Real were reigning Spanish champions and about to establish themselves on the continent in a European Cup tournament that was in its infancy.

Villalonga only spent three years in the Bernabéu hot seat, but his tenure coincided with the most successful period in the club's history. He reclaimed the 1954/55 La Liga title and lifted the Copa Latino before the realisation of Real's Holy Grail occurred a year later, when the team playing all in white lifted the first ever European Cup. Villalonga's exciting attacking team defeated French side Stade de Reims 4-3 in a thrilling final. The Spaniard, aged just 36 years and 184 days, remains the youngest manager to have won the tournament.

The following campaign, Villalonga's final season with Real, proved his most successful as he added the considerable talents of Raymond Kopa to a team already bulging with some of the finest players on the planet. He led the team to an unprecedented treble of La Liga title, the Copa Latina and a third successive European Cup. The 1957 European Cup was again won in style as Real defeated Fiorentina 2-0 in the final, announcing their arrival as the dominant force on the continent and setting themselves on the way to being the most successful side the competition has ever seen, as the team masterfully perfected by Villalonga went on to win the European Cup for the next three seasons.

A visionary who had the self-confidence to manage a team filled with such a multitude of stars, Villalonga's single-minded approach and independent streak eventually proved to be his downfall at Madrid. He believed Real had become too attack-minded and the defensive side of their game suffered as a result, particularly in domestic football. So the manager demanded that star man and Argentine ace, Alfredo Di Stéfano, play higher up the pitch, causing controversy both inside and outside of the club, with many observers questioning the merits of such an audacious move. Mutiny from within the camp came when Villalonga's relationship with assistant coach Juan Antonio Ipiña soured to such an extent that both men stopped speaking to each other. A man who was obsessed with the image of his club and those that represented it, president Bernabéu made the bold decision to sack Villalonga.

In 1957 José departed Real, taking a two-year break from coaching before his appointment as manager of his former club's city rivals, Atlético Madrid in 1959. Despite not being able to call upon the star names that were available to him at Real, the ambitious manager created a winning and attractive team that went on to defeat his former club in consecutive Copa del Generalissimo finals in 1960 and 1961. Villalonga's team also finished as La Liga runners-up in 1961 and enjoyed European success in 1962, when they defeated Fiorentina 3-0 after a replay to lift the European Cup Winners' Cup.

Villalonga's three-year rein in charge of Atlético came to an end following the Cup Winners' Cup triumph as he was appointed head coach of the Spanish national side. After just two years in charge, the manager implemented the magic of his club career at international level, leading a talented Spanish side that included the likes of star striker Luis Suárez and Josep Maria Fusté to their first major trophy, when they defeated the USSR 2-1 in the European Championship Final thanks to a late header from Marcelino Martínez. Performing with swagger and authority as tournament hosts, the Spaniards had already disposed of Hungary in the semi-finals and played with a level of belief and freedom that the national side had lacked for years and would struggle to recapture for half a century.

It was an honour that maintained Villalonga's reputation of being able to conquer the continent, as he became the first coach to win Europe's top prizes at both club and international level. This led Spaniards to christen him the 'Great King Continental'.

The manger stayed in place for the 1966 World Cup but his team struggled to recapture their previous form and after suffering defeats to eventual finalists West Germany and a combative Argentina, Spain exited the tournament in the group stage. The tournament signalled the end of Villalonga's involvement in the national team and proved to be his last act in football. He retired from the game aged 47.

The man who helped put the finishing touches to the creation of a legendary team, José Villalonga was more than just a coach lucky enough to manage a wonderfully talented group of players. He possessed the judgement and character to mould them into a successful team, giving them the confidence and presence to become winners, then serial winners. His abilities to create successful teams continued when he took charge of Atlético Madrid with considerably fewer resources and during his largely successful tenure as Spain's head coach.

In many ways, José Villalonga was the José Mourinho of his era. He possessed great presence and the ability to create winning teams that played with great belief; belief that he exuded from the touchline and in the dressing room. Like Mourinho, Villalonga was stubborn, single-minded and not afraid to cause a stir. Santiago Bernabéu may have been the man to build Real Madrid, but it was José Villalonga who added the finishing touches that instilled a winning mentality and brought both instant and lasting success to help propel the club into the forefront of the European game—a position they have barely relinquished ever since.

# 13. MIGUEL MUÑOZ

**Born:** January 19, 1922 in Madrid, Spain
**Died:** July 16, 1990, aged 68
**Clubs Managed:** Real Madrid, Plus Ultra, Granada, Las Palmas, Sevilla
**International:** Spain: 1969 and 1982-1988 (Reached the 1984 European Championship Final)
**Major Honours:** 15

A man who enjoyed great success under José Villalonga Llorente as a Real Madrid player, Miguel Muñoz went on to manage the Spanish giants to nine La Liga titles and two European Cup victories. He then came close to realising the international feats of his mentor by guiding Spain to the 1984 European Championship Final.

A serial winner who had the foresight to rebuild great teams while ensuring continued success, Muñoz remains Real Madrid's longest serving and most successful manager. His team was famed for playing entertaining football, as he utilised the attacking brilliance of some of the greatest performers of all time.

A versatile midfielder or defender, Muñoz spent the majority of his playing days with Real, winning four La Liga titles and three European Cups before hanging up his boots in 1958. A year later Muñoz spent a few months as the club's caretaker boss before being instilled as reserve team manager of the Plus Ultra side, which was Real's feeder squad.

Midway through the 1959/60 season he was promoted to the role of Real Madrid manager, succeeding the Argentine Luis Carniglia who had won a single La Liga and two European Cups in two years. Muñoz went on to blow that record out of the water in his subsequent 13 seasons in charge, signalling the start of an incessant period of trophy gathering by presiding over another European Cup victory for the Madridistas in a final considered to be the most entertaining in the competition's history.

Muñoz's team featured the magical trio of Raymond Kopa, Alfredo Di Stéfano and Ferenc Puskás and defeated German champions Eintracht Frankfurt 7-3 in a final held at Hampden Park, Glasgow. The game included four goals from Puskás and a Di Stéfano hat-trick. The victory saw Muñoz become the first man to lift the European Cup as both a player and a manager. The inaugural Intercontinental Cup was

The immaculately dressed Pep Guardiola fashioned near footballing perfection during a prolific four-year spell with Barcelona that produced 14 major trophies.

A true great as a player, Johan Cruyff was a tactical visionary who created beautiful and successful football at Ajax and Barcelona.

A hugely intelligent and tactically astute manager, Ottmar Hitzfeld delivered the European Champions League to both Borussia Dortmund and Bayern Munich.

Enigmatic, outspoken and brash, Brian Clough possessed a brilliant football mind and enjoyed unprecedented success with lesser clubs.

Sitting proudly alongside the European Cup he so desperately desired, Sir Matt Busby established Manchester United as a footballing institution.

The self-proclaimed 'special one', José Mourinho has been a prolific trophy gatherer in four of Europe's major leagues.

A double European Cup Winner, the revolutionary Ernst Happel combined great tactical awareness with an ambitious, attacking style of play.

Posing with one of the three European Cups he won, Bob Paisley took Liverpool to dizzying heights during the 1970s and '80s.

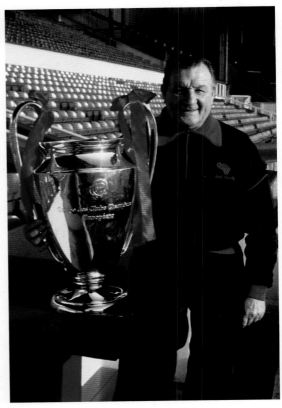

A football purest who excelled as a coach and a manger, the statesman of Dutch football, Rinus Michels, excelled at both club and international level.

Lifting the last of his 49 major honours - a 13th Premier League title for Manchester United - Sir Alex Ferguson's outstanding achievements are unlikely to be equalled.

claimed later that year as Real defeated South American Copa Libertadores champions, Peñarol, 5-1 on aggregate.

As well as that instant European success, Muñoz worked hard to instil the discipline and consistency that made Real the dominant domestic force in Spanish football, describing his vision with great simplicity as, "Success is the result of discipline and big moments coming together." He led the club to the 1961 La Liga title at the end of his first full season in charge and more Spanish championships followed. In fact, Madrid lifted the next four La Liga crowns, completing a sequence of five in a row in 1965.

The league title was surrendered in 1966 as Real focused on reclaiming their first European Cup in six years, a relative famine for Madrid. That campaign saw Muñoz's rebuilt side, minus the combined genius of Di Stéfano and Puskás, defeat holders Inter Milan in the semi-finals then Partizan Belgrade in the final thanks to goals from Fernando Serena and Amancio Amaro. It proved to be the manager's last European success with Real, but he continued his emphatic record in domestic football by leading Los Merengues to three consecutive La Liga titles in 1967, 1968 and 1969 and a final top-place finish in 1972.

Muñoz remained at the Bernabéu for a further two seasons, lifting the third Copa del Rey of his Madrid tenure in 1974 before a string of bad results led to pressure from the terraces and he departed the club. The manager modestly said he had been lucky to have coached so many top-class players, famously stating, "I have a big flower in my backside." But while he may have been fortunate, his managerial abilities and adroit manner of handling superstar performers and maintaining their hunger and desire, ensured sustained success for his teams.

He also knew when to refresh the team, meaning luck was just a minor element of his success.

Like many managers who have enjoyed a lengthy spell of glory with the same club, Muñoz was acutely aware of the need to gradually rebuild the team throughout the years. He phased out experienced world-beaters such as Di Stéfano, with whom he had played alongside and enjoyed a great friendship, to make room for an influx of hugely talented young players. During that transitional period, Real continued to dominate in Spain but found European football a harder nut to crack, which explained their six-year absence without lifting the European Cup. This run included an appearance in the 1964 Final, when they lost 3-1 to Helenio Herrera's great Inter Milan side.

Muñoz remained in Spanish club football and enjoyed short and far less productive spells with smaller clubs; Granada CF, Las Palmas and Sevilla, before the Spanish FA appointed him as head coach following the nation's disappointing display on home soil during the 1982 World Cup.

Muñoz had a six-year spell as Spain's manager, encouraging the side to play a more expressive style with greater freedom. This contributed to a memorable 12-1 thrashing of Malta in a 1983 European Championships qualification game. The Spaniards needed to win the game by an 11-goal margin to pip the Netherlands to qualification for Euro 1984 and they went on to achieve it in emphatic fashion. Following the match, Muñoz described the victory as, "The happiest day of my sporting career, and I had quite a few happy days."

Under his stewardship, Spain enjoyed good progress during the 1984 European Championships, reaching the final where they faced hosts France. However, inspired by the brilliance of Michel Platini, the French went on to lift the trophy following a 2-0 victory. In the aftermath of the European Championships, Muñoz began to integrate fresh talent into the Spain team, including the likes of Emilio Butragueño and Míchel, and secured qualification for the 1986 World Cup in Mexico. Spain began the tournament in bullish mood, thumping a highly-rated Denmark side 5-1 in a clash that saw Butragueño score four goals and secure progress to the quarter-finals. Muñoz's men met Belgium in the last eight, and were eventually defeated on penalties.

The experienced manager was afforded another opportunity to guide his country at a major tournament when he ensured qualification for the 1988 European Championships. However, Spain struggled during the competition and suffered an early exit, failing to progress from the group stages to bring an end to Muñoz's reign as coach.

While his career failed to finish with the flourish of success that it had began with, Muñoz's trophy-filled tenure in Spanish football is notable for the continued success he brought to Real Madrid over a sustained period of time. He possessed the strength of character and judgement to replace club legends, reshaping and evolving the Spanish giants while delivering an unprecedented eight titles in 10 years. Furthermore, those La Liga crowns were accompanied by success in Europe as Madrid continued to be the team to beat on the continent.

# 12. BÉLA GUTTMANN

**Born:** January 27, 1899 in Budapest, Hungary
**Died:** August 28, 1981 in Vienna, Austria
**Clubs Managed:** SC Hakoah Vienna, Enschede, Újpest, Vasas SC, Ciocanul Bucharest, Kispest, Padova, Triestina, Quilmes, APOEL FC, AC Milan, Vicenza, Honvéd, São Paulo, FC Porto, Benfica, Peñarol, Servette, Panathinaikos, Austria Vienna
**International:** Austria: 1964
**Major Honours:** 11

The revolutionary Hungarian coach managed the likes of AC Milan, São Paulo and Benfica, tasting glory in both Europe and South America and winning successive European Cups in the 1960s. One of the game's first big managerial characters, Béla Guttmann's most notable triumphs came with Benfica, guiding the Lisbon team to successive European Cup wins in 1961 and 1962. He was one of a trio of Hungarian coaches who pioneered the attacking 4-2-4 formation and the man responsible for mentoring the huge talents of the majestic Eusébio.

A qualified dance instructor with a degree in psychology, Guttmann had the theory to back up his beliefs, as well as a committed passion for attacking football. He is one of just a handful of European coaches to have enjoyed success in South America, lifting a State Championship Brazil. The much-travelled coach seldom stayed at the same club for longer than two seasons, believing that remaining for a third season was fatal. A controversial character, his arrogance and prickly demeanour instigated fallouts with many of the clubs he worked for, including Benfica which he departed and notoriously inflicted a curse upon when they refused to grant him a pay rise.

A successful footballer in his homeland, Guttmann had to flee Hungary for Vienna in 1922 to escape the anti-Semitism existing in the country at the time. He joined SC Hakoah Vienna, winning the Austrian League title before departing to play in the US, where he finished his playing days.

Guttmann returned to Europe in 1932 and coached clubs in Austria, the Netherlands and Hungary. The 1939 Hungarian League and the Mitropa Cup with Újpest were his first major honours, before the outbreak of the Second World War. During the War, his older brother was killed in a Nazi concentration camp, but Béla managed to escape to Switzerland where he was held in internment, allowing him to survive the Holocaust.

After the conflict, Guttmann returned to Hungary to coach Vasas SC before taking charge of Romanian side Ciocanul, where he insisted his salary was paid in vegetables due to food shortages in the country in the aftermath of the war. However, he soon walked out on the club following interference from a director, opting to rejoin Újpest where he won another league title before departing for their domestic rivals Kispest.

Guttmann managed smaller Italian clubs such as Calcio Padovo and Triestina Calcio before a short spell in Greece became a precursor to his appointment as AC Milan manager in 1953. At Milan he built a strong team that included the likes of Gunnar Nordahl, Nils Liedholm and Juan Alberto Schiaffino, and inspired the side to a strong start to his second season in charge. But, with the team top of the table after 19 games, the manager's ongoing disputes with the club's board led to his dismissal. He took over at Vicenza Calcio before returning to his homeland with Honvéd and then taking his first job in South America with Brazilian giants São Paulo in 1957.

In Béla's first year in Brazil his team, including the likes of Dino Sani, Mauro and Zizinho, won the São Paulo State Championship. Guttmann possessed the players to perfect the 4-2-4 system and it would act as a blueprint for generations of successful South American teams, including the Brazil national side that won the 1958 World Cup. It was a system inspired, at least in part, by Gustáv Sebes, the man who coached the hugely talented Hungarian side labelled the 'Magnificent Magyars', who famously destroyed England 6-3 in 1953 before going on to reach the World Cup final a year later.

Guttmann spent another season with São Paulo before returning to Europe to become FC Porto manager in 1958. His first season in charge ended in league success as Porto overhauled an impressive Benfica team to lift the 1959 title. It was the first of three Portuguese titles for Guttmann, but his last at Porto as he stepped down and took charge of their great rivals Benfica later that year.

At the Estádio da Luz, the Hungarian again showed his ruthless streak, sacking 20 of the club's first-team players and promoting a host of youngsters, before winning the 1960 and 1961 league titles with a team that included the hugely promising talents of Eusébio, José Águas, José Augusto, Costa Pereira, António Simões, Germano and Mário Coluna. The club's first ever European Cup was secured in 1962 when Guttmann's youngsters defeated Barcelona 3-2 in a thrilling final, which saw the 4-2-4 formation in full flow. Attacking at pace and in numbers, the manager was less concerned with the defensive side of the game and encouraged his players to outscore the opposition and to express themselves.

It was an approach that Guttmann later justified, saying, "I never minded if the opposition scored, because I always thought we could score another." That victory ensured Benfica were the first club other than Real Madrid to win the competition. The trophy was retained a year later following a memorable 5-3 win over Real Madrid, despite falling 2-0 and 3-2 behind, with the team apparently primed to ensure the same domination their opponents had previously enjoyed.

However, with the manager and the team at the peak of their powers, Guttmann requested a pay rise which was subsequently rejected by the board of directors despite the unprecedented success he had brought to the club. Guttmann promptly tendered his resignation and allegedly placed a curse on Benfica, stating, "Not in a hundred years from now will Benfica ever be European champion." It's a proclamation that remains true to this day as, despite the Portuguese giants having reached the final of seven different European competitions since the Hungarian departed the club, they have lost each of them.

After things turned sour in Portugal, Guttmann returned to South America with Uruguayan side Peñarol, but it ultimately proved a short and unsuccessful spell and he returned to Europe, being named head coach of Austria in 1964. That was another short-lived appointment as, after less than a year, Guttmann amazingly returned to Benfica, but, just as with the other four clubs he would go on to manage at the end of his career, he struggled to recapture success, eventually ending his career with FC Porto in 1973.

Much like Helenio Herrera, Béla Guttmann transformed the public perception of what a manager should be. Quite often the centre of attention, Guttmann was one of the great characters of his era, with the Hungarian often referred to as being one the first 'superstar' coaches.

The transient nature of his career perhaps proved his downfall as he managed a mammoth 23 teams in 13 countries during his 40-year coaching career. Guttmann had the happy knack of creating teams in his image and ensuring his attacking philosophy came to life on the pitch. He wanted his players to play their natural game and to rely upon their skills and their instinct. He gave them freedom to perform, unburdened by pressure or expectation.

Perhaps his intensity was both a strength and a weakness, as it produced short bursts of brilliance during which his players were captivated by his character and his methods. But it also saw Guttmann and those around him eventually burnt out and alienated, leading to his frequent departure from various roles despite enjoying success. The man himself had his own views on managers, labelling them as lion tamers and saying that a coach "dominates the animals, in whose cage he performs his show, as long as he deals with them with self-confidence and without fear. But the moment he becomes unsure of his hypnotic energy, and the first hint of fear appears in his eyes, he is lost."

Whether he was a managerial free spirit, a mercenary looking for his next pay cheque or a simply a trouble-maker, Béla Guttmann's insistence on attacking football and ability to maximise the talents of the players at his disposal were summed up in his first spectacularly successful spell at Benfica. If the Hungarian had remained with the Portuguese team he put on the footballing map, surely further trophies would have followed and he would have ranked even higher on this list.

# CHAPTER 7
## MANAGERS 11 – 9

# 11. JOCK STEIN

**Born:** October 5, 1922 in Burnbank, Scotland
**Died:** September 10, 1985, aged 62
**Clubs Managed:** Dunfermline Athletic, Hibernian, Celtic, Leeds United
**International:** Scotland: 1965 and 1978-1985
**Major Honours:** 25

Affectionately revered and highly regarded both inside and outside of football, Jock Stein was the prototype of the hugely passionate, inspiring and vastly successful Scottish manager that has dominated British football for more than half a century. His achievements were impressive enough, but his legacy extended to influencing and shaping some of the most successful bosses to have graced the game, including the likes of Bill Shankly and Sir Alex Ferguson.

A larger-than-life presence and character, Jock Stein created the first dynasty of dominance that Scottish football had experienced, guiding Celtic to nine successive league titles and taking them to the Promised Land in 1967, when the Glasgow giants became the first British club to lift the European Cup. These achievements were all the more notable due to the style and manner in which they were realised.

Stein was a passionate believer in his teams playing entertaining, attacking football, seeing it as his duty to create a sporting spectacle the public would relish. Towards the end of his career, Jock memorably stated, "Without fans who pay at the turnstile, football is nothing. Sometimes we are inclined to forget that. The only chance of bringing them into stadiums is if they are entertained by what happens on the football field." The Scotsman was also determined to blood youngsters and created a hugely successful team made entirely of locals.

Before turning professional as a footballer, Stein worked as a coalminer while playing at amateur level. It provided a grounding and work ethic that shaped his career in the game, his principles and his belief in the huge importance of team spirit and morale. Stein played professionally for Welsh side Llanelli Town before returning to his homeland with Celtic in 1951. Trophy success followed before Jock was forced to retire from the game six years later, having sustained serious ankle injuries.

Stein went on to coach Celtic's reserve side, when he first had the opportunity to work with a generation of talented youngsters, including Billy McNeill, Bobby Murdoch and John Clark, who would become the lifeblood of the club. He took his first managerial role with Dunfermline in 1960. After turning around the fortunes of a team struggling at the wrong end of the table, Scottish Cup success followed a year later and with consistently high league finishes, Stein guided the club into European football. He achieved notable progress in the UEFA and Cup Winners' Cups, reaching the quarter-finals of the latter in 1962.

In 1964, the highly rated Scotsman was appointed Hibernian manager but remained at Easter Road for less than a season, albeit after a successful spell, leaving Hibs close to the top of the table and in the semi-final of the Scottish Cup. He had also won the Summer Cup and recorded a famous 2-0 friendly victory over Real Madrid. However, the lure of a return to Celtic proved too strong and he joined the Bhoys in March 1965.

Stein developed a reputation for being ahead of the game in terms of maximising the talents of his players by advocating a high-energy, fast-tempo style of play. He was also one of the first managers to have a significant involvement in training sessions and the first Protestant to take charge of a club embraced in Catholicism. Stein's philosophy, married with the size and greater draw of Glasgow Celtic, was a recipe for prolific success.

He went on to spend 13 years at Celtic Park, winning 10 Scottish League titles, eight Scottish Cups, six Scottish League Cups and a solitary European Cup. The first of those trophies came during his opening months in charge, as Stein inspired Celtic to the Scottish Cup Final where they defeated his former club Dunfermline 3-2 thanks to Billy McNeill's winning goal. This was Celtic's first Scottish Cup in 11 years and their first trophy in eight years.

Around the same time as his appointment with Celtic, Stein took charge of the Scottish national side on a part-time basis as they attempted to qualify for the 1966 World Cup. Despite positive results against the likes of Finland and Italy, the Scots failed to progress from their group and the manager stepped down to focus on club football.

Stein showed sound judgement in the transfer market, snapping up Joe McBride from Motherwell ahead of the 1965/66 campaign. The striker proved to be an excellent addition, scoring 43 goals as Celtic went on to claim the Scottish League Championship for the first time in 12 years, as well as defeating city rivals Rangers to lift the League Cup, only to lose to the same opponents in the Scottish Cup Final. The Bhoys also reached the UEFA Cup semi-finals that season, narrowly losing to Liverpool.

Domestic success continued the following campaign as Stein led Celtic to their first treble of league title, Scottish Cup and League Cup. However, more was to follow that season as the inspirational manager took the club on a European adventure, their first in the European Cup, which eventually ended with a captivating and groundbreaking victory over a hugely impressive Inter Milan side that had already won two European Cups.

Held in Lisbon, the final famously saw a clash of the defensive and negative approach of the Italians with the progressive, free-flowing and adventurous style adopted by Stein's Celtic. One of Stein's famous quotes about attacking football was, "The best place to defend is in the other team's penalty box." The inspirational manager's pre-match team talk illustrated his ability to measure and capitalise on the sense of occasion to instil confidence and a feeling of destiny amongst his players. His final words to the players before the game were; "If you're ever going to win the European Cup, then this is the day and this is the place. But we don't just want to win this cup, we want to do it playing good football—to make neutrals glad we've won it, glad to remember how we did it."

Celtic came from a goal behind to win the game, playing with great flair and bravery, and the players were later christened as the 'Lisbon Lions'. Inter had taken an early lead from a penalty that had allowed them to adopt their customary ultra-defensive style, inviting the attacking talents of Celtic on to them. Inspired by the nimble and mercurial creative talents of 'Jinky' Jimmy Johnstone on the wing, as well as the energy and passion of Bobby Lennox, Bobby Murdoch and Billy McNeil, the Glasgow club came forward in waves and waves of attacks but found a mass of Italian bodies and the inspired form of goalkeeper Giuliano Sarti blocking their path.

Their tenacity and patience was eventually rewarded when Tommy

Gemmell drove a crisp strike into the back of the net from the edge of the area after 63 minutes, before Stephen Chalmers guided the winner home from close-range with just six minutes remaining. In lifting the trophy Stein ensured legendary status as the first British manager to win the European Cup, as well as becoming the first manager to win every competition he had entered.

Another distinct achievement of the 1967 success was that the Celtic team was made up entirely of Scotsmen who had all been born within 30 miles of Glasgow. Many of them had been developed at Celtic and moulded into a truly great team by the manager. After the match, Stein was in euphoric mood, stating, "There is not a prouder man on God's earth than me at this moment. Winning was important, aye, but it was the way that we have won that has filled me with satisfaction. We did it by playing football. Pure, beautiful, inventive football. Our objective is always to try to win with style."

The 1967/68 campaign brought another League and League Cup and saw Celtic take part in the Intercontinental Cup against Racing Club of Argentina in a controversial trio of matches. The Scottish side faced intense provocation as the Racing players fouled and spat at them before eventually winning a third play-off game 1-0 in Montevideo.

Stein's men failed to defend their European title but continued to impress domestically, securing further league titles, including another treble in 1969; a feat the club would fail to repeat for another 32 years. A year later, Celtic reached their second European Cup Final under Stein, following a two-legged semi-final victory over Don Revie's Leeds United. However, the Bhoys lost the final 2-1 to Feyenoord at the San Siro in Milan. That was the last time that Stein led the club to a European final despite reaching two further semi-finals. Since that clash, Celtic remain the only Scottish club to have reached a European Cup Final.

An awesome ninth successive league title was secured in 1974 as the rest of Scottish football struggled to keep pace with Celtic to such an extent the Football League was reconstructed a year later. In 1975, Stein was seriously injured in a car accident. He came close to death and missed most of the 1975/76 campaign, which saw Celtic end the season trophyless. His return to the dugout for the 1976/77 brought a 10th league title and another Scottish Cup.

The following season saw Celtic struggle for the first time during Stein's tenure and he was persuaded to stand down from his position. The club's greatest ever manager was offered a management role in Celtic's pools company, rather than on the board of directors. Hurt by the snub, he opted to leave the club and take up a new challenge south of the border as Leeds United boss.

It proved a disappointing move for

Leeds and Stein, as the Scot inherited a team in steady decline following the Don Revie years and the controversial Brian Clough tenure. Stein failed to inspire the club above mid-table mediocrity in a spell that provided a culture shock following the glory-filled European adventures he'd experienced with Celtic. The Scottish FA soon approached Leeds, seeking permission to offer Stein the vacant managerial post with the national team. However, Leeds Chairman Manny Cussins refused their request, which prompted the in-demand manager to tender his resignation, bringing an end to his spell with Leeds after just 44 days; the exact same short-lived tenure as Brian Clough.

Stein's official appointment as Scotland manager came on his 56th birthday and he went on to defeat Norway 3-2 at Hampden Park in his first game in charge. He began by selecting only English-based Scottish players but vowed to call-up those from north of the border in the future. He also brought a more considered, tactically aware approach to the national side. Failure to qualify for the 1980 European Championships, then losses to Northern Ireland and England in the British Home Championship drew media criticism, but Stein remained at the helm and went on to guide the Scots to the 1982 World Cup. However, a win against New Zealand, draw with the Soviet Union and loss to Brazil saw them miss out on qualification from the group stage on goal difference.

Scotland missed out on the 1984 European Championships but looked on course to qualify for the 1986 World Cup following a crucial 1-1 draw with Wales in Cardiff. The draw ensured the Scots finished second on goal difference and set up a play-off clash with Australia, a tie that would eventually be won to secure safe passage for another major tournament.

Sadly, Stein wouldn't have the opportunity to lead his country into another World Cup as tragedy struck during the closing minutes of the draw with Wales. He suffered a heart attack and died shortly after the game, aged 62. The players and the coaching staff, including Stein's assistant Alex Ferguson, were heartbroken by the loss of their manager, mentor and a man they held in such high esteem and affection. The future Manchester United manager would later express his huge admiration for Stein, crediting the approach and wisdom of the great man in his own development, saying, "I am proud to say that I knew Jock Stein as a manager, as a colleague and as a friend... he was the greatest manager in British football... men like Jock will live forever in the memory."

Ferguson went on to guide the team into the 1986 World Cup, but Stein's legacy in the game extended immeasurably beyond qualification for the tournament. That legacy was one of unbridled success at Celtic, achieved by a side playing with a creative spark and swagger seldom evident in British teams. His insistence on producing entertaining, attacking football ensured that the achievements became hugely celebrated and admired all over Europe. In fact, Celtic's relentlessly creative display in the 1967 European Cup Final had a huge impact on football on the continent, with the previously respected defensive catenaccio style becoming less popular for a number of years.

A man who had the knack of transforming struggling teams into successful ones, while developing the natural talents of players and making shrewd additions at the right time, Stein showcased all of the attributes possessed by the very finest managers. The Scotsman was innovative and light years ahead of his time when it came to preparation, strategic approach and psychology. He was a natural judge of character and knew how to treat players as men, both collectively and individually. In the era of a trio of great Scottish managers, which also included Bill Shankly and Matt Busby, Jock Stein won the most trophies of all three and became the first to succeed in Europe's premier club competition.

Shankly famously labelled Stein as "immortal" following the 1967 European Cup success, emphasising not only the significance of that individual achievement but also the accumulation of a life's work. Although the great Scot's mortality was so suddenly and tragically realised in a literal sense as he died doing what he loved in 1985, in a metaphorical sense, Jock Stein has remained immortal and one of the greatest managers and football men that the game has ever seen.

# 10. HELENIO HERRERA

**Born:** April 10, 1910 in Buenos Aires, Argentina
**Died:** November 9, 1997, aged 87
**Clubs Managed:** Puteaux, Stade Français, Real Valladolid, Atlético Madrid, Málaga, Deportivo de la Coruña, Sevilla, Belenenses, Barcelona, Inter Milan, AS Roma, Rimini
**Major Honours:** 17

The antithesis of Jock Stein in terms of philosophy and the style with which his hugely successful Inter Milan operated, and the man he faced in the 1967 European Cup Final, Helenio Herrera was another extremely prolific manager. The Argentine enjoyed a great record in Europe, winning 14 major trophies with clubs such as Barcelona, AS Roma and in, particular, Inter Milan, where his team became known as 'Grande Inter'. However, to simply label Herrera as a defensive coach is inaccurate as his Barcelona side played some spellbinding attacking football.

Born in Argentina to Spanish parents, Herrera and his family immigrated to Morocco when he was just four. He went on to adopt French citizenship and play football in the north African country for RC Casablanca before transferring to French side CASG Paris in 1932. He appeared for several French clubs before and after World War II, eventually becoming player-manager of Puteaux in 1944. A year later, Herrera's playing days came to an end as he opted to focus on his managerial career, departing Puteaux for Stade Français, a club he had played for on two separate occasions.

Success was far from instantaneous for Herrera who endured three trophyless seasons with Stade before the president opted to sell the club. In turn, the Argentine moved to Spain to take charge of Real Valladolid, then Atlético Madrid, where he won the La Liga Championship in 1950 and 1951. Further spells came with Malaga, Deportivo de La Coruña and Sevilla before Herrera spent two seasons coaching in Portugal with CF Os Belenenses.

A return to Spain followed and Herrera was appointed head coach of the mighty Barcelona. He went on to match and exceed the domestic success he had enjoyed with Atlético Madrid, lifting successive La Liga titles in 1959 and 1960, wrestling domination of the league away from the great Real Madrid side of the era. He also claimed a Copa Del Rey, then enjoyed his first European honours, winning the 1958 UEFA Inter-Cities Fairs Cup after beating a London XI 8-2 in the final. The competition had run across the course of three seasons. Herrera again lifted the same trophy two years later following a 4-1 aggregate victory over Birmingham City.

All of these successes were realised by playing the sort of attacking and entertaining football associated with the Catalan club. His innovative tactical approaches, including playing inside-forwards in the normally defensive wing-half positions, saw Barcelona comprehensively destroy the majority of their opponents, with the 1958/59 title-winning season seeing Barcelona score 96 goals in 30 games. Despite such impressive achievements, the much-travelled manager left the Nou Camp after just two years in charge following a disagreement with the club's star player, Ladislao Kubala, and a European Cup semi-final defeat to rivals Real Madrid.

Herrera moved to Italy and linked-up with the club that became his spiritual home, Inter Milan. He signed his midfield general at Barcelona and the reigning European Footballer of the Year, Luis Suárez, and modified a defensive formation, labelled the 'Verrou' (door bolt) to add a fifth defender, the sweeper, who operated behind two central defenders.

The tactically astute manager also made moves to ensure that the team became more dangerous on the counter-attack, utilising the energy, judgement and pace of the great Giacinto Facchetti from full-back and introducing the catenaccio style. Despite the approach being invented by an Austrian coach called Karl Rappan and previously used by Nereo Rocco, it would forever be associated with Herrera due to the modifications he made and the great success he achieved with it.

As well as his on-pitch methods, the Argentine was a pioneer of using psychology and inspirational team talks to motivate his players. He was also at the forefront of emblazoning such messages as 'Class + Preparation + Intelligence + Athleticism = Championships', at the training ground and stadium. He also encouraged players to chant them during training sessions to instil an incessantly driven winning mentality. As Luis Suárez, who played under Herrera for Barcelona and Inter Milan later expressed, "His emphasis on fitness and psychology had never been seen before. Until then, the manager was unimportant."

As many managers of his era, Herrera was a fierce disciplinarian who demanded the highest standards of his players, both on and off the pitch. His code of conduct included a ban on drinking and smoking and a fastidious control of the players' diets and their fitness. He also introduced the ritual of taking the team to stay in a hotel before games to aid match preparation. All of these aspects ensured that the uncompromising taskmaster was light years ahead of the game.

Herrera was also well aware of the impact of a vociferous home support and became one of the first bosses to refer to the crowd as the team's '12th player'. All of these innovations, combined with the excessive success he experienced, saw Herrera become one of the first managers to be regularly recognised and credited for the performance of their team, making his own headlines in the same way as the best players had done for years. Europe's great teams such as Real Madrid had been famed for their on-field stars such as Di Stéfano and Puskás, but following their manager's huge impact on the consciousness of the world game, Inter came to be known as 'Herrera's Inter'.

Helenio transformed Inter into one of the most ruthless and productive forces in Europe. The team finished third in Serie A in his first season, second in 1962, then sealed the Italian league title in 1963. Herrera wasn't finished there and took European football by storm with his revolutionary tactical approach, guiding the Milanese club to their first European Cup success in 1964, following a convincing 3-1 defeat of Real Madrid to lift the trophy thanks to a Sandro Mazzola double.

In winning the tournament, Inter became the first club to have done so without losing a single game throughout the competition. Not one to rest on his laurels, Herrera led the club to greater heights the following season, winning another Serie A title and retaining its crown as European champions following a 1-0 final victory over Benfica. This success earned the manager the title of 'Il Mago'—'the magician'. Both European Cup successes were followed up with Intercontinental Cup triumphs, with Inter defeating Argentina's Independiente in both the 1964 and 1965 finals.

Herrera's approach was hugely focused on defence, but was just as reliant on the attacking skills of Luiz Suárez and Jair who were both creative and efficient when it came to taking chances and exposing opponents on the counter attack. It's unfair to label Inter as purely a defensive unit; the side may have had the perfect defensive foundations but every player also knew the importance of their role from an attacking point of view. Full-backs were capable of playing devastating counter-attacking football. It may not have been as celebrated as the expressive nature employed by the famous Dutch and Spanish teams in the years to come, but it is without question a hugely effective system for maximising every ounce of ability from both the individual and team unit.

Inter reached another European Cup Final under Herrera in 1967 but with key play-makers, Luis Suárez and Jair out injured and their opponents Celtic swarming over them with incessant and irresistible attacking football, the two-time champions lost 2-1 despite taking an early lead. It was the first time Herrera's defensive, containing tactics had been fundamentally exposed by an opponent and he left the San Siro a year later after failing to add to his trophy tally.

His next role came with AS Roma in 1968, where he coached a young Fabio Capello and famously became the highest-paid manager in the world, receiving an estimated £150,000 a year. His first season in the Italian capital brought Coppa Italia success but following the breakdown of relations with club president, Alvaro Marchini, Herrera was sacked.

He opted to return to Inter in 1973 but couldn't recapture any of the old magic and departed after a single season in charge, as a heart attack left him unwilling to remain as a full-time coach. Following four years away from the game, Herrera returned to football in 1978, managing Rimini Calcio for a season before a similarly short spell with Barcelona, which saw him lift another Copa del Rey—his last ever major honour as a manager—in 1981.

It would be a fair comparison to label Helenio Herrera as the José Mourinho of his era, or perhaps the original 'special one'. The monikers bestowed upon him, such as 'the magician', 'the saviour' and 'the wizard', illustrate a character and an influence on the game similar to Mourinho's. The Portuguese ace has been labelled as playing 'anti-football' in relation to his defensive approach and while this term didn't exist during Herrera's era, it is an adequate description of the style of his Inter Milan side. Also, like Mourinho, Herrera wasn't opposed to taking credit for his team's victories, as well as the blame for disappointing results and performances, as he became one of the first coaches to openly attempt to take pressure away from his players.

His ability to find success with more than one system and, in particular, two such markedly different philosophies, shows his adaptability, footballing knowledge and great managerial prowess. The style he adopted at Inter was one that became the blueprint for Italian football and the customary approach taken by teams all over the continent in European competition.

Much like Mourinho, controversy followed Herrera in equal abundance to success, with his fierce training regime putting the health of his players at risk, including the aforementioned Giulano Taccola. When Taccola fell ill before a game, the Roma doctor found a heart murmur. Herrera allegedly kept this information from the player who later collapsed in the changing room following a training session two weeks later. There were also accusations of match-fixing and the manager doping his players with many reporters labelling him 'the pharmacy cup coach'.

Thus, Helenio Herrera remains one of the game's most polarising football managers. He will never go down as one of the most loved managers and the memories of his successes and his style are rarely held in great affection, but his undeniable talent, backed up by a hugely impressive record, ensures his reputation as one of the most revered and respected bosses of all time.

The Argentine is also as responsible as any of his peers or any man that went before him for shaping the role of the football manager as the talisman and figurehead of the club. Without Herrera's impact the high regard in which managers have become held would have been a more gradual process. Quite simply Helenio Herrera was an innovator, a trailblazer and a true winner.

# 9. VICENTE DEL BOSQUE

**Born:** December 23, 1950 in Salamanca, Spain
**Clubs Managed:** Real Madrid B, Real Madrid, Besiktas
**International:** Spain: 2008-present day (Won the 2010 World Cup and the 2012 European Championship)
**Major Honours:** 9

A serial trophy winner at both club and international level, Vicente del Bosque claimed La Liga titles with Real Madrid as well the World Cup and European Championship double with Spain. A man whose achievements aren't often as celebrated as they should be, del Bosque perhaps suffers from perceptions of his introverted character and his good fortune of being able to select some of the finest players of their generation in the two most prolific teams he has managed. Both of those perceptions may have cost him his job at Real Madrid, when, despite enjoying sustained success, the club chose to replace him with a bigger name manager in the belief that the players were primarily responsible for the achievements.

Del Bosque's top-10 ranking in this book is primarily due to his ability to have enjoyed ultimate success as both a club and international manager, dealing with the weight of expectations to win Champions League crowns with Real Madrid and Spain's first World Cup. In fact, he is currently the only manager to have won the triple crown of World Cup, European Championship and Champions League. The understated manner in which he has realised these achievements, while managing the egos of some of the biggest names in football and finding a tactical approach and a formation to utilise their talents, has seen his teams become more important and more prominent than the personality of the manager; an occurrence that is often a rarity in the modern game.

A talented all-round midfielder as a player, del Bosque made more than 400 appearances in the Spanish top flight, enjoying greatest success at Real Madrid, where he won five La Liga titles, four Copa del Reys and a European Cup runners-up medal. He was also capped 18 times by his country and a part of Spain's 1980 European Championships squad.

Del Bosque began his managerial career in the youth ranks at Real Madrid, coaching the club's B team and experiencing brief spells as the caretaker boss of the first team on several occasions. He was finally given the opportunity to take up the reins for a more sustained period in November 1999, after John Toshack's star-studded team had endured a disappointing start to the season. Del Bosque gradually improved matters while inspiring Madrid to an impressive European Champions League campaign. Able to call upon the likes of Roberto Carlos, Raúl and Steve McManaman, the incoming manager negotiated the group stages of the competition before a 3-2 aggregate victory over Manchester United in the quarter-finals, when Raúl's predatory finishing skills proved key. Madrid then defeated Bayern Munich by the same aggregate scoreline in the semi-final to set up an all-Spanish final against Valencia.

Del Bosque had ensured the team was built on solid foundations, maximising the know-how and experience of the defensive-minded Spanish players such as Míchel Salgado, Fernando Hierro, Iván Campo and Iván Helguera, which allowed the attacking talents of McManaman, Nicolas Anelka, Raúl and Fernando Morientes to flourish. Since then, no successful Madrid team has contained so many Spanish players, with as many as seven Spaniards starting the Champions League Final. Two of them, Raúl and Morientes, went on to score crucial goals, alongside McManaman, as Madrid brushed aside their opponents 3-0 in the final. Del Bosque took a more measured and pragmatic approach, primarily focusing on the team unit rather than the individuals within it, but he wasn't afraid to make bold decisions, such as his inclusion of Iker Casillas in goal against Valencia in the Champions League Final at the age of just 19—the youngest goalkeeper to have started in a European Cup Final.

The 2000 European Cup success heralded the beginning of Real Madrid's most successful spell of the modern era as, under del Bosque, they won another Champions League in 2002, two La Liga titles, the Spanish Super Cup, European Super Cup and the Intercontinental Cup. In total, Vicente spent four years at the Bernabéu helm, coinciding with Real's most consistent European run in decades, as they reached at least the semi-finals in each of his seasons in charge.

In del Bosque's early Madrid tenure his team didn't play particularly adventurous football, but were well organised, slick in possession and lethal on the counter attack, thanks to the awesome goal-scoring abilities of Raúl. A manager who understood the importance of creating a balanced team, del Bosque's qualities were summed up well by former midfielder Steve McManaman, who said, "He has a very good brain in assessing what kind of footballers his players are, what kind of people we are, how we all work together. He is scrupulously fair-minded... his skill is in subtly weighing up how the team could tick."

In 2000, the culture of the Spanish giants changed immeasurably as the charismatic Florentino Pérez was appointed president, signalling the beginning of a spending spree that saw Real sign some of the biggest names in world football and led to the team being dubbed 'Los Galacticos'. Del Bosque may have been the manager but the man identifying the targets and completing the deals was Pérez , and the likes of Luís Figo, Zinedine Zidane and Ronaldo all arrived at the club for astronomic transfer fees.

With a wealth of attacking options at his disposal, del Bosque was able to field an imperious looking side and the 2001 La Liga title was claimed by a seven-point advantage. The 2003 title was also delivered when the full force of Figo, Zidane and Ronaldo came to the fore, with the latter finishing as the club's top scorer in the league with 23 goals. In between those domestic successes, del Bosque's men enjoyed additional Champions League success, claiming the 2002 crown with a 2-1 victory over Bayer Leverkusen in a final that featured a moment of technical brilliance from Zinedine Zidane who powered a seemingly impossible left-footed volley into the net to secure the trophy.

With Real returned to the forefront of European football and again a force in the Champions League, del Bosque had transformed the fortunes of a club that had only flirted with the continent's primary competition since their domination of the 1950s and '60s. The manager, later aided by significant investment, helped to put Madrid back on top of the game.

The 2003 La Liga crown proved to be the Spaniard's last trophy at Real as he was shown the exit door in the immediate aftermath of the title celebrations with Florentino Pérez feeling he was no longer the right man for the job. After turning down the chance to remain at the Bernabéu as the club's technical director, del Bosque departed the club. Despite continued investment in the team and a number of high-profile managerial appointments, Real failed to win La Liga for the next four seasons and are yet to lift another European Cup following that 2002 success under the guidance of the Spaniard.

Del Bosque had been popular with the star-studded Madrid players, giving them the freedom and responsibility to express themselves on the pitch. He exuded composure on the touchline in the middle of the tinderbox pressure cooker of the Bernabéu, never visibly losing his cool, avoiding confrontations and proving himself a classy operator.

After a year out of the game, del Bosque was appointed in only his second managerial role, taking charge of Turkish side Besiktas. Despite the huge anticipation for success that followed his arrival, Vicente struggled to inspire the required performances and results and was relieved of his duties in the final few months of the 2004/05 campaign.

Having previously turned down the Spain job in 2004, del Bosque eventually took charge of the national team in 2008, succeeding European Championship-winning manager Luis Aragones at the helm, a year after a link with a return to the Bernabéu as Real Madrid coach failed to materialise. He inherited a team excessively filled with talent and strong in every department, and one that had also conquered the psychological barrier of succeeding in a major tournament. As European Championship holders, Spain were immediately instilled as one of the favourites for the 2010 World Cup, ratcheting up the pressure on their new manager.

Del Bosque guided Spain to an emphatic qualifying campaign for the 2010 World Cup, with the manager becoming the first debut international coach to win his first 10 games in charge as his team topped the group with a 100 per cent record of 10 wins from 10. Del Bosque made gradual modifications to the Spain team that had won Euro 2008, placing greater trust in the ball-keeping qualities of Xabi Alonso, Xavi and Andrés Iniesta and embracing the tiki-taka style even more than his predecessor.

A shock Confederations Cup semi-final defeat to the USA in South Africa in 2009 was a rare low-point, but by the time Spain returned to Africa a year later, they were primed for a tilt at the biggest trophy in international football. The tournament didn't start well for Spain, when they lost 1-0 to Switzerland despite dominating possession. However, wins in their next two group games set up a knockout tie with Portugal. A hard-fought 1-0 win achieved through David Villa's goal was followed by a victory by the same scoreline and through the same scorer in the quarter-finals over Paraguay, setting up a semi-final clash with an emerging German team Spain had defeated in the Euro 2008 Final. Following another tight game, largely dominated by the Spaniards, del Bosque's men again sealed a 1-0 victory, with Carles Puyol forcing home the winner as the nation reached its first World Cup Final.

Spain's opponents in the final were the Netherlands, another footballing nation that had underachieved on the biggest stage. Holland contained technically brilliant players of their own but, intimidated by the intricate passing and tempo-controlling style of their opponents, they resorted to a negative and aggressive approach, committing a series of fouls to try and break the Spaniard's rhythm. A disappointing final ended 0-0 after 90 minutes, but Spain's superiority counted in extra-time when Andrés Iniesta prodded home the winner.

Spain's success had echoed that of the Real Madrid side del Bosque had managed, with a solid defensive unit being perfectly complemented by hugely skilled midfielders who could dominate possession, and attacking players boasting incisive finishing when it mattered.

To back up that World Cup success, Spain again enjoyed an emphatic qualification route to the 2012 European Championships, winning all eight group stage matches. Buoyed by the confidence of their previous achievements and given further attacking licence, del Bosque's men played a more entertaining style of play at the tournament itself. They thumped the Republic of Ireland 4-0, drew with Italy and beat Croatia 1-0 in the group stages before a comfortable 2-0 win over France in the quarter-final and a penalty shootout victory over Portugal in the semi-finals, set them up for a final clash with Italy.

Showing similar form to the World Cup, Spain gradually improved as the tournament progressed and, with huge strength in depth, del Bosque used his squad superbly to freshen up the team, adding extra energy and attacking nous when required. All of those factors were evident in the final, when Italy were thumped 4-0 thanks to goals from David Silva, Jordi Alba, Fernando Torres and Juan Mata. It was Spain's second successive European Championship and third successive major international honour, confirming their continued dominance of the world game.

Del Bosque remained in charge following the victory and guided Spain to the 2013 Confederations Cup Final, where they were beaten by hosts Brazil. Following another successful qualification campaign his team will return to the same country to play in the 2014 World Cup, when they will again be among the favourites to lift the trophy.

Many managers have possessed world-class players, but to realise team success it takes a manager capable of blending their talents together, motivating them, selecting the correct tactics, creating a harmonious dressing room and ensuring their readiness to perform. Vicente del Bosque has achieved all of these things at the very highest level in an understated and unflappable manner. In his first 13 years as a manager he won nine major trophies, including both international and club football's premier competitions.

A man of substance whose teams play with great style, del Bosque's achievements are often overlooked and attributed to the hugely talented players he has selected. However, at Real Madrid, a similar list of stellar names has failed to recapture such sustained performances, results and trophies under each of his predecessors, which have included the likes of Fabio Capello, Manuel Pellegrini and José Mourinho. He may not get the recognition he deserves but Vicente del Bosque has been prolifically successful.

# CHAPTER 8
## MANAGERS 8 – 6

# 8. OTTMAR HITZFELD

**Born:** January 12, 1949 in Lörrach, West Germany
**Clubs Managed:** Zug 94, Aarau, Grasshoppers Zürich, Borussia Dortmund, Bayern Munich
**International:** Switzerland: 2008-present day
**Major Honours:** 25

One of the most tactically astute managers of the modern era, Ottmar Hitzfeld has enjoyed significant domestic success in every country he has coached, with his most notable achievements coming in Germany where he lifted the Champions League with both Borussia Dortmund and Bayern Munich, becoming one of only four managers to have won the competition with two different clubs. Hitzfeld also claimed seven Bundesliga titles and lifted major honours with FC Basle and Grasshoppers Zürich in Switzerland.

A trained mathematician and a qualified sports teacher, Hitzfeld's playing career was largely spent in the lower leagues of German football before he signed for Swiss top-flight side FC Basel, where he went on to claim domestic honours. He then enjoyed several seasons playing in the German Bundesliga before returning to Switzerland and eventually ending his career at FC Luzern.

At the age of 34, Ottmar took his first steps in coaching, spending a year with FC Zug in Switzerland before taking charge of

FC Aarau in 1984 and leading the club to the Swiss Cup a year later. A move to high-profile Swiss side, Grasshoppers Zürich, came in 1988 and further domestic honours followed, including the 1988 Swiss Cup, a league and cup double in 1990 and the retention of the Swiss title in 1991.

Hitzfeld's achievements were attracting the attentions of clubs across the border in Germany, including Borussia Dortmund, who appointed him as manager in 1991 after a disappointing 10th-place Bundesliga finish. Taking his trusted assistant Michael Henke with him, Hitzfeld oversaw a transformation of the club's fortunes on the pitch, leading Dortmund to a runners-up spot in the league and securing qualification for the UEFA Cup.

Borussia continued to progress under Hitzfeld, reaching the final of the UEFA Cup in 1993. The Germans eventually lost out to Juventus over two legs, but their presence ensured the club's first appearance in a major European final since 1966.

Dortmund's progress in Europe was matched by their increased consistency in the Bundesliga, winning the league title in 1995. It was the club's first major honour since lifting the 1989 German Cup, breaking Hitzfeld's duck as a trophy-gatherer in his homeland. Borussia retained their title in 1996, but their league campaign suffered during the 1996/97 season, but with good reason, as Hitzfeld guided his charges to the final of the Champions League.

As in the UEFA Cup, Hitzfeld's Dortmund faced reigning European Champions Juventus in the final. Their Italian opponents were enjoying some of their most prolific and consistent form under the guidance of Marcello Lippi. The final was played at the home ground of Dortmund's rivals, Bayern Munich, and many observers labelled the Italian team as favourites and thanks to their recent success and their list of stellar names, including Zinedine Zidane, Didier Deschamps, Alessandro Del Piero and Christian Vieri.

However, Borussia went on to control the game for large periods, as Paul Lambert and former Juventus man Paulo Sousa bossed the midfield and provided a covering blanket for the Dortmund defence that allowed the Germans to play an effective counter-attacking style.

Following the triumph, Hitzfeld was moved upstairs where he became Dortmund's sports manager, with former Parma boss Nevio Scala taking over the coaching duties and leading the Germans to Intercontinental Cup glory later that year.

Germany's biggest and most successful club, Bayern Munich, saw an opportunity and appointed Hitzfeld as their manager in 1998. It proved a shrewd move as Munich went on to lift the Bundesliga title by a record points margin at the end of Ottmar's first season in charge. The same year the club also reached the finals of the German Cup and the Champions League, signifying Bayern's first appearance in a European Cup Final for 12 years. Hitzfeld had negotiated a tough group stage, taking on the likes of Manchester United and Barcelona, before beating Kaiserslautern and an emerging Dynamo Kiev in the semi-finals to set up what proved to be a memorable final clash with Manchester United at the Nou Camp. Both clubs were chasing an unprecedented treble of domestic league and cup, as well as the European crown, and both had played impressively throughout the season. However, the final ultimately proved to be a disappointing spectacle with both Bayern and United struggling to find their usual fluidity. Munich took an early lead through a Mario Basler free-kick and looked likely to hold on to that advantage as the match approached the 90th minute. In fact, the German side came close to increasing their lead on several occasions as both Mehmet Scholl and Carsten Jancker hit the woodwork, as Munich caught United on the counter attack. However, as the match entered stoppage time, the never-say-die attitude Sir Alex Ferguson's side had become famed for led to an amazing turnaround. The English side scored twice as substitutes, Teddy Sheringham and Ole Gunnar Solskjær, scored the goals that claimed the trophy and left Bayern stunned.

Still hurting from the momentous defeat against United, Hitzfeld's men suffered further disappointment, going on to lose the German Cup Final to Werder Bremen on penalties. However, the manager didn't have to wait long to secure the trophy, as Bayern won the league and cup double the following season. The Germans again reached the later stages of the European Cup before being knocked out in the semi-finals by eventual winners Real Madrid.

A hat-trick of Bundesliga titles was completed in 2001 as Hitzfeld again led Munich to the European Cup Final, gaining revenge over both Manchester United and Real Madrid in the knockout stages of the competition. Bayern faced the previous season's runners-up, Valencia, in the final and following a closely fought contest the German club went on to win on penalties, securing their fourth European Cup and their first for 25 years. Ottmar remained at the helm to guide Bayern to Intercontinental Cup success later that year, following a 1-0 victory over Boca Juniors.

A trophyless season followed before Hitzfeld inspired another Bundesliga title from his Bayern charges and a second German Cup in 2003. But, after a disappointing 2003/04 campaign bereft of trophies and the usual stylish performance his teams had been famed for, Hitzfeld's contract was cancelled.

Despite being offered the chance to coach the German national team, Hitzfeld opted to take a break from the game. Two years later, a return to Bayern beckoned following the sacking of Felix Magath as manager. Hitzfeld inherited a team eight points adrift in the title race with 15 games remaining and couldn't turn around the side's fortunes in time to achieve anything more than a fourth-place finish. This meant the Bavarian club missed out on Champions League qualification for the first time in a decade.

The summer of 2007 saw Hitzfeld given licence to improve the Bayern squad and he spent significantly on the likes of Franck Ribéry, Luca Toni and Miroslav Klose, as established performers such as Roy Makaay, Mehmet Scholl and Owen Hargreaves departed the club. A revitalised Bayern began another spell of domestic dominance, winning the treble of Bundesliga, German Cup and German League Cup in 2008 and reaching the semi-final of the 2008 UEFA Cup. Despite such a successful season, Hitzfeld announced his plans to step down the following summer as he opted to take charge of the Swiss national side.

Hitzfeld's first international coaching assignment soon brought success as he guided the Swiss to the 2010 World Cup, famously securing a 1-0 opening win over tournament favourites and eventual winners, as well as reigning European Champions, Spain. However, a defeat to Chile and a draw with Honduras saw Switzerland exit the tournament at the group stage. Despite failing to reach Euro 2012, Hitzfeld remained in his post and led the Swiss to qualification for the 2014 World Cup.

A hugely gifted manager, tactician and motivator, Ottmar Hitzfeld's phenomenal achievements are matched by the rarity of both his longevity over two spells at Bayern Munch and his propensity for European Cup success with two of German football's biggest clubs.

The manager's first Champions League success with Borussia Dortmund remains one of the biggest shocks in the modern era of the competition and he showed great resilience and character to return from a crushing defeat in the 1999 final to inspire Bayern to lift the trophy two years later.

An uncompromising disciplinarian who prides himself on running a tight team unit, Hitzfeld is an excellent man-manager who inspires players to realise greater heights, both individually and as part of a team. He also possesses excellent judgement of a how to set up teams for different opponents and occasions, as well as the know-how to make telling tactical adjustments in the heat of the action.

Hitzfeld's record stands up against the greatest German managers of all time and saw him recently voted the best coach in Bayern Munich's history, as well as the greatest in the history of the Bundesliga. Another accolade and a succinct endorsement from a man not known for being effusive with praise, came from German legend Lothar Matthäus, who labelled Hitzfeld as "by the far the best manager of my football life".

A calculated tactician who enjoys the rare distinction of being cherished at both Borussia Dortmund and Bayern, Ottmar Hitzfeld is a statesman of German football and one of the most resourceful football bosses of the modern era.

# 7. BRIAN CLOUGH

**Born:** March 21, 1935 in Middlesbrough, England
**Died:** September 20, 2004, aged 69
**Clubs Managed:** Hartlepool United, Derby County, Brighton & Hove Albion, Leeds United, Nottingham Forest
**Major Honours:** 11

A two-time European Cup winner with unfashionable Nottingham Forest and one of the biggest characters in the English game, the incomparable Brian Clough wore his heart on his sleeve and had an aura around him that only the very best managers possess. Part of a managerial team made in football heaven, alongside his assistant Peter Taylor, Clough took two provincial clubs to heights they hadn't dared to dream of before and haven't come close to since.

The ultimate man-motivator who had the vision to transform established players into alternative positions to create an almost perfect team unit, the outspoken Englishman possessed an unswerving belief in the way football should be played and the manner in which his players should behave. His controversial views off the pitch and the frequency with which he was happy to air them ultimately cost him his dream job as England manager, but the biggest loser in that situation was the Football Association and English football, who both missed out on the man that could have positively shaped its game for years to come.

As a player, Clough was a prolific goal scorer with Middlesbrough and Sunderland, finding the net 251 times in 274 starts. He played the majority of his career in the English Second Division but still won two England caps before being forced to retire from playing in 1964, aged just 29 years old, after sustaining a serious knee injury two years earlier.

A year after his retirement Clough undertook his first managerial appointment when he was appointed Hartlepool United boss, naming Peter Taylor, a former team-mate during his playing days with

Middlesbrough, as his assistant to begin a successful association that would last for the majority of both men's careers. Inheriting a club with threadbare resources, the 30-year-old Clough became the youngest manager in the Football League. He gradually improved Hartlepool's fortunes on the field, transforming a side used to struggling at the wrong end of the table to one pushing for promotion.

The north-east minnows were in dire financial straits, but their ambitious new manager was determined to be a success and toured local pubs raising money to keep the club afloat, also mucking in with other jobs around the stadium to save money. The team gradually began to improve, going on to achieve a respectable eighth-place finish in 1967; their highest league placing for 10 years. Clough and Taylor's reputations were growing and the promising duo joined Second Division Derby County. The team they had built at Hartlepool continued to progress and achieved promotion, for the first time in their history, in 1968.

Derby had finished 17th in the second tier. Clough and Taylor failed to improve upon that placing at the end of their first season in charge, but started to show the astute moves in the transfer market they would become famed for, snapping up a good blend of exciting young talent and experienced professionals, including the likes of Roy McFarland, John O'Hare and Alan Hinton. Another major addition came in 1968 when the hardworking duo captured the signature of former Tottenham Hotspur great, Dave Mackay.

It proved an inspirational move as Clough had the foresight to transform the Scotsman from a battling midfielder into a deep-lying sweeper. With the influential Mackay in fine form and Clough able to summon greater performances and more consistency from the other Derby County players, the Rams finished top of the 1968/69 Second Division with a seven-point margin, having clocked up a 22 game unbeaten run, to gain promotion and ensure a First Division return for the first time since 1953.

The shrewd management duo weren't finished there and as the younger players in the team continued to flourish and the impressive Colin Todd was added to an extremely fluid team unit, Derby adjusted well to life in the top flight. Priding himself on playing a passing, entertaining style, drenched in the principles of fair play and respecting referees, Clough's men become one of the more entertaining sides in the English game. After two top-10 finishes, Derby were crowned English champions for the first time in their history in 1972. The Rams finished a single point ahead of Leeds United, managed by Don Revie; a manager and team that Clough came to despise, due to a style of play he perceived as dirty and underhand.

Clough was an indomitable character whose passion and presence in the dressing room, combined with an extremely sharp and astute mind, saw him become a master motivator. With Taylor's more measured and observant approach, as well as his ability to pick the perfect players to complement the team, Derby belied their position as one of the lesser clubs in the top flight and regularly outplayed the traditionally more successful sides of the era.

As well as setting up teams well tactically, Clough had a penchant for transforming his team's performances and subsequent results. Quick-witted and as opinionated as any Englishman to have been involved in football, 'Cloughie', as he was affectionately known, became a journalist's dream, providing incisive and cutting sound bites and insight into his managerial philosophy.

First Division title success saw Derby qualify for the European Cup for the first time and they went on to enjoy great success, defeating the likes of Benfica and Spartak Trnava to reach the semi-finals where they were controversially beaten 3-1 on aggregate by Italian giants Juventus. After the game, Clough claimed the Italian club had bribed the match officials following harsh bookings of Roy McFarland and Archie Gemmill and a lack of action taken against some aggressive treatment by the Italians particularly angered the manager and caused him to label their opponents "cheating bastards".

Despite the club's continued progression, that sort of controversy was far from rare and trouble was brewing in paradise as Clough's increasingly brash behaviour began to infuriate Derby's chairman, Sam Longson. A series of events saw the two single-minded men continuously clash, including Clough and Taylor agreeing a record transfer fee of £225,000 for Leicester City's David Nish without consulting the Derby board, and Clough's amazing outburst towards the club's fans following a 2-1 over Liverpool in 1972 when he said, "They started chanting only near the end when we were a goal in front. I want to hear them when we are losing. They are a disgraceful lot."

Longson apologised on behalf of his manager and a wedge continued to be driven between the two men as Clough's media presence increased and he continued to make offers for players from other clubs, including West Ham United's Bobby Moore, without notifying the board. In October 1973, Sam Longson called for the sacking of both Clough and Taylor. However, both men offered their resignation leading to widespread consternation from fans, who demanded that the board stand down with both men reinstated. Eventually Longson and the board won the power struggle and Clough and Taylor moved onto pastures new.

During his six-year spell at Derby, Clough was transformed from a hugely promising and enthusiastic young manager into a streetwise, domineering presence, both in and out of the dugout.

His sense of justice and the way football should be played had progressed from controlling matters on the field to looking to have an impact on the wider game and the authorities running the sport. He was the first British manager to become a media sensation, both during interviews and as a television pundit and newspaper columnist, ensuring a wide-reaching platform for his opinions. Clough also flourished into a top-class manager during his Derby tenure, lifting two league titles and showing the tactical awareness to continue to improve the team and enjoy progress in European competition.

Upon leaving Derby, Clough and Taylor took charge of Third Division Brighton & Hove Albion, with Clough opting to leave the south coast club after just eight months to take up the irresistible and hugely controversial challenge of succeeding Don Revie at Leeds United. It was a move that shocked the world of football and put the first strains on the previously sound relationship between Clough and Taylor.

Having been so fiercely critical of Revie, Leeds United and several of the players individually, the move to Leeds appeared to be one verging on professional suicide for Clough. His history of attacking the club and their methods, as well as a manager that the players were hugely loyal to, left Brian in an almost hopeless situation. Following a disastrous 44-day spell in charge at Elland Road, which saw many of the players that had been dedicated to Revie alienated and the team record their worst start to a season for 15 years, he was relieved of his duties.

Clough and Taylor were reunited in the East Midlands just months after the Leeds debacle when they joined another small provincial side in the Second Division, Nottingham Forest. A club of similar stature to Derby County, Clough and Taylor soon reshaped the squad with Taylor continuing to find the right players at the right time for Clough to mould into a hungry, passionate and winning team unit.

At the end of his first full season in charge, Clough guided Forest into the First Division by virtue of a third-place finish. An interview for the England job came following Don Revie's controversial departure in 1977, but the FA went with the perceived safer choice of Ron Greenwood. Undaunted, Clough returned to club football even more determined to succeed. His team then took the top flight by storm during the 1977/78 season finishing top of the pile and seven points clear of second-placed Liverpool to lift the club's first ever First Division title. In the process, Clough became only the third manager, and one of just four in the history of the game, to have won the English Championship with two different clubs.

The 1978 League Cup was added following a 1-0 victory over Liverpool.

Perhaps learning from his acrimonious departure from Derby and stung by the episode with Leeds United, Clough toned down his controversial comments and lessened his media work during his time with Nottingham Forest to concentrate on building his second great team.

During Forest's title defence in 1978/79, Clough and Taylor spent a British record £1m to bring the attacking talents of Trevor Francis to the club from Birmingham City. It proved to be money well spent, as although the league title was surrendered to Liverpool, Forest went on to reach the 1979 European Cup Final where they defeated Sweden's Malmö FF by a solitary goal, scored by Francis. That European Cup triumph saw Forest become only the third English club to have lifted the famous trophy, having knocked out holders Liverpool on their way to the final. Clough remains the only manager to have guided a team to European Cup glory just a year after being promoted to the top flight.

The capture of Francis was just the latest in a long line of hugely successful transfer signings, which also included England's match-saving goalkeeper Peter Shilton, the ever-reliable John McGovern, who became club captain and Kenny Burns who was solid at the back and provided a goal threat going forward. The new additions brought the best out of the players that Clough had inherited, such as Ian Bowyer, Martin O'Neill and the highly skilled John Robertson, who became a key creative force.

A year later, Forest amazingly reached a second consecutive European Cup Final and defeated SV Hamburg 1-0. This time the winning strike was forced home by John Robertson, while Shilton gave a stunning display of goalkeeping to keep their opponents at bay and give Forest the distinction of becoming only the second English team, after Liverpool, to have retained the trophy.

During this period, Forest also achieved a record-breaking unbeaten run that gave their manager great satisfaction, as they went 42 league games without defeat between 26 November, 1977 and 9 December, 1978. It was a record that stood until 2004 when it was beaten by Arsène Wenger's Arsenal.

With the challenges of Europe continuing to burden their domestic campaign, Forest lost the 1980 League Cup Final to Wolverhampton Wanderers and finished the 1979/80 season in fifth place. As Clough began to break up his successful team and bring in new high-profile additions, such as Justin Fashanu and Asa Hartford, a gradual slump slowly began to set in. In 1982, Peter Taylor retired from football as his relationship with Clough had become increasingly strained. Within a few years their friendship had soured completely. Regretfully for both men, that relationship was not rekindled before Taylor's death in 1960, something that haunted Clough for the rest of his life.

The impact of Taylor's departure on Forest and Clough may not have been immediate but without his right-hand man and confidant to bounce ideas off, and most notably to offer scouting advice on new signings, the club and their manager were arguably never the same again.

A couple of disappointing seasons followed the second European Cup success. The club continued to challenge at the top of the table, for the remainder of the decade, finishing third in 1984 and 1988 and enjoyed further progress in Europe, reaching the semi-finals of the UEFA Cup in 1984, losing a tie to Anderlecht that was shrouded in controversy regarding the alleged bribery by the Belgian club.

Forest remained in the top flight under Clough but it took until 1989 for them to win their next significant trophy when they lifted the League Cup following a 3-1 victory over Luton Town. It came during a season in which the Nottingham club came close to the title, eventually finishing third, and reached the semi-final of the FA Cup in which they were defeated by Liverpool in a tie dominated by the tragedy of the Hillsborough disaster.

Another League Cup followed in 1990 when Forest defeated Oldham Athletic 1-0 in the final before Clough's men reached the final of the FA Cup, the only major tournament the manager was yet to win, in 1991. Facing Tottenham at Wembley, Forest took the lead through a thunderous Stuart Pearce free kick, but the Londoners came back through Paul Stewart before an extra-time own goal by Forest's Des Walker gifted Spurs the trophy.

A further Cup final loss came a year later as the Tricky Trees were defeated 1-0 by Alex Ferguson's emerging Manchester United in the 1992 League Cup. It proved to be the last high-point of Clough's Forest tenure. The team and the club continued to stagnate as their legendary manager failed to keep up with revolutionary changes enveloping the professional game in England, as money became more important and an influx of foreign players entered the Premier League.

The newly rebranded division's first season kicked-off in 1992/93 and it proved to be a nightmare for the Nottingham club. Following a campaign strained with struggle that saw the team almost exclusively occupy bottom place in the table, they dropped out of the division, marking the first relegation of Clough's career. Before the demotion, he had already announced his decision to step down from the Forest hot seat and retire from the game.

Cloughie's later years had been clouded by ill-judgement, partially influenced by his continued battle with alcoholism, meaning that a sustained decline was inevitable. Not all of the blame can be laid at the manager's door, however, as the club failed to progress off the pitch and despite having competed with England's biggest clubs on the field, they never came close to matching them in terms of infrastructure and investment; two elements that become increasingly important in football.

Arguably the biggest personality to have graced the English game due to his charisma and penchant for a controversial opinion, Clough was quite simply one of the greatest manager's the English game has ever seen and alongside, Bob Paisley, he remains one of the most talented English bosses of all time. To have taken two provincial clubs with such limited resources from relative mediocrity to the top of the English game, and in Nottingham Forest's case, sustained European success, is a remarkable achievement. The style with which these successes were realised, with attractive, entertaining football and with a fair play a prerequisite of any Brian Clough team, ensured that those glories remain even more honourable.

It is important to distinguish between the impact of Clough the manager with that of Clough and Peter Taylor as a managerial partnership. Both men complemented each other perfectly, covering each other's weaknesses and sharing a footballing philosophy and a vision to create teams that led to great success at Derby County and Nottingham Forest. Without Taylor at his side, Clough continued to keep Forest in the top flight and added further domestic trophies but the magic that had seen them lift the European Cup twice had seemingly dried up.

Undoubtedly Clough's is also a career that featured its fair share of regret and missed opportunities, including the circus-like spell at Leeds, the despair of taking a club he had built up to such glories down to relegation and the ongoing disappointment of not being given the chance to manage his country. In a period in which England struggled to make any impact on the international game, often missing out on qualification for major tournaments, it's almost criminal Clough wasn't given the chance to fulfil his ultimate ambition and manage the England national side. The outspoken boss clearly paid for his brash character and his tenacious approach to challenging authority.

Clough's success is also notable due to the fact that he achieved it without managing one of English football's biggest clubs. Had he been afforded the resources of Manchester United, Liverpool or Arsenal it would have been interesting to see what he could've accomplished. It's also worth considering the records of both Nottingham Forest and Derby County before and since his tenures in charge.

Before Clough, the highlight of Derby's history had been a solitary FA Cup success in 1946 while after his departure, it hasn't got any better than a 1975 First Division title claimed under Clough's former star-signing Dave Mackay.

Forest's pre-Clough record was only notable for two FA Cup victories, in 1898 and 1959, while following his retirement, the club have mostly played outside of the Premier League.

Clough was an expert man-manager who understood how to deal with the unique intricacies of each of his players, as he later illustrated, saying, "I don't need a boring book by Freud to show me how to [read people]. I've been doing it since day one in management. The art of management is knowing your own players, and I'm not talking about whether someone has a better right foot than left. I'm talking about really knowing them, knowing what sort of person you've got on your hands. And I don't remember Freud winning a European Cup Final."

It was just one of a succession of famous quotes that provided a vivid glimpse into the self-confidence possessed by Clough and the secrets of his success. Other quips included his less than modest reflection on his on record, when he said, "I wouldn't say I was the best manager in the business. But I was in the top one," and "Rome wasn't built in a day. But I wasn't on that particular job."

Assessing all of his considerable strengths and occasional weaknesses, it's clear that Brian Clough remains a footballing enigma whose impact on all areas of the game is unlikely to ever be matched.

# 6. SIR MATT BUSBY

**Born:** May 26, 1909 in Orbiston, Scotland
**Died:** January 20, 1994, aged 84
**Clubs Managed:** Manchester United
**International:** Great Britain: 1948 and Scotland: 1958
**Major Honours:** 13

The man who built and rebuilt Manchester United transforming a club struggling both on and off the pitch following World War II and the Munich Air Disaster, Sir Matt Busby created a footballing philosophy and dynasty that saw United become one of the most famous and popular clubs in the world, while lifting multiple domestic honours and the Holy Grail of the European Cup.

Like his modern-day equivalent, Sir Alex Ferguson, Sir Matt Busby's success at Manchester United was matched by longevity and an immeasurable impact on the entire club. The 'Godfather of Old Trafford' possessed a passion for thrilling, attacking football and trusted in the talents of youth with great enthusiasm. Both facets contributed to carving out Manchester United's celebrated worldwide reputation.

Manchester United quite simply wouldn't have been Manchester United without Sir Matt Busby. More than a manager, more than a figurehead, he came to symbolise everything great about the club.

Like many of the finest Scottish managers, Busby was a miner's son who followed his father down the pits in his youth, before beginning a career in professional football. Busby went on to appear for United's great rivals, Manchester City and Liverpool, winning an FA Cup with the former and making a single international appearance for his country before the Second World War interrupted his progress. After the war, having served as a football coach in the army's Physical Training Corps, Busby was offered the assistant manager's role at Liverpool, but wanting to be his own man and take full control of a team, something he insisted upon during discussions with Old Trafford directors, he opted to accept Manchester United's managerial proposition, taking charge of the club in 1945.

Busby discovered a club in disarray as Old Trafford had been devastated by German bombers during the War, leaving United without a home and adequate training facilities. The Reds were struggling financially and had to play their home matches at Manchester City's Maine Road ground while Old Trafford was rebuilt.

One of Busby's first acts as United manager was to appoint the enthusiastic and visionary Welshman, Jimmy Murphy, as his assistant. Both men relished their involvement on the training pitch with the players, as Busby enjoyed a more hands-on coaching role than traditionally adopted by British managers.

As well as his determination to bring young talent through, Busby wasn't averse to making significant moves in the transfer market to transform the club from a mediocre mid-table side to one challenging at the top. In came the likes of the veteran Scottish winger Jimmy Delaney to supplement a team that already included Johnny Carey, Stan Pearson, Jack Rowley and Charlie Mitten. Busby also improved the side by transforming the careers of John Aston and Johnny Carey, whom he converted into full-backs, and by placing greater focus on attacking wingers, Delaney and Mitten, to ensure the team played with pace and width, as he implemented a progressive passing style that brought greater consistency.

Following a fourth-place finish in 1946, Busby guided United to runners-up spot behind Liverpool a year later, and he repeated that in three of the next four seasons. In that period, Busby claimed his first honour as Manchester United boss, lifting the 1948 FA Cup thanks to a 4-2 final victory over Blackpool. Busby's first great team peaked in 1952 when they won the First Division title, the club's first Championship in 41 years and a success that proved a watershed in United's history.

The team had featured one of the first youngsters to graduate through the Busby and Murphy academy, as future captain Roger Byrne was given his chance during the title charge. However, it remained an ageing team and Busby was abundantly aware that he needed to freshen things up. To achieve that, the Scotsman opted to put his trust in youth, selecting teenagers that had impressed on the training pitch, such as Bill Foulkes, Jackie Blanchflower, Albert Scanlon, David Pegg and the incomparable Duncan Edwards; a huge talent who Busby built his team around and who became an England regular at the tender age of 18. Other youngsters were waiting in the wings, such as future World Cup winners, Bobby Charlton and Nobby Stiles, ensuring that Busby's vision of selecting a team filled with players schooled at Old Trafford could become a reality.

It was only a matter of time before such a talented group would break into the first-team picture and Busby was a man both brave and bold enough to select them, emphasised by his famous quote, "If you don't put them in, then you can't know what you've got!" As well as introducing locally sourced talent, Busby possessed a keen eye for the abilities of youngsters based at other clubs, bringing in the likes of Johnny Berry and Tommy Taylor.

In between his impressive record with United, Busby also managed Great Britain during the 1948 Summer Olympics, where his team reached the semi-finals, losing to eventual silver medallists Yugoslavia.

Further success followed back at Old Trafford as Busby's young team, christened as the 'Busby Babes', began to dominate established First Division teams, playing a brand of attacking football inspired by youthful exuberance and adventure that captured the public's imagination. The youthful team went on to win the 1956 and 1957 First Division titles, narrowly missing out on a league and FA Cup double in '57 after losing to Aston Villa in the final. Everything clicked into place at Old Trafford during the 1955/56 season as a United team with an average age of just 22, steamrollered the Division, claiming the title by a significant 11-point margin.

The championship was retained a year later by a eight points, with the team scoring more than 100 goals. Busby's vision for the club had become a reality and his reflection of that achievement was filled with pride; "From the very start I had envisaged making my own players, having a kind of nursery so that they could be trained in the kind of pattern I was trying to create for Manchester United."

Busby often spoke of finding the players to fit into the type of 'pattern' he wanted to play and the 'Babes' team was the perfect representation of that. The 1956 title gave the club the chance to play in the recently launched European Cup competition. A visionary who was aware of the importance of keeping pace with football on the continent, Busby was determined to take United into Europe but faced significant obstruction from the English Football Association. Undeterred and following the intervention of FA Chairman Stanley Rous, the manager led his charges into Europe during the 1956/57 campaign.

United became the first English team to take part in the European Cup and Busby's young players adapted well, defeating the likes of Borussia Dortmund and Athletic Bilbao to set up a semi-final clash with reigning champions Real Madrid. The English team lost, but the experience gained in Europe whetted Busby and the players' appetites for the continental game.

With Manchester United riding the crest of the wave, Matt Busby's maturing youngsters looked set to take charge of the English and European game for the next decade, but tragedy struck during the 1957/58 campaign. A plane carrying United home from a European Cup quarter-final victory over Red Star Belgrade in Yugoslavia stopped to refuel at Munich's Riem Airport. Adverse weather conditions in Germany led to two aborted take-off attempts for the BEA Elizabethan aircraft carrying the Manchester United party, as the plane failed to gain enough momentum while surging down the runway. During a fateful third and final attempt the plane hurtled down the runway before crashing through a fence, into a house and bursting into flames.

Many passengers were killed instantly, while others such as Busby suffered serious, life-threatening injuries and were transported to a nearby hospital. The manager was at death's door and had his last rites read to him on more than one occasion. He had suffered fractured ribs, a punctured lung and leg injuries but wouldn't discover the true magnitude of the tragedy until weeks after the crash. In total, eight Manchester United players were killed, including the talismanic, influential and irreplaceable Duncan Edwards, while others were injured too severely to maintain a professional football career. The heart had been ripped out of Manchester United and a team that promised to be the next great side to dominate European competition had been devastated years before its prime.

As Busby recovered from his injuries, Jimmy Murphy, who had been on international coaching duties with Wales during the crash, kept the club afloat as United continued to fulfil their league and cup fixtures for the remainder of the campaign. Boosted by the goodwill of a nation and the sympathies of the world, a patched-together United side of emergency signings and reserve team players went on to reach the 1958 FA Cup final, where they were narrowly defeated by Bolton Wanderers. Busby was a spectator at the final ahead of his eventual return to the dugout, when he would have to rebuild the club for a second time, a task he wrote about in his autobiography, *Soccer at the Top—My Life in Football*, stating; "I was determined to keep the name of Manchester United on people's lips. We had always to look as if we were doing something. Having been the greatest we would not settle for anything less, and our supporters deserved nothing less."

Exactly what that immensely talented group of young men could have gone on to achieve will never be known. The potential lost was immeasurable and Busby believed they would have been one of the best teams ever seen, later saying; "I am convinced that I could have sat back and watched this collection of infants pile up a list of championships and cups for years to come. They were surely the greatest group of young footballers in one team ever gathered together."

Busby later had a spell as Scotland's interim manager, taking charge for two games and giving future United star Denis Law his first international cap. Before Law arrived at Old Trafford, alongside other astute signings such as David Herd and Albert Quixall, Matt began building a new team from the Munich survivors, which included heroic goalkeeper Harry Gregg, uncompromising defender Bill Foulkes and the hugely talented Bobby Charlton.

A final magical ingredient was then added when a young Northern Irishman by the name of George Best signed following a successful trial. The varied yet hugely compatible attacking trio of Best, Law and Charlton became the fabric of a gloriously entertaining pattern woven by Busby as each player possessed creativity, goal-scoring threat and the ability to win matches singlehandedly. Given the nickname of the 'Holy Trinity', Best, Law and Charlton, ably supported the by the grit of Nobby Stiles and the passing range of Paddy Crerand, went on to return United and Busby to the pinnacle of the game.

Progress was more gradual than instant as the Red Devils rediscovered their form season by season. Often struggling for consistency in the league, United tasted their first trophy success in 1963 when, inspired by the goals of Law and Herd, they defeated Leicester City 3-1 in the FA Cup Final. The league championship was secured two years later, allowing the club to participate in the European Cup for the first time since the tragedy of Munich. Busby remained resolute and determined to realise his goal of lifting the European Cup, a feat that had taken on deeper meaning since the tragedy of Munich.

The 1965/66 European campaign ultimately ended in disappointment as United were defeated by Partizan Belgrade in the semi-finals.

In an era when only the champions of each country were afforded passage into the European Cup, United had to win another league title just to earn the right to compete for Busby's Holy Grail and, following a year without a trophy, the 1967 title was delivered. This time United wouldn't be denied in Europe as they famously defeated Real Madrid in the semi-finals, thanks to a crucial and unlikely goal from Bill Foulkes. Madrid had tried to entice Busby to be their manager years earlier but the Scotsman remained loyal to United, as he later explained; "Mr Bernabéu and the officials there said it would be a tremendous salary and they would make Madrid a heaven for me. I eventually said to Mr Bernabéu that I was very grateful but my heaven is here in Manchester."

Having defeated Madrid, United set up a final tie against Benfica at Wembley. After a closely fought game ended 1-1 after 90 minutes, the Reds went on to destroy their opponents in extra-time, scoring three goals through Best, Brian Kidd and, fittingly, Munich-survivor Bobby Charlton, who netted his second of the game to seal a 4-1 victory and the first European Cup in Manchester United's history.

Emotional scenes followed as Busby finally got his hands on the trophy that he had strived and suffered so hard for. Ten years after the sadness of Munich, the club had finally conquered European football. After the game, Busby spoke emotionally to the media, attempting to sum up the gravity of the players' achievement; "They've done us proud. They came back with all their hearts to show everyone what Manchester United are made of. This is the most wonderful thing that has happened in my life and I am the proudest man in England tonight."

That season's league title was lost to local rivals Manchester City but few at Old Trafford were too concerned. The European Cup was the club's destiny and it had been realised in emphatic fashion. Busby remained as the team's manager for another season as United came close to retaining their European crown, eventually bowing out to AC Milan in the semi-final, before their manager stepped away from the dugout to take up a seat on the club's board. In his final season United played against Argentinean side Estudiantes in the Intercontinental Cup in what turned out to be a gruelling two-legged encounter that saw Busby's men viciously provoked for large periods of both games, before eventually losing 2-1 on aggregate.

Busby remained at the club as director and his former player, Wilf McGuinness, succeeded him. The great man was on hand to offer advice to the younger manager when required but his presence at the club proved too much for McGuinness and future managers such as Frank O'Farrell to deal with, as United failed to recapture anything close to the sort of success experienced under the Scotsman until several decades later. Busby was enticed into returning to the Old Trafford dugout in 1970 for a brief spell and remained as a director until his appointment as club president in 1982.

It took until 1993 for Manchester United to lift the English league title again and it was again a Scot with a similar background and footballing principles that led the club to the Promised Land; Alex Ferguson. The only United manager to match and eventually surpass Busby's achievements in terms of trophies, and a man just as focused on developing young players and succeeding in Europe, Ferguson returned the club to the peak of the game, just as Sir Matt had done during his first 24-year reign in charge. The great man himself was able to witness the securing of that first league title in 26 years under Ferguson, but died a year later, missing out on United's reclamation of the European Cup in 1999 as the Reds defeated Bayern Munich in the final on what would have been his 90th birthday.

The man described as 'Mr Manchester United' did more than anybody to establish the club as arguably the most famous and best supported sporting institution in the world. His presence remains influential at Old Trafford, both metaphorically as well as literally in the tangible forms of the bronze statue outside the ground and the road leading to the stadium christened as the Sir Matt Busby Way.

The 'Sir Matt Busby way' became the Manchester United way as he established a philosophy and legacy that has seen the club remain as one of the biggest in the world, long after he stepped down as manager. Matt Busby epitomised everything that was great about Manchester United. His vision to create teams that played entertaining, attacking football that thrilled the masses left an indelible mark on British football, as did his philosophy to trust the talents of young players and his foresight to chase success in European football.

Busby's achievements in building and re-building Manchester United, creating three great teams, each of which dominated domestically, and then inspiring the club to become England's first winners of the European Cup are legendary. The number of European crowns and league titles that his Busby Babes could have accumulated had they not been so instantly taken away in the tragedy of Munich is impossible to predict.

But, with many of those youngsters already having made the breakthrough into international football, it's not unreasonable to suggest that they could have gone on to dominate Europe in the same way as the great Real Madrid team that they had run so close during the 1957 European Cup.

On the night of Busby's death, one of his greatest signings, Denis Law, paid a fitting tribute to his former manager, saying, "He was probably the greatest manager English football has seen, a visionary who took an English club into Europe when most people thought it unwise. He proved he was right. He built great teams in the 1940s, the '50s and the '60s but, more important, he was a true gentleman to everyone, from the playing stars to the ground staff."

Law's comments illustrate how Busby ensured that Manchester United retained the feeling of being a family club, despite their ever-increasing stature, and made Old Trafford and enjoyable place for players to play football, express themselves and in-turn bring immeasurable joy to the thousands of supporters that watched them. In that sense, Busby was the original football patriarch; a father figure to the players and the father of Manchester United. As with many of the celebrated figures in this book, Sir Matt Busby was more than a great manager, he was also the creator of a great football club.

------------------------------------------------------------------------------------------

# CHAPTER 9

## MANAGERS 5 AND 4

# 5. JOSÉ MOURINHO

**Born:** January 26, 1963 in Setúbal, Portugal
**Clubs Managed:** Benfica, União de Leiria, FC Porto, Chelsea, Inter Milan, Real Madrid
**Major Honours:** 20

Enigmatic, a one-off and arguably the most opinion-splitting manager of all time, the controversy courting, self-titled 'Special One' has tasted league and European glory with some of the biggest clubs in European football, consistently lifting major honours in Portugal, England, Spain and Italy and enjoying a fast-tracked and almost unprecedented managerial career.

José Mourinho's tactical awareness and ability to draw the absolute maximum in terms of effort, skill and loyalty from his players has seen him raise teams to heights beyond what many may have believed possible. Despite never playing

to a high level professionally, Mourinho's understanding of top players' needs and the different psychologies of the range of characters that he has coached set him apart as one of the most forward-thinking bosses of the modern era.

His larger-than-life personality and ability to conduct the media to his tune, while often behaving right on the edge and often across the line of what is deemed acceptable by the authorities, is all a veneer implemented to draw attention and pressure away from his players and to wage psychological warfare with his rivals.

A modest playing career saw the

football-obsessed Portuguese appear for four of the more minor, lower league teams in his homeland before he went on to study sports science at university in Lisbon. He held down various jobs, including as a PE teacher, a youth team coach with Vitória de Setúbal, a scout for Ovarense and assistant manager of Estrela da Amadora.

Mourinho's first opportunity to work at a major club came in 1992 with Sporting Lisbon when Bobby Robson was appointed manager and José was hired as his interpreter. The young and hungry Portuguese was seen as the ideal candidate for the role due to his coaching knowledge and desire to be as involved as much as possible in everything that the manager did. Mourinho bonded instantly with Robson and the pair discussed tactics and coaching principles as José sought to capitalise on every ounce of experience and advice the Englishman had at his disposal.

When Robson moved on to FC Porto, Mourinho followed him and his involvement with the players and the coaching side of the game continuously increased, to the extent that he became assistant manager. The team enjoyed great domestic success, prompting Barcelona to appoint Robson as their new manager in 1996. Again, Mourinho followed him, especially learning Catalan for his latest assignment, and his influence on tactical briefings, analysis of opponents and during training sessions grew further.

He became an important member of the coaching set-up and was retained as assistant manager when Robson became director of football and Louis van Gaal was appointed Barça manager. Under the Dutchman, Mourinho was again given the opportunity to continue his coaching scholarship.

The Portuguese was determined to become a manager in his own right and after a spell as Benfica assistant boss he was awarded the top job in September 2000, replacing the departing Jupp Heynckes. Mourinho began well until political wrangling behind the scenes saw the new president, Manuel Vilarinho, state that he planned to replace the manager with his favoured candidate. After Mourinho's requests for a contract extension were turned down, the headstrong coach tendered his resignation and went on take up the manager's role at União de Leiria.

In charge of one of the smaller clubs in Portugal, Mourinho led his new employers to their highest ever league finish, having taking the reins with seven games of the season remaining. His first full campaign with União saw them challenge at the top of the table, spending much of the year above the likes of Porto and Benfica. His record soon drew the attention of bigger clubs and Porto appointed him as manager in January 2002.

José guided the team to 11 wins from their last 15 games to ensure a third place finish before confidently predicting that he would make the team champions the following season. It was the sort of bold statement that Mourinho would become famed for, but as with many of his predictions, it wasn't without substance. After identifying the existing Porto players he wanted to shape his team around, Mourinho made a host of successful moves in the transfer market, signing the likes of Paulo Ferreira, Edgaras Jankauskas and Maniche.

Mourinho's pre-season preparations saw Porto embrace a more scientific training approach as he increased the players' fitness to ensure that they could succeed with the fast-tempo, high-pressing style of play that he wanted to implement. Many of the signings he made where the type of strong, quick and naturally athletic players that would come to form the basis of his most successful teams. Porto sealed the 2002/03 Portuguese Primeira Liga title with an impressive 27 wins from 34 games to accrue a record total of 86 points, finishing 11 points clear of second-placed Benfica. Porto also lifted the 2003 Portuguese Cup before reaching the final of the UEFA Cup that same year, when they faced Martin O'Neill's Celtic in the final.

Mourinho's first taste of a European final came at the end of his first full season as Porto coach and at the tender managerial age of just 40. His team's energetic, counter-attacking style of play led to a 3-2 victory over the Scottish team, achieved thanks to goals from Derlei and Alenichev.

In 2003, Porto narrowly lost the European Super Cup 1-0 to AC Milan but claimed the Portuguese Super Cup. The 2003/04 league title defence became a procession as Mourinho's team finished the season with a perfect home record and eight points clear of their nearest challengers, securing the championship with five weeks to spare. Benfica defeated the champions in the Portuguese Cup but Mourinho had his eye on a greater prize; the European Champions League.

With Porto having already announced their return to the top table of continental football with UEFA Cup glory, it was now time for their formidable manager to make his presence felt in Europe's premier club competition. Following an impressive route to the last 16 knockout stages, which saw them progress from a group that included Real Madrid, Porto defeated Sir Alex Ferguson's Manchester United to continue their progress. Mourinho used his tactical nous to overhaul Ferguson's men 3-2 on aggregate thanks to a last-ditch goal from Costinha that inspired Mourinho to surge down the Old Trafford touchline, joining the celebrations in front of the Porto supporters in a move that brought the emerging manager into even sharper worldwide focus.

His team then defeated Lyon and Deportivo la Coruña to reach the final, where they were paired with AS Monaco. A tight contest was predicted, but Porto dominated the encounter from start to finish, grabbing the opening goal through Carlos Alberto and then picking their opponents off on the counter attack to increase their lead through Deco and Alenichev and complete a 3-0 victory that saw Mourinho deliver the club's second European Cup and their first for 17 years.

Mourinho had made the decision to leave Porto following the Champions League final. He had plenty of options from some of the biggest clubs in Europe but opted to move to England to take charge of the emerging London side, Chelsea, who were being transformed into a club regularly challenging for major honours thanks to the significant investment of their owner Roman Abramovich.

The Portuguese became one of the highest-paid managers in the world and memorably announced his arrival in England in his first press conference, saying, "Please don't call me arrogant, but I'm European champion and I think I'm a special one." The title 'The Special One' was immediately awarded to him by the English media; a label that has remained throughout his career. However, it's a description that has some foundation as Mourinho proved during his first season in England when, buoyed by a huge transfer outlay that saw Chelsea invest more than £70m on players, the Blues went on to win the 2004/05 Premier League title.

Playing a high-tempo and maximum-energy style of play, based on a solid and reliable defence and midfield, Chelsea powered past opponents, going unbeaten in the league at home and losing just a single game all season to amass a record points total of 95, finishing 12 points clear of runners-up Arsenal. It was the club's first English title since 1955 and saw Chelsea set a record for fewest goals conceded in a single Premier League season. The League Cup was also secured but Mourinho was denied a second consecutive Champions League crown after Liverpool knocked Chelsea out in the semi-finals.

The 2005/06 season brought more domestic success as Chelsea retained their Premier League crown, this time with a tally of 91 points that featured 15 wins from the team's first 16 matches, to complete Mourinho's fourth consecutive domestic title-winning campaign. The manager's demeanour on the touchline and during press conferences became more and more controversial, both in domestic and European football, as he verbally attacked officials and stories of illegal approaches to several players, including Arsenal's Ashley Cole, became prevalent.

The hugely successful honeymoon period between Mourinho and Chelsea began to show signs of strain during the 2006/07 season as they were beaten to the title by Manchester United. The Champions League again ended in disappointment for Chelsea, once more at the hands of Liverpool, who disposed of the London club on penalties in the semi-finals.

The FA Cup was delivered, thanks to a 1-0 win over Manchester United that saw Mourinho realise the feat of lifting every single English trophy, as well as the League Cup, but there were allegations surrounding a souring of the manager's relationship with Abramovich. Reports began to surface that the owner, rather than Mourinho, had sanctioned the £30m signing of Ukraine striker Andrei Shevchenko and that the Portuguese was feeling increasingly undermined by the presence of sporting director Frank Arnesen and the later appointment of Avram Grant as director of football.

Mourinho remained in position for the start of the 2007/08 season which started in relatively disappointing manner despite Chelsea's 3-2 defeat of Birmingham City setting a new record of 64 consecutive home league matches without defeat. Following a loss to Aston Villa, a 0-0 home draw with Blackburn Rovers and 1-1 home draw against Norwegian team Rosenborg BK, in front of a half-empty Stamford Bridge, Mourinho announced his decision to leave the club in September 2007.

Chelsea fans were distraught as the club had lost the most successful manager in its history. With Avram Grant named as his successor, the Blues continued to impress, running Manchester United close in the title race and finally reaching the final of the Champions League, something Mourinho had missed out on.

Mourinho was appointed Inter Milan manager in 2008, succeeding the departing Roberto Mancini. Inter had won the last four Italian Serie A titles but failed to make an impression in Europe. José's first season began with Italian Super Cup success and ended with another league title as they topped Serie A with 84 points, finishing 10 clear of their nearest challengers. However, Inter exited the Champions League in the quarter-finals following a tame defeat to reigning Champions Manchester United.

José soon caused a stir off the pitch in Italy, instigating controversial relationships with the media and several feuds with rival managers. Undaunted, his team continued to dominate, winning the Serie A title by another 10-point margin to claim their second successive domestic championship under Mourinho.

The Portuguese schemer made crucial additions such as Thiago Motta and Wesley Sneijder to the midfield and Diego Milito and Samuel Eto'o in attack that helped the team finally make their mark in Europe. After successfully negotiating the group stages, Inter were paired with Mourinho's former club Chelsea in the last 16 and the Portuguese again showed his excellent tactical knowledge to defeat the English club 3-1 on aggregate.

CSKA Moscow were comfortably beaten in the quarter-finals to set up a high-profile semi-final clash with holders Barcelona. It was the first time in seven years that Inter had reached that stage of the competition and it coincided with

Mourinho becoming the first manager in history to take three different clubs to the semi-finals of the Champions League.

After an emphatic 3-1 victory over Pep Guardiola's men at the San Siro, the return leg at the Nou Camp was shrouded in controversy as Inter were reduced to 10 men following the harsh 28th-minute dismissal of Thiago Motta. Mourinho came to the fore on the touchline, emotionally prompting his players, haranguing the officials and ensuring a formation was in place to frustrate their opponents.

Despite a late Gerard Piqué goal a resolute Inter lost just 1-0; a defeat that saw the team progress to the final and was labelled by Mourinho as "the most beautiful defeat of my life". As the final whistle pierced the cauldron of hate that the Nou Camp had become, Mourinho embraced the moment by sprinting on to the pitch to celebrate with his players.

The 2010 Champions League Final, Inter's first in the competition for 38 years, pitted Mourinho against Bayern Munich and Louis van Gaal. Both teams were vying for a treble, with Inter having already secured the Serie A title and the Italian Cup thanks to 1-0 victory over Roma. The final was played at Real Madrid's Bernabéu Stadium and produced an end-to-end encounter between two athletic and tactically aware teams. On the night the difference between the two sides was the craft of Wesley Sneijder and the unerringly cool finishing of Diego Milito,

who scored in each half to ensure a 2-0 victory for Inter.

The treble was secured; the first time by an Italian club. It meant Mourinho had lifted his second Champions League crown in just six years. As he celebrated at the Bernabéu, Mourinho knew that the famous stadium would be his next home, as he had accepted arguably the toughest managerial appointment in European football and was appointed Real Madrid manager ahead of the 2010/11 season.

Real were blessed with a wealth of world-class talent, including Cristiano Ronaldo and the new manager soon put his stamp on the team, signing the German pair of Sami Khedira and Mesut Özil, Argentine winger Ángel di María and Chelsea defender Ricardo Carvalho.

With Real, Mourinho faced the daunting task of delivering the club's first Champions League since 2002 and dethroning a Barcelona side from becoming one of the greatest of all time. Having operated with a more defensive style at his previous clubs, Mourinho's Madrid played a more fluid attacking game that centred on the considerable goal-scoring talents of Cristiano Ronaldo, whose game was reaching unprecedented heights and saw him placed alongside Barcelona's Lionel Messi as the greatest player in the world.

However, it was Messi and co that inflicted the first serious wound on Mourinho's Madrid tenure when they triumphed 5-0 in his first El Clásico encounter at the Nou Camp. Barcelona went on to finish four points ahead of their great rivals to lift La Liga and knocked Real out of the Champions League in the semi-finals. During the home leg, unhinged by Pepe's red card and Mourinho's dismissal to the stands, Madrid were the victim of two pieces of individual brilliance by Messi and lost 2-0. A 1-1 draw at the Nou Camp in the second leg saw Real bow out of the competition to the eventual winners, but it had been the furthest stage that Madrid had reached since 2003.

Mourinho's first season didn't end trophyless as Real gained some semblance of revenge over the Catalan club by defeating them 1-0 in the Copa del Rey Final to end Madrid's run of 18 years without winning the competition. Further domestic success followed during the 2011/12 campaign as Real were the model of consistency, winning La Liga and leaving Barcelona trailing in their wake. The champions won 32 of their 38 league matches, including a telling 2-1 defeat of Barcelona at the Nou Camp, lost just twice and clocked up an emphatic 100-point total to set numerous records and finish nine points clear of Barça. It also ended the club's four-year drought without the title.

Madrid reached the semi-finals of the Champions League but were denied on penalties by Bayern Munich as the club's 10th European Cup continued to elude them. Mourinho signed an extended contract at the end of the 2011/12 season and began the following campaign with another trophy, as Barcelona were defeated on away goals in the Spanish Super Cup, meaning that the Portuguese ace had won every domestic competition available to him in his first two years at the Bernabéu. He also became the first manager to have claimed every possible domestic competition in four separate European leagues.

Barcelona were again Real's main rivals during the 2012/13 campaign, but this time Mourinho faced a different foe in the dugout as Pep Guardiola had stepped down to be replaced by his assistant Tito Vilanova. Barça remained an equally formidable opponent and with Madrid rife with internal problems and dressing room difficulties, the Catalans regained La Liga at a canter, reaching the 100 total set by Real a season earlier and finishing 15 points clear.

Madrid again reached the latter stages of the Champions League, but the semi-finals were once more their undoing as they were defeated 4-3 on aggregate by Borussia Dortmund. It proved to be Mourinho's last season with Real as his relationships with prominent players such as Sergio Ramos, Iker Casillas and eventually Cristiano Ronaldo seriously broke down. These issues, combined with the continued public attacks on officials, which included claims that Barcelona received favourable treatment from UEFA, as well as a distasteful attack on Tito

Vilanova when he was still Barcelona's assistant coach the previous season, left the Madrid board convinced that Mourinho was no longer the right man for the club.

His last game in charge was a Copa del Rey Final loss to city rivals Atlético Madrid which prompted Mourinho to label the 2012/13 the worst of his career. A few days after that defeat, the manager's departure from the club was confirmed. It was a parting of ways that had become inevitable, and led to weeks of speculation about where José's next coaching assignment would take him, with a return to England at either Manchester United, Manchester City or Chelsea deemed most likely.

On 3 June 2013, it was announced that Mourinho would be returning to Chelsea, with the Portuguese seemingly having patched up his differences with Roman Abramovic. The Special One labelled himself as the 'Happy One' upon his return to the club and will be determined to add more silverware to the trophy cabinet, as well as his third Champions League crown.

Quite simply, both on and off the pitch, José Mourinho is a box office attraction. A unique individual who uses his flamboyant and single-minded character, often perceived as arrogance verging on conceit, as a front to protect his players and to ensure that the focus of the pressure remains on his shoulders, the hugely decorated manager has become an expert at manipulating the media and controlling the minds of his players.

His weaknesses are few, but remain significant enough to question his all time standing in the game. His strategy has primarily been to utilise physicality, strength and speed, alongside great teamwork and belief and for the most part it has worked spectacularly. Many argue that his negative tactics are too one-dimensional and his teams have lacked the sort of flair of some of the most celebrated sides of recent years; a notion put into sharp perspective when considering his main rival in recent seasons has been the majestic modern-day Barcelona.

Great teams don't become great simply because of their entertainment value, and Mourinho has developed a habit of building hugely consistent, match-winning sides at every club he has managed. An expert communicator and a meticulous planner, whose obsessive knowledge of opponents usually gives his teams the edge, Mourinho's attention to the smallest of details borders on obsession.

José's early successes at Porto and Chelsea came when the group of players he marshalled subscribed to his theories and responded to his instructions to the nth degree. A similar trust in his approach was experienced at Inter Milan and players at all three of those clubs came to be consumed by loyalty to their manager, feeling a deeper connection due to Mourinho's rapport with them, generated by private conversations and text messages that transformed their mindset and made them believe they were capable of achieving even greater heights than they'd ever imagined.

A fitting example of that relationship was provided by former Inter defender Marco Materazzi, who was filmed sobbing in Mourinho's arms following the Champions League victory and ahead of his manager's departure, and later said, "Those tears were because I had lost a friend. With José, I had a wonderful relationship not only because I enjoyed playing for him but because he gave me the feeling of being important."

At Real Madrid, a team filled with world stars eventually came to question the Mourinho method, but José still maintained his record of winning a trophy in every season he has managed. Three years is the maximum tenure that the Portuguese has remained at a single club, indicating that his intense and rigorous approach may have a shelf-life.

While he may continue to split opinions, few can argue with the facts. Now 50-years-old, Mourinho has won an incredible 20 trophies in the last 11 years, enjoying considerable success in four different countries. He has become the youngest manager to win the Champions League with two different clubs and to have been involved in 100 games in the competition. If he continues to hoist silverware and break records at the same pace over the next 10 years there's every chance that José Mourinho could go on to become the greatest manager the game has ever seen.

# 4. ERNST HAPPEL

**Born:** November 29, 1925 in Vienna, Austria
**Died:** November 14, 1992, aged 66
**Clubs Managed:** ADO Den Haag, Feyenoord, Sevilla, Club Brugge, Harelbeke, Standard Liège, SV Hamburg, FC Tirol Innsbruck
**International:** Netherlands: 1978 (Reached the 1978 World Cup Final); and Austria: 1991-1992
**Major Honours:** 17

Ernst Happel enjoyed significant domestic success in the Netherlands, Belgium, Germany and Austria, as well as winning the European Cup twice. He was also in charge of the beautifully innovative Dutch team that reached the final of the 1978 World Cup. The Austrian showed great intelligence and flexibility to succeed in different countries and became the first manager and one of only four to have lifted the European Cup with two different clubs.

Famed for his often incoherent interviews and simple team talks, and for the cigarette that seemed permanently to hang from his mouth, Happel was a tactical genius who understood how to maximise the talents of the players at his disposal while negating the strengths and exploiting the weaknesses of their opponents. Although he may often have mumbled, the Austrian was, in fact, an expert communicator, but not necessarily verbally. When it came to dealing with his players he ensured that they understood his tactical messages, messages that were mostly delivered through meticulously planned and perfectly implemented training sessions that focused on different strategies. German legend Günter Netzer, who while working as general manager for SV Hamburg, brought Happel in as first team coach, said, "Happel was able to explain to every player what exactly he wanted from him. The back four, pressing, offside trap... all of that he was able to explain. Not with words; he never spoke and when he spoke you were not able to understand him. But his training practices directly went into the flesh and bone of every player."

A skilful defender, Happel started his professional career with Rapid Wien, making his first-team debut at age 17 and going on to spend 14 years with the club in two separate spells. He won the Austrian Championship on six occasions and was named in Rapid's team of the century in 1999. He also played club football for Racing Club de Paris and earned 51 caps for Austria, appearing in two World Cups.

Happel's first coaching assignment came with Dutch club ADO Den Haag in 1962. Inheriting a team marooned at the bottom of the first division and one of the smaller sides in the Netherlands, success wasn't instant for the Austrian but he went on to transform the team into regular top-four finishers and eventually claimed the Dutch Cup in 1968 via a 2-1 victory over Ajax, having reached the final three times in his first four years in charge. It was with Den Haag that Happel cultivated his high-tempo, aggressive pressing game that depended on his players possessing great levels of stamina and placed great importance on dominating and controlling the midfield. His methods and his progress soon attracted the attentions of one of the country's biggest clubs, Feyenoord, who he took charge of two years later.

At Feyenoord Happel made his first significant impact as a coach, guiding the team to European Cup glory at the end of his debut season in charge when they defeated Celtic 2-1 after extra time in the 1970 final, thanks to goals from Rinus Israël and Ove Kindvall. Happel's men had defeated the likes of AC Milan and Legia Warsaw en route to the final in which they claimed the club's first major European honour. They failed to retain their Dutch title, however, finishing runners-up to Ajax, but winning the European Cup for the first time—the first Dutch club to do so, which more than made up for it.

As reigning European champions, Feyenoord faced Estudiantes de La Plata in the Intercontinental Cup and went on to win the tie 3-2 on aggregate, making them the first Dutch team to have won the competition. The Rotterdam club didn't enjoy the same success in the European Cup as they attempted to retain their trophy, suffering a shock first-round exit at the hands of Romanian champions UT Arad. Happel's men went on to reclaim the Dutch Eredivisie title from Ajax by a four-point advantage to signal the first league title of the emerging manager's career.

However, after two trophyless seasons, the Austrian's time with Feyenoord came to an end in 1973. The Rotterdam club had never finished outside of the top-two positions during his time in charge and he had taken them to the greatest success in their history. Happel began a short and uneventful spell with Spanish side Sevilla before moving on to Club Brugge in Belgium halfway through the 1973/74 season. It took the Austrian just a couple of years to create another winning team that wasn't just successful domestically, but also made waves in European football.

His first trophy with Brugge was the 1975/76 Belgian League title as his charges lost just six of their 36 games and finished four points ahead of second placed Anderlecht. It was the first of three successive league titles delivered by Happel, with the 1976/77 championship also being secured by a virtue of a four-point advantage over Anderlecht. The following season, Brugge pipped the same rivals by a single point, giving the manager the Belgian title in each of his three seasons at the helm.

The Belgian Cup was also secured in 1977 and Happel's high-energy outfit reached the 1976 UEFA Cup Final, where they faced Bob Paisley's impressive Liverpool side and lost a thrilling two-legged encounter 4-3 on aggregate. Two years later, Brugge continued to make their mark on the European game, becoming the first Belgian club to reach the final of the European Cup. Their impressive march towards the final featured victories over Panathinaikos, Atlético Madrid and Giovanni Trapattoni's Juventus to see them paired again with Liverpool, at that point the reigning European Champions, in the showpiece encounter.

In a tight game, Liverpool's Kenny Dalglish was the difference between the two sides as his smartly taken strike proved the only goal of the game. It was a blow to Happel who was always introspective but measured in a defeat. He was a deep thinker who valued the lessons learnt from losing as character and career defining, and once said, "It is not important why you win. You have to know why you have lost."

Despite that high-profile loss to Liverpool, Happel's achievement of taking a traditionally smaller club from one of the less-prominent football nations to such a level on the European stage was a considerable one, emphasised by the fact that no other Belgian club has managed to reach the final of the European Cup or the Champions League since Brugge's exploits in 1978.

During the 1977/78 season Happel was also appointed as the head coach of the Netherlands national team ahead of the 1978 World Cup to be held in Argentina. He departed his role with Brugge following the European Cup Final defeat to focus on preparations for the tournament. Happel was dealt a major blow when the team's talismanic star player, Johan Cruyff, refused to play in the competition in protest at Argentina's dictatorship, but he was still able to select from a squad that included the considerable talents of Johan Neeskens, Johnny Rep, Arie Haan, Ernie Brandts and Ruud Krol. His calm demeanour combined with steely focus and determination got the best out of those players, many of whom were traditionally big characters with plenty of opinions.

Things began well in Argentina as the Dutch completed a routine 3-0 over Iran before enduring a disappointing draw with Peru and suffering a shock defeat to Scotland. Qualification for the next group stages was secured by virtue of a better goal difference than the Scots. The Netherlands improved in the next group stage. Facing tougher opposition they went on to record an emphatic 5-1 victory over Happel's native Austria, a hard-fought 2-2 draw with West Germany and then a crucial 2-1 win against Italy to secure top spot in the group and passage to the final, where they faced hosts Argentina in Buenos Aires. Ahead of the game Happel, who was famously a man of few words, was said to have given the following pre-match team talk; "Gentlemen, two points," referring to the fact that teams received two points for a win at the time and indicating the simplicity with which he wanted them to approach the game.

In an engaging final filled with attacking football, Argentina took a first-half lead through the tournament's top-scorer, Mario Kempes, before the Dutch levelled matters through substitute Dick Nanninga to force the game into extra-time. Although the width of post was all that denied them from victory in stoppage time after the 90 minutes when Rob Rensenbrink's close range strike crashed back off the woodwork to safety. However, in the extra-period, buoyed by the home crowd, Argentina scored through Kempes and Daniel Bertoni to secure the trophy. Defeat meant that the Dutch had been losing finalists in consecutive World Cups; beaten by the host nation on both occasions.

After coming so close to lifting the biggest honour in international football, Happel departed his post with Holland after the tournament, opting to return to Belgian club football to take charge of Harelbeke; one of the smaller clubs in the top flight. It proved to be a short-lived reign as Ernst moved on to Standard Liège in 1979. Happel took Liège to a second place finish in 1980 before lifting the Belgian Cup and Belgian Super Cup a year later.

In 1981 Happel took his first job in German club football when he was appointed manager of SV Hamburg where he enjoyed arguably his most successful period. He ended his first season as a Bundesliga champion, beating FC Köln and Bayern Munich into second and third place respectively. Happel also guided Hamburg to the 1982 UEFA Cup Final where they were defeated 4-0 on aggregate by Sven-Göran Eriksson's Göteborg.

Happel built on that promising start the following season, as Hamburg retained their Bundesliga crown, albeit on goal difference over Werder Bremen, before guiding the club to just the second European Cup final in their history. His team blazed a trail throughout the tournament, clocking up impressive victories over the likes of Dynamo Berlin, Dynamo Kiev and Real Sociedad before facing Giovanni Trapattoni's impressive Juventus side in the final. In what proved to be a tight and cagey encounter, Happel's team came out on top thanks to a single goal from Felix Magath to secure the club's first European Cup; an achievement that remains the greatest moment in the club's history.

Happel's Hamburg set an impressive unbeaten record when, between 16 January, 1982 and 29 January, 1983, the team remained undefeated in the ultra-competitive Bundesliga for 36 games. The European Cup victory provided entry into the Intercontinental Cup Final but Hamburg lost out to Brazilian side Grêmio, also tasting defeat in the European Super Cup before going on to surrender their Bundesliga title to VfB Stuttgart on goal difference the following season.

Happel's impact on the club was later summarised by Horst Hrubesch, who played under the Austrian for Hamburg, recalling the day the new manager arrived. "He came into the dressing room and I thought somebody had switched the light on. My team-mates felt the same."

The following two campaigns, 1984/85 and 1985/86, also ended in disappointment as the team slumped to fifth- and seventh-place league finishes. The 1986/87 season brought an improvement as second place was secured as well as the first German Cup of Happel's career. The trophy was claimed following a 3-1 victory over Stuttgarter Kickers. It remains Hamburg's last major honour to date and Happel's last at the club, as he departed on a high. Ernst Happel remains quite considerably Hamburg's most successful manager, thanks to the two Bundesliga titles and one European Cup he delivered to a club that had only ever won six German titles and two European trophies in their history.

Upon leaving Germany Happel returned to Austria and took up his first coaching assignment in his homeland, when he took charge of Swarovski Tirol in 1987. Ernst guided the club to an Austrian League and Austrian Cup double in 1989 and his team defended their league title a year later. He departed Tirol in 1991 after being offered the chance to coach the Austrian national side; a post he commenced in 1992. However, it proved to be a tragically short spell in charge for Happel, as he was diagnosed with lung cancer and died in November 1992, just days before Austria faced Germany in a game that ended 0-0 and was played with Happel's cap laid upon the Austrian bench in the dugout throughout the match. The Prater Stadium that hosted the fixture was later renamed Ernst Happel Stadium.

The honours claimed by Happel are notable enough to see him make this list, but considering that they were won with smaller, less fashionable and traditionally less successful clubs, such as Feyenoord and SV Hamburg, which he also led to European glory, his achievements take on even greater significance. The second European Cup triumph also came 13 years after the first, indicating how Happel was able to progress his managerial skill through different eras. Taking into account the 1978 World Cup and how close his Ducth side came to winning the trophy, Happel's record is even more impressive.

During his 30-year managerial career, Happel showed immense versatility and became one of football's great thinkers and planners. His approach to training sessions revolutionised the attitudes and effectiveness of the majority of players he managed. But he also had an unwavering love for the game and a passionate belief that football should be an entertaining spectacle, which led to his sides playing with great creativity and ambition. Happel's coaching philosophy can be summed up in a collection of memorable quotes, including; "I'd rather win 5-4 than 1-0!", "If we want to succeed, we have to accept risks", and, "People love a player with ideas, because at the end of the day, the crowd want to be entertained. And with football being only a game, it has to be enjoyable, too."

Ernst Happel was one of the most influential coaches of his or any era. He combined great tactical awareness with an ambitious, attacking style of play that made his teams both engaging and entertaining to watch. Many managers have statues outside the grounds of the teams they have managed, some have stands named after them, but it's a mark of Ernst Happel's considerable skill that there is a whole stadium in his honour.

# CHAPTER 10

## MANAGERS 3 AND 2

# 3. BOB PAISLEY

**Born:** January 23, 1919 in Durham, England
**Died:** February 14, 1996, aged 77
**Clubs Managed:** Liverpool
**Major Honours:** 20

Liverpool's most successful manager, Bob Paisley won 20 trophies in nine years while in charge of the domineering red machine of the 1970s and '80s, including three European Cups; an achievement that remains unmatched by any manager.

Paisley maintained the winning mentality created by Shankly at Anfield and went on take the team to new levels of performance, using simple motivational methods, placing trust in his players on the pitch and creating a deep family atmosphere at the club. The Englishman spent almost 50 years at Liverpool, firstly as a player and then a physiotherapist before becoming part of the coaching set-up under Shankly and eventually taking over as manager.

Born in Durham, Paisley, like many of the successful managers celebrated in this book, had an upbringing heavily entrenched in the mining community, with his father and later, Bob himself, working at the local pits. Paisley began his football career as a player with Bishop Auckland, going on to sign for Liverpool in 1939. His playing days were interrupted by the Second World War but he was part of the Liverpool team that secured the 1947 First Division title and was made club captain in 1951. Paisley ended his playing career three years later but remained at Anfield as reserve team coach and physiotherapist. The club was in decline, having suffered relegation to the second tier and remained in the doldrums until Bill Shankly's appointment in 1959. The fiery Scotsman returned Liverpool to the First Division and a succession of trophies were delivered, alongside regular participation in Europe, before he retired in 1974.

Having become a more prominent member of the coaching staff throughout Shankly's tenure, when the manager utilised the club's boot room to host complex coaching discussions between his backroom staff, Paisley, aged 55, was quickly appointed as successor. After his attempts to persuade Shankly to remain in charge failed, the reluctant managerial genius was determined to take the club forward despite the daunting task of replacing one of the most formidable forces the English game has seen. The transition was, on the most part, an extremely smooth one, as Liverpool seamlessly promoted from within to maintain the continued flow of trophies through the 1970s and early '80s. In terms of personality both men were polar opposites, but they shared a kindred passion for the game and a similar drive to succeed, even though Paisley's was nowhere near as conspicuous as his predecessor's.

Placing great emphasis on the importance of the team unit, Paisley's training methods were relatively simple, with players often taking part in fiercely competitive five-a-side matches that were a legacy of the Shankly era rather than working on tactical preparations. However, they fostered a winning mindset, a never-say-die attitude and an extremely tight bond, as Paisley himself alluded to; "One of the things I keep reminding players is that when you're lost in a fog, you must stick together. Then you don't get lost. If there's a secret about Liverpool, that's it."

There was little fog on the horizon at Anfield as his next nine years in charge brought at least one trophy a season. His first, the 1974/75 campaign, was probably the least successful with just the 1974 Charity Shield delivered as Liverpool finished runners-up to Derby County in the First Division. A year later, Paisley made up for that disappointment by guiding the team to the 1975/76 championship. The Reds also won the 1976 UEFA Cup, defeating Club Brugge of Belgium to lift the club's second European trophy, heralding the beginning of the most successful period in the club's history.

The 1976/77 campaign brought another league title but also saw Liverpool progress to the final of the European Cup for the first time in their history thanks to an impressive campaign that included victories over Saint-Étienne and FC Zürich. Liverpool faced Udo Lattek's German champions Borussia Mönchengladbach in the final and went on to win 3-1 in Rome thanks to goals from Terry McDermott, Tommy Smith and Phil Neal. It meant Liverpool had become only the second English and third British team to lift the trophy, after Manchester United and Celtic respectively, and it announced the Reds' arrival on the world stage. Paisley become the first Englishman to have managed a European Cup-winning team. Manchester United were the only team that prevented Liverpool from lifting an unprecedented treble of League, European Cup and FA Cup that season, defeating their great rivals 2-1 in the Cup Final at Wembley.

The victory over Mönchengladbach also marked Kevin Keegan's last game for Liverpool as he opted to join SV Hamburg in Germany. A resourceful manager with a keen eye for youth and players operating at a lower level, Paisley had already brought the likes of Phil Neal, Terry McDermott, Joey Jones and David Johnson into the team and turned them into top-class performers. He had also shown great judgement of his players' abilities after scrutinising them at close quarters, emphasised by the tactical masterstroke of converting Ray Kennedy from a powerful striker into a left midfielder.

Inevitably, Paisley was prepared for Keegan's exit and moved quickly to sign Celtic star Kenny Dalglish. The Scot complemented the existing team perfectly and soon became the pivot for the majority of Liverpool's attacks, using his supreme hold-up play, close control and great vision to link-up with team-mates and score countless memorable and crucial goals. Dalglish scored the winner in the 1978 European Cup Final when he was expertly sent clear by his combative countryman,

Graeme Souness, and calmly slotted the ball past the onrushing FC Brugge goalkeeper to seal a 1-0 win and second consecutive European Cup for the Reds. The 1977/78 First Division title was lost to Brian Clough's emerging Nottingham Forest side, who went on to hamper Liverpool's progress in the European Cup, as they knocked them out of the 1978/79 competition.

Despite European disappointment, Liverpool went on to break domestic records during the 1978/79 campaign, capturing the title with a total of 68 points—at a time when just two points were awarded for victory—and conceding only 16 goals in 42 matches. The defensive side of the game was a big part of Paisley's success but his number one mantra was to ensure that Liverpool kept possession of the ball, playing small passing triangles and showing expert movement to progress up the pitch. One of his most famous sayings was, "It's not about the long ball or the short ball, it's about the right ball," indicating the importance of players understanding the game, being comfortable in possession and making the right decisions.

It was a philosophy of football that Paisley had pioneered from behind the scenes as coach alongside Shankly, with the 'pass and move' style becoming inextricably linked with Liverpool's greatest successes. He also understood the necessity for the team to play a more patient, slower-tempo style of play to succeed in Europe.

Another league title, Liverpool's fourth in succession, came in 1980, but the hat-trick of European Cup crowns eluded the manager and the club until 1981, when they defeated Real Madrid 1-0 in the final thanks to a goal from Alan Kennedy; the same year that Liverpool also won the League Cup; adding another trophy to the Paisley collection. The 1980/81 season saw the Reds finish in fifth place, but it only proved a blip, as Liverpool regained their crown at the end of the 1981/82 campaign and also retained the League Cup.

Paisley continued to refresh his team with emerging young talent, either primarily developed at the club such as Ronnie Whelan, or expertly plucked from the lower leagues, such as the prolifically consistent centre forward, Ian Rush. The manager continued to build a team not only for the present, but also for the future. A visionary who knew that even the greatest teams had to be broken up and that plans had to be made for a future that may not include him, Paisley also completed the insightful signings of Alan Hansen, Graeme Souness, Craig Johnston, Mark Lawrenson, Bruce Grobbelaar and Steve Nicol during his time in charge; bringing some of the greatest players to have worn the red shirt into the club.

The 1982/83 campaign would be just as successful and ultimately proved to be Paisley's last as manager. Liverpool went on to retain the league title, their sixth under the Englishman during his nine seasons in charge and another League Cup; the only time a club has ever won that particular competition in three successive seasons. Paisley opted to retire from football at the end of the season, ending a spell of 44 years at the club. Liverpool again promoted from within, appointing Joe Fagan as boss, and the team built by Paisley went on to win another European Cup in 1984.

Bob was appointed to the board of directors, later acting as an advisor to Kenny Dalglish during his tenure as player-manager and manager, and remained at the club as a director until ill health forced him to step down in 1992.

The level of Paisley's sustained success during a spell of less than a decade is remarkable and his almost immaculate record was summed up well by the man himself when he famously commented, "Mind you, I've been here during the bad times, too—one year we came second!" In total he claimed 20 trophies, which included six league titles and four European accolades, comprising three European Cups. Liverpool also finished as league runners-up twice during his tenure. The FA Cup was the only trophy that eluded him, but the team's incredible form in Europe makes that almost an afterthought.

As well as trophies, Paisley clocked up plenty of records during his time in charge, including the all time record of going 85 home games unbeaten in all competitions. This remarkable run featured 63 league matches and stretched over three years. He also handled the gradual transition from one great team to another by introducing younger talent at the right time and constantly evolving the team's style of play to become more fluid. Paisley also possessed great reading of the game and understanding of finding solutions for problems as matches developed, He became one of the first managers to successfully utilise substitutes as impact players who could make the crucial difference when it mattered. For example, striker David Fairclough frequently left the bench to score match-saving and winning goals, earning him the nickname 'Super Sub'.

An understated, softly spoken and humble character, Bob Paisley also displayed great warmth and possessed a sharp sense of humour, as highlighted by many of his famous quotations which included; "I tell you something, they shot the wrong Kennedy," following an unsteady Liverpool debut for future European Cup winner Alan Kennedy. Despite those occasionally pointed observations, the players held Paisley in the highest esteem, with Kenny Dalglish later summing up the great feeling he held towards the manager, when he said, "There was only one Bob Paisley and he was the greatest of them all. He went through the card in football. He played for Liverpool, he treated the players, he coached them, he managed them and then he became a director.

"He could tell if someone was injured and what the problem was just by watching them walk a few paces. He was never boastful but had great football knowledge. I owe Bob more than I owe anybody else in the game. There will never be another like him."

While Graeme Souness is equally emphatic in his assessment of the man that brought him to Liverpool; "When you talk of great managers there's one man at the top of the list and that's Bob Paisley."

A man whose humble nature made him less of a standout character and who famously preferred to let his team do the talking for him, Bob Paisley didn't need the hype and focus on his individual methods and successes that other great managers have enjoyed, in fact, he sought to avoid it. When your team speaks so emphatically for your abilities and what you have created, in many ways, words are unnecessary.

Paisley's achievements in such a short space of time are unlikely to be matched. While it can be argued that his career in the managerial forefront wasn't a lengthy one and that he only achieved success with a single, well-established club, the nine years he spent with Liverpool were the equivalent of a near-perfect managerial masterclass. He didn't possess a perfect record in the European Cup, actually crashing out of the tournament in the opening round on two occasions, but his record of winning the trophy on three occasions remains unsurpassed.

While Bill Shankly recreated Liverpool Football Club, implemented a new philosophy and a desire for excellence, Bob Paisley completed the job. He added finishing touches by realising that excellence on a consistent basis and turning the club into a relentless winning machine for the best part of two decades, including both his time in charge and the legacy of talented players that he left for his successor, Joe Fagan.

Shankly may have built Liverpool and turned them into a footballing institution but Bob Paisley made them the benchmark for all English teams and many in Europe to aspire to.

# 2. RINUS MICHELS

**Born:** February 9, 1928 in Amsterdam, Netherlands
**Died:** March 30, 2005, aged 77
**Clubs Managed:** Ajax, Barcelona, Los Angeles Aztecs, FC Köln, Bayer Leverkusen
**International:** Netherlands: 1974, 1984-1985, 1986-1988 and 1990-1992 (Won the 1988 European Championship and reached the 1974 World Cup Final)
**Major Honours:** 13

Many managers have been described as innovators and pioneers in this book, but as the brainchild behind making the theories of 'total football' a reality, Rinus Michels is arguably the most influential and inspiring boss when it comes to coaching and implementing a specific style of play. His methods: of planting seeds of thought in the minds of other future greats such as Johan Cruyff and in-turn Pep Guardiola, meant Michel's tactical brilliance has survived several generations, remaining just as relevant now as it was in the 1970s and '80s.

It's too simplistic to suggest that without Michels there would have been no Barcelona dream team under Johan Cruyff and in turn none of the Guardiola-inspired Barça brilliance of recent seasons. But it's fair to assume that neither of those teams and those eras would have been quite the same without the original principles practised by the great Dutchman.

Rinus guided the Netherlands to their first and so far only major honour, winning the 1988 European Championship, as well as overseeing their progress into the final of the 1974 World Cup. He also enjoyed domestic and European glory with the likes of Ajax and Barcelona while implementing approaches that would serve both clubs supremely well for decades to come.

A one-club man as a player, Rinus Michels spent his entire career with Ajax, winning two Dutch Eredivisie titles and making five international appearances for the Netherlands. A hard-working striker who was strong in the air, Michels went on to play 264 league games for the Amsterdam club, scoring 122 goals. However, a year after lifting his second Dutch title in 1958, Rinus was forced to retire from the game, aged 30, after suffering a back injury.

Having worked as an amateur coach for JOS, his first job back in professional football saw him return to Ajax as head coach in 1965. This heralded the beginning of arguably the most successful era in the club's history as he took a team that had been struggling at the wrong end of the table and hadn't won a Dutch league title since 1960, to the pinnacle of European football. As well as winning a succession of trophies, Michels also nurtured some of the greatest players in the club's history into the first team, shaping the careers of Dutch greats such as Johan Cruyff and Johan Neeskens and building the perfect unit to showcase their abilities.

At the end of his first season in charge, Ajax won the 1966 Eredivisie title; an honour Michels reclaimed for the next three seasons, adding three Dutch Cups to complete a tally of seven domestic trophies during his six-year spell in charge.

It was with Ajax that Michels first brought the notion of 'total football' to prominence. The revolutionary tactical approach required players to be comfortable with performing in a variety of positions on the pitch and having the technical ability and tactical intelligence to do so. The system also focused on the team both attacking and defending as one, incorporating the high-pressing techniques that have recently been taken to new levels by today's Barcelona.

His predecessor at the club, English coach Vic Buckingham had introduced the early principles associated with the strategy. Buckingham also spotted Cruyff's outrageous talents and gave the future great his first-team debut and introduced the pre-cursers of the famed Ajax youth academy; something the Englishman also developed during the early 1970s at Barcelona. Another Englishman, Jack Reynolds, who managed Ajax between 1928 and 1940 and 1945 and 1957, deserves a mention when considering the notion of 'total football', as he introduced similar theories during his time in charge, which coincided with part of Rinus Michels's Ajax career.

Michels took those beliefs, blended with his own, and perfected them into a devastatingly successful philosophy. Up until his appointment, Dutch football had generally been considered conservative, bordering on defensive, but Michels' modifications permanently transformed the culture and the perception of the

Netherlands, establishing their reputation as one of the great football nations.

The visionary's Ajax revolution began with the introduction of Henk Groot, Co Prins and Gert Bals to the team, as he selected players that were able to fit seamlessly into his total football style. He was also bold enough to sacrifice some exceptionally talented performers if they couldn't adapt to his system.

Michels' first Eredivisie title at the end of the 1965/66 season was delivered at a canter, with Ajax finishing seven points clear of second-placed Feyenoord, winning 24 of the 30 games they played and losing just twice. The second consecutive title again saw Feyenoord as their main challengers, but Michels's men claimed the championship by five points. The team's attack reached new levels, scoring 122 goals in 34 league games; a figure that remains a Dutch national record and one that featured a total of 33 goals from a preciously talented Johan Cruyff, who at 20 years old was already the clear star of the team. Another milestone followed as Ajax lifted the 1967 Dutch Cup to complete the league and cup double for the first time in their history. The 1968 title was also secured after Ajax overhauled Feyenoord, leaders for most of the season. This followed a devastating run of form at the end of the campaign.

While dominating domestically, Ajax was also gaining vital European Cup experience, reaching the quarter-finals of the 1967 competition thanks to a 7-3 aggregate victory over Liverpool and narrowly losing out to the great Real Madrid during a tie settled in extra time a year later. The team continued to progress in the tournament and reached the final in 1969, where they faced Italian champions AC Milan. Ajax had already accounted for FC Nuremberg, Benfica and Spartak Trnava but found Nereo Rocco's Milan a tougher nut to crack as the Italians ruthlessly utilised their effective counter-attacking style to win the game 4-1.

The crushing defeat taught Michels and his players a tough lesson. The Italians' contrasting, more defensive and physical style had exposed certain weaknesses and after the 1968/69 Dutch title was also lost to Feyenoord, the manager set about rebuilding a more resilient, yet equally skilled team. In came the likes of Dick van Dijk, Gerrie Mühren, Nico Rijnders and Ruud Krol as more youthful exuberance was added to the line-up.

Michels's revitalised team went on to cruise to the 1969/70 Eredivisie title, winning 27 of their 34 games and scoring 100 goals. They overcame an improving Feyenoord side, led by Ernst Happel, that went on to win the 1970 European Cup. Playing in the UEFA Inter-Cities Fairs Cup that same season, Ajax reached the semi-finals but were knocked out by English side, Arsenal.

However, the Amsterdam giants and their manager wouldn't have to wait much longer to enjoy their own taste of European glory, as they reached another European Cup Final in 1971. Ajax had defeated notable sides such as Celtic and Atlético Madrid to set up a final clash with Greek champions, Panathinaikos. The showpiece, at Wembley Stadium, proved to be a one-sided affair as Michels' side cruised to a 2-0 victory thanks to goals from Dick van Dijk and Arie Haan. It was the club's first European Cup victory and came in the same season as another Dutch Cup was also secured. However, Ajax missed out on an unprecedented treble after their old foes Feyenoord finished four points ahead of them to lift the Eredivisie title.

Michels opted to bow out on a high, swapping Holland for Catalonia as he was appointed manager of Spanish super club, Barcelona. His successor at Ajax, Stefan Kovács maximised the sheer quality of the team he was left, lifting the elusive treble of European Cup, Dutch Championship and Dutch Cup in 1972, as well as the Intercontinental Cup later that year and a third successive European Cup and another league title in 1973.

Success wasn't instant for Michels at Barcelona, with his only major honour coming following the capture of Johan Cruyff from Ajax in 1973, when Barça won the La Liga title a year later. It was a signing that, alongside the appointment of Michels, helped shape the future of Barcelona and formalise the club's belief in fast-paced, possession football that relied upon the technical excellence of every player in the team. While Michel's legacy at the Nou Camp wasn't significant in terms of silverware, it certainly was in terms of philosophy and his capture of Cruyff was arguably the most influential event in the club's history.

After securing the Spanish title, Michels rejected the chance to compete for another European Cup, opting to leave Barcelona to take charge of the Netherlands national team ahead of the 1974 World Cup. The Dutch squad was hugely influenced by Michels' Ajax team and was packed with potential, including the exciting proposition of the majestic Cruyff approaching his peak years.

The finals were held in West Germany and saw the Netherlands competing in just their third World Cup. Michels's continued belief in 'total football' allowed one of the most entertaining and aesthetically pleasing international sides of all time to flourish on the biggest stage. The team played with great width provided by pacey wingers and attacking full-backs, all operating around the supremely skilled and intelligent pivot provided by Cruyff. The Dutch comfortably progressed from their group, defeating Uruguay and Bulgaria and drawing with Sweden, scoring six goals and conceding just one.

The second round brought significantly tougher opposition, but the Netherlands still emerged at the top of their group, winning all their games against Argentina,

East Germany and reigning champions Brazil. Winning the group saw Holland paired with hosts West Germany in the final. Johan Neeskens gave the Dutch an early lead from the penalty spot and Michels's men created several gilt-edged chances after dominating large parts of the game and the majority of possession. However, facing a typically resilient West Germany team, the Dutch were made to pay for missed chances as Paul Breitner levelled matters on 25 minutes, also from the penalty spot, before the prolific Gerd Müller grabbed the winner just minutes before the interval.

Before the final, Michels had avoided defeat in his first nine games as Dutch manager, an impressive feat considering the level of opposition his team had faced and that his side had scored 14 goals and conceded just once in six matches. They had captivated the world with a form of breathtaking attacking football that celebrated and maximised the talents of one of the finest footballers of all time.

Michels opted to step down following the tournament. His time in charge had heralded arguably the greatest ever Dutch team, whose near-perfect teamwork and ability to operate as a fluid unit brought them the nickname of the 'Clockwork Oranje'. Michel's team revelled in the beliefs of binding individual instinct and imagination with team cohesion and became revered for their style of play. The team remain arguably the greatest international side to have missed out on lifting the World Cup.

He returned to Ajax a year later, but Rinus failed to add to his previous silverware and again departed Amsterdam for Barcelona in 1976, this time remaining at the Nou Camp for two seasons, which culminated in Copa del Rey glory in 1978. Michels then coached in the North American Soccer League, taking charge of the Los Angeles Aztecs between 1979 and 1980. After the ill-fated division suffered financially, Michels returned to Europe to take charge of German side FC Köln between 1980 and 1983, winning the German Cup in his last season in charge.

In 1984 the highly regarded coach returned to the international arena when he was reappointed as Dutch manager for a short spell before making way for Leo Beenhakker and again being appointed in 1988 ahead of the European Championships to be held in West Germany.

As in 1974 he inherited a team filled with top-class players, including the AC Milan trio of Marco van Basten, Ruud Gullit and Frank Rijkaard, and Michels soon blended them into a fantastically fluid team unit. However, the tournament began badly for the Dutch, who were defeated 1-0 in their opening game by the USSR. A 3-1 victory over England, inspired by an emphatic Marco van Basten hat-trick, followed before a slender 1-0 victory over the Republic of Ireland ensured the team's progress as group runners-up.

Next up was a highly anticipated semi-final clash with West Germany, the team that had defeated the Dutch and Michels in the 1974 World Cup Final. The Germans, who went on to win the 1990 World Cup, were an equally strong side and contained a selection of stellar names that included Jürgen Klinsmann and Lothar Matthäus. But, on this occasion, it was the Netherlands that triumphed following an 89th-minute winner from van Basten, which secured a 2-1 victory and progress to the final.

The Soviet Union stood between the Dutch and their first international trophy. Erasing memories of their opening day defeat against their opponents, the Netherlands dominated the game, scoring a first half header through the powerful yet brilliant Gullit, before van Basten added gloss to the scoreline with one of the finest goals ever to have graced the international scene, when he lashed a spectacular first-time volley from an seemingly impossible angle into the roof of the net to secure a 2-0 victory and the European Championships for Holland.

Michels stepped down after the tournament, opting to return to German club football with Bayer Leverkusen. A single trophyless season followed before the Dutchman returned for his fourth spell as coach of the Netherlands in 1990. Michels secured qualification for the 1992 European Championships, held in Sweden, and looked to succeed with a largely similar squad that had triumphed four years previously, albeit with a collection of youthful additions that included Dennis Bergkamp. Some of the old magic remained, as the Dutch recorded group stage victories over Scotland and a crushing 3-1 defeat of Germany. But that impressive performance wasn't built upon and the Netherlands exited the tournament at the semi-final stage following a penalty shootout defeat to Denmark, the eventual winners of the tournament. It proved to be Michels's last act as a manager, as he announced his retirement following the tournament, having left an indelible and almost unrivalled mark on the game.

Extremely intelligent, Rinus Michels developed a reputation of having an authoritarian style of management, which saw him nicknamed 'The General', a label later emphasised by his famous quote about the importance of winning the battle during a football match; "Professional football is something like war. Whoever behaves too properly is lost."

That warring, battling belief was in direct contrast to the beautifully creative style that Michels' greatest teams displayed. Another famous quote from the legendary manager, provides a greater indication of his approach and his views on the complex role of a football manager; "It is an art in itself to compose a starting team, finding the balance between creative players and those with destructive powers, and between defence, construction and attack—never forgetting the quality of the opposition and the specific pressures of each match."

Rinus Michels was a forward thinker who believed in attacking football, a great defensive work ethic and a huge commitment to training. Total football may have been perceived as being of great beauty, but Michels understood as well as anybody that for that beauty to flourish, it required hard work, discipline and the perfection of the ugly side of the game.

As well as the impressive haul of trophies delivered at club level, particularly at Ajax, where he built one of European football's truly great teams from relatively modest foundations, Rinus Michels also enjoyed significant success at international level, winning the European Championships and coming close to World Cup glory. He also implemented a philosophy, a way of playing and an approach to introducing young players into a single system that left a lasting legacy with both Ajax and Dutch football in general.

One argument against the Dutchman is that he could have won so many more major honours if he had remained in post at Ajax and the Netherlands for longer periods, missing out on successive European Cups at club level and the opportunity to take his European Championship winners into a World Cup on the international scene. But he left both teams in extremely rude health and created an impressive platform for others to build upon.

His total football principles and emphasis on intelligent positioning and movement are still evident in the modern era. This is particularly prevalent at his former club Barcelona, where the almost indelible mark of his guiding hand remains conspicuously clear on the club's tactical and philosophical blueprint. One man who went on to embody Michels's innovative approach on the field of play was Johan Cruyff who used his supreme ability and understanding of the game to prompt teammates operating in a flexible kaleidoscopic of different positions and roles that saw defence seamlessly transform into attack and vice versa.

Cruyff was given a freedom to express himself on the pitch, roaming around different areas to find space and the positions most likely to damage opponents, in a similar manner to modern day greats Cristiano Ronaldo and Lionel Messi. Cruyff went on to emblazon those same principles upon his own managerial career, creating similarly captivating and successful teams, particularly during his time with Barcelona. After Michels's death, Johan had the following to say about his mentor, "He put the Netherlands on the map in such a way that everybody still benefits from it. With him, results came first, but quality of soccer was number one. Both as a player and as a trainer there is nobody who taught me as much as him."

Further praise, and an appreciation of his methods came from the rampaging full-back of his 1974 Netherlands side, the great Ruud Krol, who said, "He covered all the ground before a match, but most of all he gave you a sense of freedom. You never went on the field weighed down by what you had to do. He recognised your ability and he gave you some respect that in the heat of the game you would do the right thing. He didn't give you a plan that had to be slavishly followed. He said we were good enough players to understand what was required."

Michels's methods had huge impacts of some of the other true greats of the European game, including his 1988 European Championship final match-winner, Marco van Basten, who calls his former manager "the father of Dutch football".

Rinus Michels was not only a forward thinker, but a man who inspired great thought and consideration of his methods for future generations of coaches and managers. His legacy to the game was greater than trophies, gloriously entertaining football and memorable moments. The Dutchman introduced an ideology that has been as wide-reaching and impactive as anything else implemented by his contemporaries. He saw football in a different way and prompted a new dawn of tactical thinking around some of the most simple yet hugely effective approaches.

In essence, Michels provides the best example of combining the abilities of a great coach and a great manager; an extremely rare blend that many of his contemporaries and those mentioned elsewhere in this book simply do not possess.

Arguably his standout quality was his ability to not only revolutionise the game and introduce new tactical approaches, but to do so while achieving significant success at both club and international level. Many managers created and revolutionised clubs, Rinus Michels did so with the footballing culture of a whole country. In that sense, the Dutchman was a one-off.

# CHAPTER 11
## THE GREATEST MANAGER

## SIR ALEX
# FERGUSON

**Born:** December 31, 1941 in Glasgow, Scotland
**Clubs Managed:** East Stirlingshire, St Mirren, Aberdeen, Manchester United
**International:** Scotland: 1985-1986
**Major Honours:** 49

On 8 May, 2013 an announcement made by Manchester United rocked the football world. The club released a statement confirming Sir Alex Ferguson was to retire from his role as the club's manager, inspiring weeks of tributes to the man deemed by many observers to have been quite simply, the greatest manager of all time. After 26 years of near perfect management, his success-filled reign of domination had come to an end.

Statistically, Sir Alex is far and away the most successful manager in the history of the British game. He transformed Manchester United, a club without a league championship for 26 years, to a record 13 Premier League crowns, as they became the most prolific title winners in the English game. The club now has a total of 20 top-flight championships, eclipsing Liverpool's achievements.

Ferguson also returned United to the Promised Land in Europe, winning three European trophies, including two Champions Leagues; the first of which, in 1999, formed part of an unprecedented treble of league, FA Cup and Champions League successes. His achievements at

Old Trafford are extraordinary; winning a huge amount of trophies, revolutionising an ailing club both on and off the pitch and placing United at the top of world football. When Ferguson's successes in Scotland with Aberdeen are taken into account, his candidacy as the greatest manager ever becomes even more prominent.

An expert psychologist, man-motivator and tactician, Ferguson was more driven and determined than anyone he encountered. His hunger for sustained and repeated success and desire to constantly improve, ensured that both he and Manchester United remained at the forefront of football as it developed into the modern era. He embraced change, yet remained faithful to his core principles around work ethic, attitude and the way the game should be played.

The Glasgow-born Ferguson began as an amateur striker for Scottish club Queen's Park before joining St Johnstone, then Dunfermline in 1964, when he turned professional. Strong in the air and a capable finisher, Ferguson helped Dunfermline challenge for the Scottish First Division before being signed by his boyhood team, Glasgow Rangers, in 1967. Despite a promising start, Ferguson's career at Rangers ultimately ended in disappointment and he departed for Falkirk after just two years. Alex became player-coach with the club, but lost those responsibilities when John Prentice became manager. He moved to Ayr United,

before hanging up his boots aged 32 in 1974 and an embarking upon his first managerial role with East Stirlingshire; a club that, as the man himself would famously later recall, only had eight players and not a single goalkeeper.

Despite a relatively impressive start to his East Stirlingshire career, Ferguson spent less than a year with the club, opting to join St Mirren; a traditionally bigger outfit that at the time were placed below his team in the league.

The hungry young manager remained at St Mirren for the next four years, transforming a team marooned in the bottom half of the Second Division into First Division (Scotland's second tier) champions in 1977. He implemented a strong scouting network and put great trust in youth, assembling a team with an average age of 19. St Mirren played expansive, attacking football and were on course to develop into a top-flight force. However, following a disagreement over club finances and an alleged approach for his services from Aberdeen, Ferguson was dismissed from his post in 1978. He took the decision to an industrial tribunal but lost and later took up the reins at Aberdeen, leaving St Mirren to suffer the ignominy of being the only club to have ever sacked Alex Ferguson.

A blusterous force of nature, whose stance as a tough disciplinarian was soon becoming renowned in the Scottish game, Alex Ferguson took charge of Aberdeen in

June 1978. The Dons had been a prominent top-flight club for decades but had struggled to break the stranglehold of the Glasgow giants, Rangers and Celtic, and had only lifted the Scottish Championship once in their history, back in 1955.

Aberdeen had finished the previous season in second place but Ferguson had inherited an ageing team; one that he was keen to redevelop as quickly as possible. Without significant financial resources, the new manager turned to youth to transform the club's fortunes. A staunch advocate of developing his own players, Ferguson introduced the likes of Jim Leighton, Alex McLeish and Gordon Strachan and expertly blended them with slightly more experienced performers, such as Willie Miller and Mark McGhee.

His first season in charge ended with a fourth-place finish and exit at the semi-final stage of both domestic cup competitions. A harsh taskmaster, who demanded the highest of standards from his players while placing great value on hard work and discipline, Ferguson also gave his young team the licence to express and enjoy themselves by playing attacking, high-tempo football. In combining all of these traits he created a team with a ruthless winning mentality that matched his own.

Another famous Ferguson trait in evidence during his Aberdeen tenure was his propensity to create a siege mentality at the club, claiming the media were biased towards Rangers and Celtic. This fostered an amazing team spirit that served his club well when they ousted their Glasgow rivals from the top of the table and themselves became the team to be shot at.

Despite a slow start, Aberdeen went on to claim the 1979/80 title, finishing a point ahead of second-placed Celtic. It was the first time that the Scottish League had been won by a team other than Rangers or Celtic for 15 years. Ferguson's men also reached the final of the 1980 Scottish League Cup but were defeated by Dundee United following a replay.

The 1980 success was the first of three league championships the Dons won under Ferguson. They won back-to-back titles in the 1983/84 and 1984/85 seasons. Aberdeen also enjoyed domestic cup success, lifting the Scottish Cup on four occasions, including three in successive seasons, and the League Cup once.

Ferguson also led Aberdeen to European success for the first time in the club's history during a memorable 1982/83 European Cup Winners' Cup run, which saw the Dons overcome Swiss club FC Sion, Albania's Dinamo Tirana and Lech Poznan of Poland in the opening rounds. This set up a meeting with German giants Bayern Munich in the quarter-finals. Following a battling 0-0 draw in Germany, Aberdeen put on a feast of attacking football in the home leg, winning the tie 3-2 on aggregate, with another youngster introduced by Ferguson, John Hewitt, grabbing the winning goal.

Hewitt and Aberdeen weren't finished there and following a comfortable 5-1 win over Belgian side Waterschei Thor in the semi-finals, Ferguson's team faced the might of Real Madrid and their manager Alfredo Di Stéfano in the final. On a rain-drenched night, the Dons recorded a famous victory over the Spanish megastars, winning 2-1 after extra time thanks to a Hewitt diving header. Aberdeen became just the third Scottish team to lift a European trophy, after Celtic and Rangers, and went on to defeat SV Hamburg in the 1983 European Super Cup, which meant they became the only Scottish club to have lifted more than one European trophy; a record they still hold.

The Dons came close to retaining their Cup Winners' Cup crown but were defeated 2-0 on aggregate by Porto at the semi-final stage of the 1983/84 competition. After Ferguson's third league title success in 1985, the following campaign was deemed by many as a failure, despite the team winning the Scottish Cup and League Cup. This simply emphasised how the manager had transformed the club's expectations. That double-cup-winning season proved to be Ferguson's last full campaign at Pittodrie, as the job of his life, the opportunity to resurrect Manchester United, was about to be offered to him.

During Ferguson's seven years in charge, Aberdeen won 10 major honours, including three league championships and two European trophies. The club won more trophies under Ferguson than during the rest of their 110-year history, with 10 of the 18 major honours the club has achieved won under his tenure.

The summer of 1986 saw Ferguson manage the Scotland national team at the World Cup in Mexico. Having worked as assistant to the great Jock Stein, who had been of great influence to him, Ferguson took up the reins after Stein collapsed and died of a heart attack at the end of a qualifying game against Wales.

Alex successfully negotiated a two-legged play-off match with Australia to secure qualification for the tournament. However, hampered by the country's searing heat, as well as a tough group containing West Germany, Denmark and Uruguay, the Scots struggled in Mexico and failed to progress to the knockout stages. Ferguson stepped down after the tournament to refocus on club football and on 6 November 1986 his new assignment was confirmed with English giants, Manchester United, a club struggling to live up to the huge expectations of recreating their past glories.

Ferguson became Manchester United's prime target once Ron Atkinson had been sacked following a disappointing start to the 1986/87 campaign. Ferguson's work ethic and philosophy appealed to a United board hoping to have finally found a man able to match the extremely high standards set by the legendary Sir Matt Busby in the 1950s and '60s.

A manager who wanted an input in every part of the club, Ferguson continued to show at United that he was a fantastic organiser with an incessant work ethic who strived for perfection in all areas. He also sought to ensure the club, despite its magnitude and standing in the game, retained a family atmosphere, while also raising standards around training, scouting and youth development.

Success would be far from instant for Alex Ferguson at Old Trafford. Despite a promising initial start and significant investment in the transfer market, the team's fortunes actually took a turn for the worse for a number of years. Manchester United under Ron Atkinson had been an entertaining team, capable of playing brilliant football and tasting success in the cup competitions, but had struggled for consistency in the league. Many of the more notable players, including Norman Whiteside, Paul McGrath and Bryan Robson, were a part of a significant drinking culture that existed at Old Trafford.

Ferguson moved to eliminate a lack of discipline in many of his players by demanding higher standards both on and off the pitch. United had dropped to second from bottom in the table under Atkinson, but Ferguson managed to stabilise their 1986/87 campaign and finish a solid 11th place. The summer of 1987 saw several new arrivals at Old Trafford, including Steve Bruce, Brian McClair and Jim Leighton, as Ferguson tried to shape a team that could challenge at the top end of the table. It had the desired effect as United ended the 1987/88 campaign in second place, but without realistically challenging champions Liverpool, who strolled to the title.

Further key signings followed, including Mark Hughes in 1988, but the following campaign proved to be a disappointing one, with United finishing 11th in the league and the cup competitions failing to provide any inspiration. Even more significant transfer activity followed in the summer of 1989 as the likes of Neil Webb, Mike Phelan, Paul Ince and Gary Pallister all joined United, the latter in a club record £2.3m deal. However, the 1989/90 season brought the first major low for Ferguson as his team were thumped 5-1 away to local rivals Manchester City and went on to suffer a sequence of eight games without a win, including six defeats. The club was hovering above the relegation zone and the media and certain sections of the United support began to call for Ferguson's head.

However, many fans remained patient and hoped, if not truly believed, the Scotsman would turn things around. The club directors remained calm and, well aware of Ferguson's hard work behind the scenes transforming the club's infrastructure, backed their manager. The decision-makers had witnessed progress in a number of areas and remained confident Ferguson's vision for the club matched theirs. The manager and the fans needed something positive to cling to and looked towards the 1990 FA Cup for respite from their travails in the league.

Following a run of seven games without a win, United faced Nottingham Forest in a tough-looking FA Cup third round tie. The world's oldest cup competition represented the club's only chance of silverware that season. United went on to record a scrappy 1-0 victory thanks to a goal from local youngster, Mark Robins, one of a number of home-grown players given their debut by Ferguson.

It proved to be the game and the goal that ignited Manchester United's season, breathing new life into the team. Ferguson's men went on to reach the final where they faced Crystal Palace at Wembley. After a first thrilling encounter ended 3-3, with United's goals coming from Bryan Robson and Mark Hughes, the final went to a replay, which United won 1-0 through Lee Martin's strike to claim the first trophy of the Ferguson era and set the club on the way to unparalleled future years of success.

The manager showed his ruthless ability to make key decisions to benefit the team and the type of big game judgement that would serve him well in the future. He dropped goalkeeper Jim Leighton, a man he had brought to the club from Aberdeen for the Cup Final replay in favour of on-loan Les Sealey.

United's young team continued to improve in the league, but the cup competitions helped them sustain that progression. They were beaten finalists in the 1991 League Cup and went on to reach the final of the European Cup Winners' Cup that same season, the first in which that English clubs had been permitted to play in continental competition since the Heysel Stadium disaster in 1985.

United faced a star-studded Barcelona managed by Johan Cruyff that would become European Champions a year later. The English team raced into a two-goal lead thanks to a Mark Hughes brace and withstood late pressure from the Catalan giants to seal a 2-1 victory. It was just United's second European honour and saw Ferguson add to the Cup Winners' Cup he had previously claimed with Aberdeen.

While returning to European success was a key achievement for United and their manager, the league title remained the Holy Grail. Ferguson's team, buoyed by the significant additions of Paul Parker and Peter Schmeichel, were edging closer and closer and completed their first sustained title challenge during the 1991/92 season, before eventually being pipped by Leeds United in the final weeks of the season. United maintained their record of lifting silverware in consecutive seasons by winning the League Cup for the first time in the club's history with a 1-0 victory over Brian Clough's Nottingham Forest. United also defeated Red Star Belgrade to lift the European Super Cup.

As well as clever signings in the

transfer market, Ferguson continued to trust in youth and the early 1990s saw the emergence of two of the most exciting players seen at Old Trafford for generations, as the lightning-quick and tantalising talented Lee Sharpe and Ryan Giggs burst onto the scene. A slow start to the 1992/93 season was quickly addressed by Ferguson when he completed the key signing of the enigmatic Eric Cantona from Leeds United in what proved to be a bargain £1.2m fee.

Cantona proved to be the final figure of flair United needed. He was a player who had the imagination to unlock defences with a beautifully weighted pass, a gravity-defying flick or spectacularly timed shot. The fans soon took to the Frenchman, whose physical presence and body language on the pitch portrayed an individual blessed with great confidence. The Frenchman had the courage and strength of character to express his natural talent under the greatest of pressure; qualities that crucially rubbed off on his team-mates as they went on to win the inaugural Premier League title and the club's first English championship for 26 years. United finished 10 points ahead of second-placed Aston Villa and played some breathtaking football throughout the campaign.

Ahead of the 1993/94 season, Ferguson made one key addition to his squad, capturing the fiery, yet supremely talented, Roy Keane from Nottingham Forest.

Irishman Keane added energy, physicality, attitude and skill to a team already brimming with all of those qualities and United went on to dominate the division and retain their title. The Red Devils added the FA Cup following a comprehensive 4-0 victory over Chelsea at Wembley, to claim the league and cup double for the first time in the club's history.

The 1994/95 season was a rare blip on the radar for Ferguson and United as, deprived of Eric Cantona due to a long-term ban, they surrendered their league title on the final day of the season to big-spending Blackburn Rovers, managed by Kenny Dalglish. Rather than search for the solutions to his team's shortcomings in the transfer market, Ferguson did quite the opposite, making the controversial decisions to let key performers and fans' favourites Mark Hughes, Paul Ince and Andrei Kanchelskis depart the club.

However, the canny Scotsman had a quintet of tricks up his sleeve, as he placed his trust in youth to the most significant degree in his career, blooding a group of teenagers that would go on to dominant English football for the best part of the decade. United's youth team had been attracting attention for the winning the FA Youth Cup for the first time since the days of Matt Busby, all the while playing with attacking verve and style. Ferguson knew the time was right to introduce the stars of his ever-improving youth set-up into the first team, and in came Gary and

Phil Neville, Nicky Butt, Paul Scholes and David Beckham to join regular starter Ryan Giggs and the relatively young Roy Keane in the line-up.

Despite being famously derided by some pundits and seriously questioned by elements of the United support, it didn't take long for the world of football to realise that Ferguson's bold decision was an undoubted masterstroke, as the youngsters, dubbed in the media as 'Fergie's Fledglings' showed maturity and ability beyond their years.

Lee Sharpe, who was signed by Ferguson as a teenager and became one of the first young players to be given a chance in the first team, spoke to the author in 2013 about his memories of playing under Sir Alex. "He was always brave enough to give young lads a try. He went through a few groups of young lads and I was part of a couple of those. The other strengths were the passion, the focus and the drive of the man.

"If he could, I think he would work 24 hours a day, seven days a week. He watches reserves, teams you're going to play and players he wants to sign. As a man away from the pitch he was a lot like a father figure for the young lads, not so much when you were on the pitch, he didn't care who you were or how old you were at that point!

"But, off the pitch ... I had viral meningitis and the press had a few bad things to say about me. He looked after me and sent me home to my mum and dad. He's also looked after me with contracts and he's been fantastic. He's a tough man to play for on the pitch but off the pitch, he's a real gentleman."

United, aided by the return of Eric Cantona and the continued improving goal-scoring exploits of Andy Cole, went on to lift the 1995/96 Premier League title, their third in four seasons and defeat bitter rivals Liverpool in the FA Cup Final to complete a second double in three years. It was the season that saw United claw back an impossible looking points deficit from runaway leaders Newcastle United as Ferguson started to use psychological mind games aimed at rival managers, such as Newcastle boss Kevin Keegan. Keegan famously reacted angrily to the Scotsman's comments which questioned the motivations of Leeds United and Nottingham Forest in matches against Newcastle, showing a lack of control that revealed a man and a team under intense pressure.

Another league title was delivered in 1996/97, but United bowed out of the European Champions League at the semi-final stages following a two-legged defeat to eventual winners Borussia Dortmund. Ferguson's side had failed to make an impression in the tournament in the early '90s, but with the younger players gaining more and more experience of continental football and the intelligent additions of the likes of Ronny Johnsen and Ole Gunnar

Solskjær, the Manchester club were getting closer and closer.

Eric Cantona's shock retirement in May 1997 and a serious injury sustained by Roy Keane during the 1997/98 season saw United's progress stutter, as Arsène Wenger's brilliant Arsenal side beat them to the league title following an impressive late-season surge. Teddy Sheringham had been signed to replace Cantona but the following summer saw Ferguson invest even more significantly in his squad, spending heavily on Jaap Stam, Jesper Blomqvist and Dwight Yorke. Stam and Yorke proved to be particularly inspired signings as United battled with Arsenal throughout the 1998/99 season for both the Premier League title and the FA Cup.

The two teams met in a memorable cup semi-final reply, which saw United claim an unlikely victory after extra-time with 10 men, thanks to a penalty save from Peter Schmeichel and a remarkable individual goal from Ryan Giggs. The title race went down to the final day of the season when United defeated Tottenham Hotspur to wrestle the Premier League crown back from north London.

United defeated Newcastle United in the FA Cup Final to seal Ferguson's third double, but the manager and the players had a bigger prize on the horizon as the club prepared for the European Cup Final for just the second time in its history. The Red Devils had successfully negotiated a tough-looking Champions League group that featured Bayern Munich and Barcelona, before disposing of Inter Milan and Juventus in the quarter- and semi-finals to set up a final clash against Bayern Munich, in a match held at Barcelona's famous Nou Camp Stadium.

Ferguson's players were on the verge of making history. No British team had ever won a treble of the three major trophies, but United were now just 90 minutes, and perhaps a little bit of stoppage time, away from achieving that feat. With Keane and Scholes suspended, Ferguson had to reshuffle his pack for the final, selecting David Beckham in a more central role, bringing Jesper Blomqvist in on the left wing and shifting Ryan Giggs to the right. The adjustments and perhaps the nerves of the occasion unsettled United in the opening exchanges and Bayern took an early lead when Mario Basler's deflected free-kick left Peter Schmeichel stranded.

The English club struggled to make an impression on the game and went in behind at half-time. During the interval Alex Ferguson's motivational speech famously included the line, "At the end of this game, the European Cup will be only six feet away from you and you'll not even be able to touch it if we lose. And for many of you that will be the closest you will ever get. Don't you dare come back in here without giving your all."

The manager's words and his second-half substitutions eventually did the trick as replacement Teddy Sheringham grabbed a close range equaliser in the first minute of stoppage time. The Red Devils weren't finished there and when another corner was won two minutes later, David Beckham whipped in another beautiful delivery, which was flicked on by Sheringham and prodded into the roof of the net by the other substitute, Ole Gunnar Solskjær. Peter Schmeichel went on to lift the trophy as United reclaimed the title as Europe's premier club.

After the game, Ferguson described his teams' never-say-die spirit by famously saying, "I can't believe it. I can't believe it. Football, bloody hell. But they never gave in and that's what won it."

United won the 1999 Intercontinental Cup, defeating Palmeiras in the final and competed in the inaugural World Club Championship in Brazil. Their Premier League title was later retained, a feat achieved again in 2001, giving the Red Devils three successive league titles for the first time in their history; becoming just the fourth side to have done so.

The 2001/02 season saw United again spend significantly in the transfer market, with Dutch striker Ruud van Nistelrooy and Argentine play-maker Juan Verón brought into the club. It was also announced that year would be Ferguson's last season as Manchester United manager, with the Scotsman having decided to retire from the football at the end of the campaign at the age of 61.

The final of that season's Champions League was to be played in Glasgow, and ever the romantic, Ferguson possibly envisioned another European Cup victory in his hometown as the perfect crowning glory to his managerial career. However, that wasn't to be the case as United were sent crashing out of Europe in the semi-finals by Bayern Leverkusen and lost the title to Arsenal with Sir Alex later announcing that he'd had a change of heart and would continue at the Old Trafford helm, well into his 60s.

Ferguson brought young England defender Rio Ferdinand from Leeds United in the summer of 2002 as he began to build another great Manchester United team. He went on to seal the 2002/03 Premier League title, his eighth as manager, after an excellent end-of-season run, inspired by the goals of duo van Nistelrooy and Paul Scholes.

Manchester United finished third when Arsenal claimed the 2004 Premier League, but the Old Trafford club won the FA Cup, overcoming Millwall in the final. It was the first time United had dropped outside of the top two positions since the inception of the Premier League as the team was entering a period of transition that would see them fail to win another league title until 2007.

Academy graduates such as Wes Brown, Darren Fletcher and John O'Shea were featuring in the team more regularly and Ferguson made two significant young additions to his team, first in 2003 when a twinkle-toed Portuguese winger called Cristiano Ronaldo was captured from Sporting Lisbon and a year later, when the prodigiously talented English striker Wayne Rooney was signed from Everton. Both players would form the basis of Ferguson's next great team, but it took time for them to find the consistency to regularly challenge for major honours.

As well as a strong Arsenal side, United and Ferguson's progress was stalled by the emergence of Chelsea. Bankrolled by Russian billionaire Roman Abramovic and with José Mourinho as manager, the west London club went on to dominate the Premier League during the 2004/05 and 2005/06 campaigns. United came close to another FA Cup in 2005, but despite a performance inspired by the youthful exuberance and technical brilliance of Rooney and Ronaldo, the Red Devils failed to convert the abundance of chances they created against opponents Arsenal and went on to lose the final on penalties. Ferguson had a painful 2005, with United ending the campaign trophyless. That year Chelsea won the Premier League, Arsenal the FA Cup and Liverpool claimed an unlikely Champions League crown.

There was also uncertainty at boardroom level at Old Trafford with the Glazer family taking over the club, leveraging their purchase of United with huge sums of debt. Ferguson went on to establish a good and trusted working relationship with chief executive David Gill and the Glazers, and defended the club's owners. Despite the fans' concerns, the trophies continued to roll into the Old Trafford cabinet. However, many believe that this sustained success was in spite of the Americans' presence, rather than because of it and mainly thanks to the miraculous brilliance of the manager.

The 2005/06 season was another campaign of transition for United, as Roy Keane left the club in controversial circumstances and Ruud van Nistelrooy was given a less prominent role. During these transitional years, the Champions League continued to be a challenge for Ferguson's developing team. The lowest point came in 2005, when United failed to make it through the group stages, as many of the younger players struggled to adapt to the demands of playing for the club.

Ferguson had to react to the power and purpose of Mourinho's Chelsea, who had set an impressive precedence with solid defence and prolific scoring. Chelsea had started both title-winning seasons in top form, with United traditionally timing their peak fitness and performance later in the campaign to ensure a good run-in. In response, Ferguson adjusted his team's pre-season preparations ahead of the 2006/07 campaign, ensuring everybody at the club was made aware of the importance of a quick start to the season.

Buoyed by a League Cup final victory over Wigan Athletic in 2006, which was achieved thanks to the goals, pace and movement of Rooney, Ronaldo and Louis Saha, United looked set for another chapter of success. Ferguson hoped the League Cup, as in 1992, would act as a catalyst to galvanise and foster confidence amongst his players.

United enjoyed the positive start they needed to the 2006/07 season, winning their first four Premier League games for the first time, with Rooney and Ronaldo emerging into regular match winners, ably supported by the steadying and assured influences of Michael Carrick and the evergreen Paul Scholes and Ryan Giggs in midfield. The squad was backed up by one of the best back fives in the club's history, which featured Edwin van der Sar in goal and Gary Neville, Patrice Evra, Nemanja Vidic and Rio Ferdinand in defence.

Chelsea remained a noteworthy rival, but United continued to churn out match-winning displays both at home and away, with both Rooney and Ronaldo, as well as Ole Gunnar Solskjær, returning from long-term injury, and Henrik Larsson, an inspired loan signing, all contributing key goals and performances.

November 2006 brought the 20th anniversary of Ferguson's appointment as Manchester United manager and his team went on to celebrate that landmark at the end of the season by lifting the Premier League title, finishing six points ahead of Chelsea. It was the club's ninth championship under Ferguson, but they were denied what would have been a unique fourth league and cup double when Chelsea defeated them 1-0 after extra time in the 2007 FA Cup Final. United enjoyed an improved European campaign, reaching the semi-finals of the Champions League following a thumping 7-1 home victory over Roma that showed just how far the likes of Rooney and Ronaldo had come. Ferguson's third great team looked primed and ready to secure more silverware.

The summer of 2007 saw Ferguson invest heavily in the likes of Nani, Anderson, Owen Hargreaves and Carlos Tévez. It gave Ferguson an almost unrivalled collection of creative midfield and attacking talents that would allow United to excel both domestically and in the continent.

Despite a slow start to the 2007/08 season, the Red Devils went on to challenge for the title once again. Arsenal were considered their major rivals for the Premier League following José Mourinho's early season departure from Chelsea. However, the Blues went on to recover their form, and Chelsea took United all the way in both the league and in Europe. In a season inspired by the prolific goal-scoring form of Cristiano Ronaldo, both teams were level on points ahead of the final day of the season with the Red Devils ahead thanks to their superior goal difference. United won 2-0 against Wigan Athletic as Chelsea drew with Bolton Wanderers. It was Ferguson's 11th Premier League title and set up United's second European Cup Final under his guidance, just a few days later, when they faced Chelsea in Moscow.

In an end-to-end game played in torrential rain, United bossed the first half and took an early lead through a Ronaldo bullet header but Chelsea clawed them back in the second period through Frank Lampard's deflected effort to force extra time. The game went to penalties and United looked set to lose when Ronaldo's missed penalty gave Chelsea captain, John Terry, the chance to win the game. However, he slipped and the ball slide off the post and went wide.

United levelled matters before taking a sudden-death lead through Giggs, who was making his 759th appearance for the club, breaking Sir Bobby Charlton's all-time record, calmly slotted his penalty home. Chelsea's Nicolas Anelka then had to score to keep his team in the game, but his tame penalty was comfortably saved by Edwin van der Sar, to ensure the second Champions League of Ferguson's tenure and his fifth European trophy, in total. In the process he also became just the third British manager to win the European Cup on more than one occasion.

The Premier League title was retained in 2008/09, meaning United had drawn level with Liverpool's record of 18 English league titles and had become the only team in English history to have won three consecutive titles on two occasions. The Red Devils also lifted the World Club Cup, beating Ecuadorian club LDU Quito 1-0 in the final and defeated Tottenham Hotspur to lift the League Cup. United again reached the final of the European Cup, where they faced Pep Guardiola's Barcelona side. Ferguson's team began the final in positive mood and had the better of the game, before a tactical reshuffle from the Catalan giants saw Samuel Eto'o move into a wide position. Eto'o went on to score the opening goal of the game with Lionel Messi doubling Barcelona's advantage to seal a 2-0 victory.

The 2009/10 season ultimately ended in disappointment despite the delivery of another League Cup following a 2-1 victory over Aston Villa. The league title was lost to Chelsea on the final day of the season and Bayern Munich knocked United out of the Champions League.

In December 2010, Ferguson became the club's longest serving manager, overtaking Sir Matt Busby's previous record of 24 years, one month and 13 days at the helm. United went on to reclaim the Premier League title at the end of the 2010/11 season, finishing nine points clear of nearest challengers Chelsea and an emerging Manchester City to surpass Liverpool's benchmark of 18 titles.

United again reached the final of the Champions League, where they were once more pitted against Guardiola's almost peerless Barcelona. The Wembley showpiece proved to be a chastening experience for Ferguson's men as the

Catalan side were vastly superior and passed and probed their way to an emphatic 3-1 victory.

Adjustments were required to the United playing staff in the summer of 2011 as key performers van der Sar, Scholes and Gary Neville left. In came a younger generation, including David de Gea, Phil Jones and Ashley Young, as the manager again attempted to build for the future. It was a season of further landmarks, as Ferguson celebrated his 70th birthday, had the North Stand at Old Trafford named after him, managed his 1,000 Manchester United league game and clocked up his 100th Champions League victory.

United began the campaign in impressive, goal-scoring form as they featured another generation of talented home-grown players, including Tom Cleverley and Danny Welbeck, and achieved several notable results, including an 8-2 victory over Arsenal. But their open style of play and ferocious desire to attack saw them pay a heavy price in a local derby clash with Manchester City at Old Trafford. City, managed by Roberto Mancini and now firmly installed as title contenders following significant investment in the team, tore 10-man United to shreds, hitting five goals in the second half to win the game 6-1. The defeat was Ferguson's heaviest in charge of United and an experience he labelled as one of the most humiliating of his career.

The goals conceded that afternoon ultimately proved to be crucial at the end of the season. Manchester City had led the table for much of the campaign, but faltered in the final few months, allowing United to build up an eight-point lead with just six games remaining. However, the club stuttered against the likes of Everton and Wigan, before losing another key Manchester derby, this time away at City, to send Mancini's men top of the table on goal difference. The final day saw United needing a minor miracle with City hosting relegation threatened Queens Park Rangers and the Red Devils travelling to Sunderland. United got the 1-0 win they needed and came agonisingly close to lifting an unlikely title as City slipped 2-1 behind at the Etihad Stadium. However, two late goals, including a stoppage-time winner from Sergio Agüero, meant City were champions and United ended second on goal difference.

Entering his 70s, Ferguson remained hungry, focused and keen to face the challenge provided by Manchester City. He again invested heavily in the summer of 2012, capturing the prolific Robin van Persie from Arsenal. The Dutch striker proved to be an inspired signing and his goals took United to a record extending 20th league title and their 13th Premier League crown under Ferguson. United dominated the division, topping the table for most of the campaign and eventually finishing 11 points clear of runners-up Manchester City. Ferguson's team was knocked out of the Champions League in the last round of 16 by Real Madrid in controversial circumstances, as Nani was harshly sent off with United in front in the second leg to leave Ferguson apoplectic on the touchline and reportedly "too angry" to attend the post-match press conference.

Towards the end of the season, the reason for Ferguson's bitter disappointment at that Real Madrid defeat became clear when he announced his decision to retire from football. This meant that European Cup exit ended his last chance of lifting the famous trophy for a third time, an achievement that would have seen him draw level with Bob Paisley on three European Cups. It is one of the few accolades Ferguson missed out on during a truly majestic managerial career.

Sir Alex Ferguson's retirement signalled the end of an era, both for Manchester United and football in general. He had been synonymous with Manchester United for more than a quarter of a century and represented a generation of football supporters' only knowledge of a Manchester United manager.

Ferguson was made a director and club ambassador of Manchester United and played a big part in selecting his successor, David Moyes, indicating that he is still likely to be a significant presence in the corridors of power at Old Trafford.

Tributes following the announcement were plentiful and glowing, with the likes of UEFA president Michel Platini labelling Ferguson as "a true visionary", Sir Bobby Charlton describing him as "the greatest manager there has ever been", and Bryan Robson, who said, "You've got to say that he's been the greatest club manager there's ever been anywhere in the world. When you think that he's rebuilt probably four or five squads to be successful—and what he did at Aberdeen as well. Because of that record he's got to go down as the best."

Ferguson's European record may be criticised in some quarters, but had he been able to field his strongest team in the 1992/93 and 1993/94 Champions League competitions, when the number of 'foreign' players in each was limited, and if his team's regular appearances in modern Champions League finals hadn't coincided with the emergence of one of the greatest teams in living memory in Barcelona, he surely would have added to those two European Cups, two European Cup Winners' Cups and single European Super Cup.

In club football he won almost every honour available to him. Only the UEFA Cup proved elusive; which is hardly surprising considering his teams seldom played in that competition. The successes he achieved usually came in captivatingly entertaining fashion, but Ferguson has become accustomed to winning in many different ways, either with adventurous, powerful and beautifully crafted attacking football, or with caution born from a solid defensive unit. He has won by dominating matches or leagues and leading from the front all season, or by coming back from almost certain disappointment with a late surge of form or late goal to win league titles and crucial cup ties.

Other accolades include a record number of English league titles for a single manager, being the only manager to win the League and Cup double in both England and Scotland, and being the most recent manager to win a Scottish Championship with a club outside the Old Firm. He is also the only manager to have led a team to a top-three league finish in 20 consecutive seasons, a feat he realised with Manchester United between the 1991/92 and 2012/13 campaigns, finishing a total of 22 seasons in the top three; featuring 13 first-place finishes, five runners-up spots and three third-place finishes.

Ferguson's accumulation of trophies marks him out as the most successful manager in British if not world history. With Aberdeen and Manchester United, the Scotsman presided over a total of 49 major honours. His list of achievements are unlikely to be ever be surpassed. As a manager and as a man, Sir Alex Ferguson left an indelible mark and legacy on the culture and the fabric of British football.

His longevity at a club of the magnitude of Manchester United is remarkable. To remain at Old Trafford for 26-and-half years, producing success after success and rebuilding and reinventing new teams to maintain that glory, is an astonishing

feat. His teams have also played a high-tempo attacking style that has been a fitting tribute to the traditions of Manchester United. Both United and Aberdeen performed with creativity, bravery and commitment, featuring young players reared through the club's youth system.

From last-gasp equalisers at Wembley to late winners at the Nou Camp, extra-time drama at Villa Park, to Rio Ferdinand's winner in the manager's last game in charge of the club at Old Trafford, Ferguson's reign has been inextricably linked with delayed and decisive drama, making his successes even more captivating.

Ferguson was never afraid to make big, often controversial decisions. He dropped prominent players, including the likes of David Beckham and Wayne Rooney, for big games and allowed fans' favourites and those seemingly at the peak of their powers, such as Paul Ince, Ruud van Nistelrooy and Jaap Stam, to leave.

Van Nistelrooy, whose exit from Old Trafford came after a souring of his relationship with Ferguson, spoke to the author in 2013, following a charity match between Manchester United and Real Madrid legends, to provide a glimpse into Sir Alex's standing in the game.

Talking of Ferguson's visit to the Real Madrid dressing room following the game, van Nistelrooy said, "Everybody had his autobiography and asked for his signature. Everybody was there, like Zinedine Zidane and Luís Figo. He's got such unbelievable respect throughout the football world and beyond. It was a highlight of my career to work with him for five years and learning from him. He got the best out of me."

An indomitable force of nature in the dugout and in the dressing room, Ferguson's personality and fierce competitive instincts alone would have made him a winner, but combined with all of his other traits, including his intelligence, and abilities to judge a player and mould a team, ensured that he was a world class football manager.

The mantra that one player could never be bigger than the club, remained loud and clear throughout Ferguson's career, even though he created and celebrated a collection of world renowned superstars. He did, however, know how to massage the egos of some of his brightest lights, affording the likes of Eric Cantona and Cristiano Ronaldo extra licence both on and off the pitch. He understood that when dealing with football genius, it's important not to control them too much, instead to channel them properly to allow their talents to flourish.

At both Aberdeen and Manchester United, the manager's psychology proved key for those both inside and outside of the club. Defending his players to the hilt in public and creating a 'them against us' siege mentality was a stable of Ferguson's motivational techniques. He was constantly able to reinvent his team and his own approach to the rapidly changing world of football, adapting the way he dealt with the players and his attitudes towards training, preparation and tactics.

The way 'Fergie' transformed United on and off the pitch ensured that the club became even more popular and renowned all over the world. He also created several winning teams and safeguarded United's future in the greatest traditions of the club by constantly trusting in youth.

The charismatic serial winner, known by many as 'the Boss', has been more than simply United's manager. He has been the club's leader, figurehead and the man that has epitomised everything that the Red Devils are famed for. Success hadn't always been guaranteed at Old Trafford, but under Ferguson it was demanded. Fleeting glimpses of failure would be temporarily tolerated and used to re-motivate his players for the next challenge, as he always sought a reaction from his players in adversity.

He knew that the fans were desperate for success when he first arrived in 1986, having suffered for decades watching their great rivals Liverpool dominate domestically and in Europe. Ferguson was abundantly aware the Merseyside club were the benchmark and his aim was to not only match what Liverpool had achieved, but to surpass it, as the famous quote he made in 2002 showed; "My greatest challenge is not what's happening at the moment, my greatest challenge was knocking Liverpool right off their f***ing perch."

Looking at the managers that Ferguson has finished above in this book is a pretty good indication of his standing in the game, and when considering some of the leading British lights that could possibly rival him, it becomes clear that the Scotsman eclipses each of them in different ways. As well as enjoying success with one of the world's biggest clubs, Ferguson also tasted the type of glory with a provincial club that Brian Clough experienced with Derby County and Nottingham Forest, as he won league titles and conquered Europe with Aberdeen.

Like Sir Matt Busby and Bill Shankly, Ferguson also transformed and revolutionised clubs, taking Manchester United from mid-table mediocrity to complete dominance of the English game. The records of Shankly and Bob Paisley at Liverpool are hugely impressive, particularly Paisley, who won three European Cups. But when the joint record of both men is compared with Ferguson, it's the Manchester United man whose achievements become even more notable. In total, Shankly and Paisley managed Liverpool for a 24-year period. In that time, they won three European Cups, nine domestic titles, two UEFA Cups, two FA Cups and three League Cups. In his 26 years at Old Trafford, Ferguson won two Champions Leagues, 13 domestic titles, a European Cup Winners' Cup, five FA Cups and four League Cups, and that's without adding his achievements at Aberdeen.

However, it may not solely be history that judges Sir Alex as the greatest, rather the future, as it remains to be seen what his successor David Moyes can achieve with the same players and resources, as he attempts to follow the hardest act in football history.

In Ferguson's final game at Old Trafford, fittingly accompanied by the presentation of yet another Premier League title, the song played as he entered the Theatre of Dreams for the final time as manager was the Frank Sinatra classic, *My Way*. If there was ever a manager that did things his way, it was Sir Alex Ferguson. His unwavering desire for success and his courage, determination and defiance to continually deliver it ensures that Ferguson stands out as one of football's most unique and enduring characters, as well as the greatest manager the game has ever seen.

# STATISTICS

## THE GREATEST MANAGERS—THE TOP 30…

30. Nereo Rocco
29. Sir Bobby Robson
28. Mário Zagallo
27. Jupp Heynckes
26. Otto Rehhagel
25. Fabio Capello
24. Carlo Ancelotti
23. Louis van Gaal
22. Valeriy Lobanovskyi
21. Udo Lattek
20. Pep Guardiola
19. Bill Shankly
18. Arrigo Sacchi
17. Johan Cruyff
16. Giovanni Trapattoni
15. Marcello Lippi
14. José Villalonga
13. Miguel Muñoz
12. Béla Guttmann
11. Jock Stein
10. Helenio Herrera
9. Vicente del Bosque
8. Ottmar Hitzfeld
7. Brian Clough
6. Sir Matt Busby
5. José Mourinho
4. Ernst Happel
3. Bob Paisley
2. Rinus Michels
1. Sir Alex Ferguson

## A FULL LIST OF CLUBS AND COUNTRIES MANAGED AND HONOURS WON

Major honours include pre-season contests, such as the English Community Shield and the Italian, Spanish and German Super Cups, but not lesser, now defunct domestic trophies such as the English Full Members Cup or the Texaco Cup. League titles are only recognised for the top two divisions of each country. In terms of European competition, the European Super Cup is recognised as a major honour, but the Intertoto Cup is not.

### NEREO ROCCO

Clubs: Triestina, Treviso, Padova, AC Milan, Torino, Fiorentina

Honours:

**AC Milan**

Italian Serie A: 1961/62, 1967/68

Italian Cup / Coppa Italia: 1972, 1973, 1977

European Cup: 1963, 1969

European Cup Winners' Cup: 1968, 1973

Intercontinental Cup: 1969

**Total Honours: 10**

## SIR BOBBY ROBSON

Clubs: Fulham, Ipswich Town, PSV Eindhoven, Sporting Lisbon, FC Porto, Barcelona, PSV Eindhoven, Newcastle United

Country: England

Honours:

**Ipswich Town**
FA Cup: 1978
UEFA Cup: 1981

**PSV Eindhoven**
Dutch Eredivisie: 1990/91, 1991/92

**FC Porto**
Portuguese Primeira Liga: 1994/95, 1995/96

**Barcelona**
Spanish Cup / Copa del Rey: 1997
Spanish Super Cup / Supercopa de Espana: 1996
European Cup Winners' Cup: 1997

**Total Honours:** 9

## MÁRIO ZAGALLO

**Clubs:** Botofogo, Fluminense, Flamengo, Al-Hilal, Vasca da Gama, Botafogo, Bangu

**Countries:** Brazil, Kuwait, Saudi Arabia, United Arab Emirates, Portuguesa

**Brazil**
World Cup: 1970
Confederations Cup: 1997
Copa America: 1997

**Botafogo**
Taca Brasil: 1968
Rio de Janeiro State Championship: 1966/67, 1967/68
Guanabara Cup: 1967, 1968

Total Honours: 8

Jupp Heynckes

**Bayern Munich**
German Bundesliga: 1988/89, 1989/90, 2012/13
German Super Cup: 1978, 1990, 2012
European Champions League: 2013
German Cup / DFB-Pokal: 2013

**Real Madrid**
European Champions League: 1998
Spanish Super Cup / Supercopa de Espana: 1997

**Total Honours:** 10

## OTTO REHHAGEL

**Fortuna Düsseldorf**
German Cup / DFB-Pokal: 1980

**Werder Bremen**
German Bundesliga: 1987/88, 1992/93
German Cup / DFB-Pokal: 1991, 1994
German Super Cup: 1988, 1993, 1994
European Cup Winners' Cup: 1992

**Kaiserslautern**
German Bundesliga: 1997/98
German Bundesliga 2: 1996/97

**Greece**
European Championship: 2004

**Total Honours:** 12

## FABIO CAPELLO

**AC Milan**
Italian Serie A: 1991/92, 1992/93, 1993/94, 1995/96
Italian Super Cup / Supercoppa Italiana: 1992, 1993, 1994
European Champions League: 1994
European Super Cup: 1994

**Real Madrid**
Spanish La Liga: 1996/97, 2006/07
**AS Roma**
Italian Serie A: 2000/01
Italian Super Cup / Supercoppa Italiana: 2001
**Total Honours: 13**

## CARLO ANCELOTTI

**AC Milan**
Italian Serie A: 2003/04
Italian Cup / Coppa Italia: 2003
Italian Super Cup / Supercoppa Italiana: 2004
European Champions League: 2002/03, 2006/07
European Super Cup: 2003, 2007

Club World Cup: 2007
**Chelsea**
English Premier League: 2009/10
FA Cup: 2010
FA Community Shield: 2009
**Paris Saint-Germain**
French Ligue 1: 2012/13
**Total Honours: 12**

## LOUIS VAN GAAL

**Ajax**
UEFA Cup: 1992
Dutch Eredivisie: 1993/94, 1994/95, 1995/96
Dutch KNVB Cup: 1993
Johan Cruyff Shield: 1993, 1994, 1995
European Champions League: 1995
European Super Cup: 1995
Intercontinental Cup: 1995
**Barcelona**
Spanish La Liga: 1997/98, 1998/99

Spanish Copa del Rey: 1998
European Super Cup: 1997
**AZ Alkmaar**
Dutch Eredivisie: 2008/09
**Bayern Munich**
German Bundesliga: 2009/10
German Cup / German DFB-Pokal: 2010
German Super Cup: 2010
**Total Honours: 19**

## VALERIY LOBANOVSKYI

Dynamo Kiev
European Cup Winners' Cup: 1975, 1986
European Super Cup: 1975
Soviet / Ukrainian League: 1973/74,

1974/75, 1976/77, 1979/80, 1980/81, 1984/85, 1985/86, 1989/90, 1996/97, 1997/98, 1998/99, 1999/00, 2000/01
Soviet / Ukrainian Cup: 1974, 1978, 1982,

1985, 1987, 1990, 1998, 1999, 2000
USSR Super Cup: 1980, 1985, 1986
Commonwealth of Independent States

Cup: 1997, 1998
**Total Honours: 30**

## UDO LATTEK

**Bayern Munich**
German Cup / German DFB-Pokal: 1971,
1984, 1986
German Bundesliga: 1971/72, 1972/73,
1973/74, 1984/85, 1985/86, 1986/87
European Cup: 1974
**Borussia Mönchengladbach**
German Bundesliga: 1975/76, 1976/77

UEFA Cup: 1979
**Barcelona**
European Cup Winners' Cup: 1982
Spanish League Cup: 1983
Spanish Cup / Spanish Copa del Rey:
1983
**Total Honours: 16**

## PEP GUARDIOLA

**Barcelona**
Spanish La Liga: 2008/09, 2009/10, 2010/11
Spanish Cup / Spanish Copa del Rey:
2009, 2012
Spanish Super Cup / Spanish Supercopa:
2009, 2010, 2011

European Champions League: 2009, 2011
European Super Cup: 2009, 2011
FIFA Club World Cup: 2009, 2011
**Bayern Munich**
European Super Cup: 2013
**Total Honours: 15**

## BILL SHANKLY

**Liverpool**
English First Division: 1963/64, 1965/66,
1972/73
English Second Division: 1961/62

English FA Cup: 1965, 1974
FA Charity Shield: 1964, 1965, 1966, 1974
UEFA Cup: 1973
**Total Honours: 11**

## ARRIGO SACCHI

**AC Milan**
Italian Serie A: 1987/88
Italian Super Cup / Supercoppa Italiana:
1988

European Cup: 1989, 1990
European Super Cup: 1989, 1990
Intercontinental Cup: 1989, 1990
**Total Honours: 8**

## JOHAN CRUYFF

**Ajax**
Dutch KNVB Cup: 1986, 1987
European Cup Winners' Cup: 1987
**Barcelona**
European Cup Winners' Cup: 1989
Spanish Cup / Spanish Copa del Rey: 1990

Spanish La Liga: 1990/91, 1991/92, 1992/93, 1993/94
Spanish Super Cup / Spanish Supercopa: 1991, 1992, 1994
European Cup: 1992
European Super Cup: 1992
**Total Honours: 14**

## GIOVANNI TRAPATTONI

**Juventus**
Italian Serie A: 1976/77, 1977/78, 1980/81, 1981/82, 1983/84, 1985/86
UEFA Cup: 1977, 1993
Italian Cup / Coppa Italia: 1979, 1983
European Cup Winners' Cup: 1984
European Super Cup: 1984
European Cup: 1985
Intercontinental Cup: 1985
**Inter Milan**
Italian Serie A: 1988/89
Italian Super Cup / Supercoppa Italiana: 1989

UEFA Cup: 1991
**Bayern Munich**
German Bundesliga: 1996/97
German Cup / German DFB-Pokal: 1997/98
German League Cup: 1997
**Benfica**
Portuguese Primeira Liga: 2004/05
**Red Bull Salzburg**
Austrian Bundesliga: 2006/07
**Total Honours: 22**

## MARCELLO LIPPI

**Juventus**
Italian Serie A: 1994/95, 1996/97, 1997/98, 2001/02, 2002/03
Italian Cup / Coppa Italia: 1995
Italian Super Cup / Supercoppa Italiana: 1995, 1997, 2002, 2003
European Champions League: 1996
European Super Cup: 1996

Intercontinental Cup: 1996
**Italy**
World Cup: 2006
**Guangzhou Evergrande**
Chinese Super League: 2011/12, 2012/13
Chinese FA Cup: 2012
**Total Honours: 17**

## JOSÉ VILLALONGA

**Real Madrid**
European Cup: 1956, 1957

Spanish La Liga: 1954/55, 1956/57
Copa Latina: 1955, 1957

**Atlético Madrid**
Copa del Generalissimo: 1960, 1961
European Cup Winners' Cup: 1962
**Spain**
European Championships: 1964
**Total Honours: 10**
**Miguel Muñoz**
**Real Madrid**
European Cup: 1960, 1966

Intercontinental Cup: 1960
Spanish La Liga: 1960/61, 1961/62, 1962/63,
1963/64, 1964/65, 1966/67, 1967/68, 1968/69,
1971/72
Spanish Cup / Spanish Copa del Rey:
1962, 1970, 1974
**Total Honours: 13**

## BÉLA GUTTMANN

**Újpest**
Hungarian League: 1938/39, 1946/47
Mitropa Cup: 1939
**São Paulo**
São Paulo State Championship: 1957
**FC Porto**
Portuguese Liga: 1958/59

**Benfica**
Portuguese Liga: 1959/60, 1960/61
Portuguese Cup: 1962
European Cup: 1961, 1962
**Peñarol**
Uruguayan League: 1953
**Total Honours: 11**

## JOCK STEIN

**Celtic**
Scottish First Division: 1965/66, 1966/67,
1967/68, 1968/69, 1969/70, 1970/71, 1971/72,
1972/73, 1973/74, 1976/77
Scottish Cup: 1965, 1967, 1969, 1971, 1972,
1974, 1975, 1977

Scottish League Cup: 1966, 1967, 1968,
1969, 1970, 1975
European Cup: 1967
**Total Honours: 26**

## HELENIO HERRERA

**Atlético Madrid**
Spanish La Liga: 1949/50, 1950/51
Copa Eva Duarte: 1950
**Barcelona**
Spanish La Liga: 1958/59, 1959/60
Spanish Cup / Spanish Copa del Rey:
1959, 1981
European Inter-Cities Fairs Cup: 1958,

1960
**Inter Milan**
Italian Serie A: 1962/63, 1964/65, 1965/66
European Cup: 1964, 1965
Intercontinental Cup: 1964, 1965
**Roma**
Italian Cup / Coppa Italia: 1969
**Total Honours: 14**

## VICENTE DEL BOSQUE

**Real Madrid**
Copa Iberoamericana (1): 1994
Spanish La Liga: 2000/01, 2002/03
European Champions League: 2000, 2002
European Super Cup: 2002
Intercontinental Cup: 2002

**Spain**
World Cup: 2010
European Championship: 2012
**Total Honours: 9**

## OTTMAR HITZFELD

**FC Aarau**
Swiss Cup: 1985
**Grasshopper Zürich**
Swiss Super League: 1989/90, 1990/91
Swiss Cup: 1989, 1990
Swiss Super Cup: 1989
**Borussia Dortmund**
German Bundesliga: 1994/95, 1995/96
German Super Cup: 1995, 1996
European Champions League: 1997

**Bayern Munich**
German Bundesliga: 1998/99, 1999/00,
2000/01, 2002/03, 2007/08
German Cup / German DFB-Pokal: 2000,
2003, 2008
German League Cup: 1998, 1999, 2000, 2007
European Champions League: 2001
Intercontinental Cup: 2001
**Total Honours: 25**

## BRIAN CLOUGH

**Derby County**
English First Division: 1971/72
English Second Division: 1968/69
**Nottingham Forest**
England First Division: 1977/78
English League Cup: 1978, 1979, 1989, 1990

FA Charity Shield: 1978
European Cup: 1979, 1980
European Super Cup: 1979
**Total Honours: 11**

## SIR MATT BUSBY

**Manchester United**
English First Division: 1951/52, 1955/56,
1956/57, 1964/65, 1966/67
FA Cup: 1947/48, 1962/63

FA Charity Shield: 1952, 1956, 1957, 1965,
1967
European Cup: 1968
**Total Honours: 13**

## JOSÉ MOURINHO

**FC Porto**

Portuguese Primeira Liga: 2002/03, 2003/04

UEFA Cup: 2003

Portuguese Cup: 2003

Portuguese Super Cup: 2003

European Champions League: 2004

**Chelsea**

English Premier League: 2004/05, 2005/06

English FA Cup: 2007

English League Cup: 2005, 2007

FA Community Shield: 2005

**Inter Milan**

Italian Super Cup / Supercoppa Italiana: 2008

Italian Serie A: 2008/09, 2009/10

Italian Cup / Coppa Italia: 2010

European Champions League: 2010

**Real Madrid**

Spanish La Liga: 2012

Spanish Cup / Spanish Copa del Rey: 2011

Spanish Super Cup: 2012

**Total Honours: 20**

## ERNST HAPPEL

**ADO Den Haag**

Dutch KNVB Cup: 1968

**Feyenoord**

Dutch Eredivisie: 1970/71

European Cup: 1970

Intercontinental Cup: 1970

**Club Brugge**

Belgian Championship: 1975/76, 1976/77, 1977/78

Belgian Cup: 1977

**Standard Liège**

Belgian Cup: 1981

Belgian Super Cup: 1981

**SV Hamburg**

German Bundesliga: 1981/82, 1982/83

German Cup / German DFB-Pokal: 1987

European Cup: 1983

**FC Swarovski Tirol**

Austrian Championship: 1988/89, 1989/90

Austrian Cup: 1988/89

**Total Honours: 17**

## BOB PAISLEY

**Liverpool**

English First Division: 1975/76, 1976/77, 1978/79, 1979/80, 1981/82, 1982/83

English League Cup: 1981, 1982, 1983

FA Charity Shield: 1974, 1976, 1977, 1979, 1980, 1982

European Cup: 1977, 1978, 1981

UEFA Cup: 1976

European Super Cup: 1977

**Total Honours: 20**

## RINUS MICHELS

**Ajax**
Dutch Eredivisie: 1965/66, 1966/67, 1967/68, 1969/70
Dutch KNVB Cup: 1967, 1970, 1971
European Cup: 1971
**Barcelona**
Inter-Cities Fairs Cup Trophy Play-Off: 1971

Spanish La Liga: 1973/74
Spanish Cup / Spanish Copa Del Rey: 1978
**FC Koln**
German Cup / German DFB-Pokal: 1983
**Netherlands**
European Championship: 1988
**Total Honours: 13**

## SIR ALEX FERGUSON

**St. Mirren**
Scottish First Division: 1976/77
**Aberdeen**
Scottish Premier League: 1979/80, 1983/84, 1984/85
Scottish Cup: 1982, 1983, 1984, 1986
Scottish League Cup: 1986
European Cup Winners' Cup: 1983
European Super Cup: 1983
**Manchester United**
FA Charity/Community Shield: 1990 (shared), 1993, 1994, 1996, 1997, 2003, 2007, 2008, 2010, 2011

English FA Cup: 1990, 1994, 1996, 1999, 2004
European Cup Winners' Cup: 1991
European Super Cup: 1991
English League Cup: 1992, 2006, 2009, 2010
English Premier League: 1992/93, 1993/94, 1995/96, 1996/97, 1998/99, 1999/00, 2000/01, 2002/03, 2006/07, 2007/08, 2008/09, 2010/11, 2012/13
European Champions League: 1999, 2008
Intercontinental Cup: 1999
Club World Cup: 2008
**Total Honours: 49**